DRAWING FOR

3-DIMENSIONAL DESIGN

CONCEPTS · ILLUSTRATION · PRESENTATION

DRAWING FOR
3-DIMENSIONAL DESIGN

CONCEPTS · ILLUSTRATION · PRESENTATION

ALAN PIPES

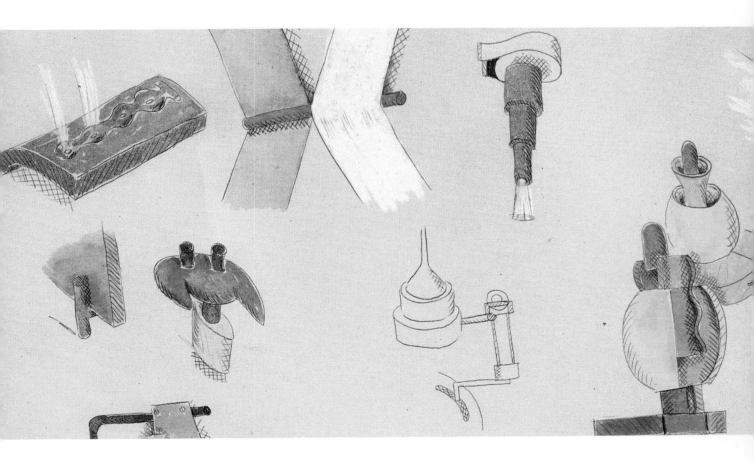

WCB Wm. C. Brown Publishers

To Shuna

First published in the U.S.A. in 1992 by
Wm. C. Brown Publishers
2460 Kerper Blvd.
Dubuque, Iowa 52001
U.S.A.

ISBN 0-697-13945-X

This book was designed and produced by
JOHN CALMANN AND KING LTD, London

Designed by Wade Greenwood Design, London
Typeset by Black Box Graphics, Maidenhead
Printed in Singapore by Toppan Ltd

Title page Part of a two-metre-long frieze entitled
"Inside-outside" by London-based designers
Daniel Weil and Gerard Taylor, drawn in 1987 for
an exhibition in Frankfurt, using watercolour,
wax crayon and pencil on wallpaper lining paper.
The designers believe that a drawing is not a passive
and calculated representation, but must convey energy
and emotion to bring the proposed product
to life in the mind of the client.

Contents

Drawing is the world's most obsessive temptation

Paul Valéry

Introduction

The love affair that architects have with the drawing is well documented. Some architects do nothing but draw; some are better known for their drawings than their buildings. Architectural drawings are rapidly becoming collectors' items, art objects in themselves.

But the designers of products – be they automobiles, hairdryers, chairs, industrial machines or pasta – also have a special relationship with drawings. For them, drawings must convey information about complex three-dimensional shapes, endowing new products which can be unfamiliar to the consumer with personality and ease of use. Buildings, on the other hand, are mostly rectilinear, seldom free-form, and their function is usually apparent.

A product designer's drawing has three main functions:

it is a means of externalizing thoughts and sorting out multi-faceted problems;

it is a medium of persuasion that sells the idea to the clients and reassures them that their brief is being satisfied;

it is a method for communicating complete and unambiguous information to those responsible for the product's manufacture, assembly and marketing.

In addition, once the product has been designed, the designer may be expected to produce further drawings – called technical illustrations – that instruct the end user in the product's operation.

This book aims to reveal and explain these crucial and fascinating aspects of the designer's skill, taking the reader through the entire design process: from initial concept sketches where the designer struggles for a solution while satisfying the constraints introduced by marketing and production people; through presentation drawings and visualizations, general arrangements and fully dimensioned detail-drawings for the parts themselves and the tools, moulds or dies required to manufacture them; to technical illustrations for use in marketing, and exploded assembly or instruction diagrams for maintenance and operation.

For the first time, computer-aided design (henceforth abbreviated to cad) will be placed in its rightful context, as just another tool – albeit an extremely powerful and versatile one – at the disposal of the designer, to be used as and when appropriate. It will be shown how cad can now be integrated

▶ Czech-born emigré and Amsterdam-based designer Bořek Šípek uses organic shapes and sculptural imagery that subvert the mechanistic perfection of "conventional" industrial design. In this study for coffee pots, "Coffee Copi," dated 1985, he used a conventional orthographic plan and elevation, rendered at a scale of 1:1 in a romantic way: "I work by trying to invent a story for everything I do," he is quoted as saying. Šípek also prefers to work intuitively rather than committing himself on the drawing board: "The pieces look so ugly in drawings," he said to Driade of his basket-weave chairs. "Let's do it with prototypes."

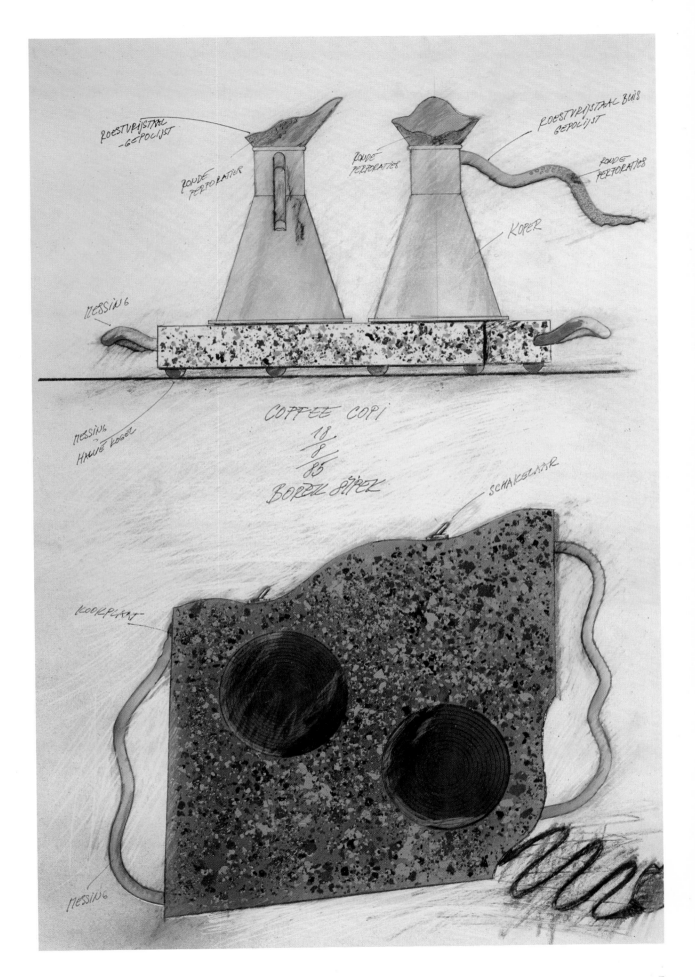

ROESTVRIJSTAAL
-GEPOLIJST

ZONDE
PERFORATIES

ROESTVRIJSTAAL BUIS
GEPOLIJST

ZONDE
PERFORATIES

ZONDE
PERFORATIES

KOPER

MESSING

MESSING

MESSING
"HALVE KOGEL

COFFEE COPI
18/8/85
BOREK STREK

SCHAKELAAR

KOOKPLAAT

MESSING

Introduction

into the design process at every stage, as an enabling technology with enormous potential for transforming the role of designers, restoring to them the control and breadth of perception over their designs that has been denied them since the demands of the industrial revolution led to the division of labour and to the fragmentation of the design-to-production cycle.

Product designers, unlike architects, have always been self-deprecating about their drawings. They make modest remarks like: "the drawing is just a means to an end, the important thing is the finished product." And when the project is over, the early exploratory drawings are often destroyed, cleared away to make room for the next job. A designer's archive will consist of photographs of the manufactured project, and perhaps of the prototype models.

Nevertheless, when pressed, designers will admit to deriving great joy from the act of drawing and are quick to praise a colleague's skill in representing on paper a three-dimensional object. The product designer's art is therefore often a hidden one.

A designer who cannot draw well is at a severe disadvantage. Despite the important role of the concept block model (many designers, surprisingly, just can't think in 3D and need something tangible they can hold and move around), the drawing is the fundamental means of externalizing ideas (talking to oneself) and then communicating those concepts to other members of the design team, to clients and managers, and on to those responsible for production.

The importance attached to design as "functional problem solving" in recent years has had the effect of relegating drawing to that of a frivolous activity, a necessary evil. *Styling* has been used as a dirty word. Post-modernism, by restoring colour, texture and ornamentation as deserving attributes of a design, has also emphasized the idea of design as differentiation. There is no such thing as the "ideal" car or jug kettle. The look of a product will change inevitably with fashion. Aesthetics is a marketable commodity. And it follows that if a design cannot be generated automatically from a functional specification, it will have to be drawn, albeit in the widest sense. A designer needs to be a paragon – proficient in a whole range of apparently disparate drawing skills.

At the concept stage, as well as being able to sort out on paper his or her own thoughts, it is crucial for the designer to be able to explain in a few economically placed lines, perhaps at a briefing meeting with the client, exactly how the as-yet-nonexistent product will look, feel and fit together and to demonstrate that all the various constraints imposed by the client's brief will be resolved.

Designers must know how to convey information about complex, often free-form, shapes. They are increasingly asked to demystify unfamiliar products, perhaps inspired by an advance in technology – such as CD players, shopping calculators and telephone answering machines – endowing them with personality and, notably with the "New American" designers who emerged in the mid-1980s, making the shapes themselves metaphors or clues for their efficient use.

A presentation drawing is something completely different. Here the intention is to show the client or financier a selection of highly rendered images, as realistic-looking as possible, so that a decision can be made to go ahead with the project. At present these are likely to be marker or pastel drawings on board. Airbrush, always the preferred medium for special presentations or very elaborate and costly work, sadly requires too much painstaking preparation and is therefore not cost-effective for the average design project with a tight deadline. In future, more and more presentation visualizations are likely to be computer-generated.

Working drawings must be produced by the design practice once the design route has been chosen. The product's component parts and sometimes even the tooling required to manufacture it must be depicted accurately and unambiguously, to standard conventions readable by engineers and patternmakers.

In short, the product designer ideally needs to be a jack of all trades – and a master of all of them, too. In practice, however, the various tasks will be devolved to those best skilled to undertake them – a good concept designer's time will not be wasted by the project leader in producing repetitive working drawings.

Paradoxically, cad – now commonplace in those design activities just prior to production, the so-called downstream activities that follow the creation of the general arrangement drawing – will prove a mixed blessing to the designer. Cad will speed up, smooth out and concatenate the design process, but will also make the designer more responsible and accountable for the integrity of the design. The cold efficiency of the cad system eliminates "draftsman's licence" from the drawing – the designer now has to work hard to resolve all the potential production problems upfront, and not leave them for the patternmaker to inherit and sort out later on down the line.

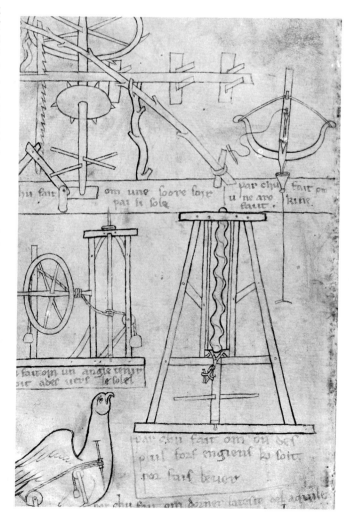

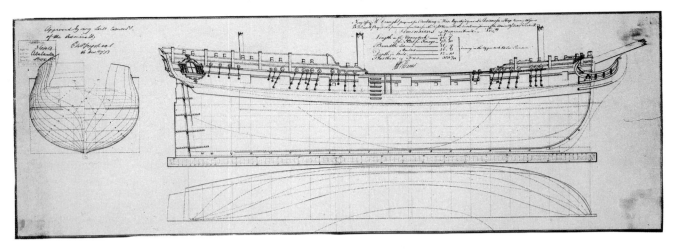

◄ The sketchbooks of the 13th-century master stonemason Villard de Honnecourt look naïve by modern standards, with his diagrammatic approach to the third dimension, but before industrialization they served as an aide memoire and a hardcopy record for the craftsman.

▲ This drawing of a sloop of 1775, the *Atalanta*, is more like a present-day engineering drawing with its arrangement of half-plan (a ship is symmetrical), front and side elevation. Conventions were already being implemented: the contours of the ribs on the front elevation are depicted stern to amidships on the left, bow to amidships on the right.

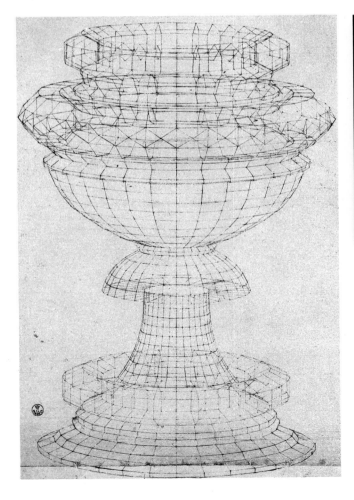

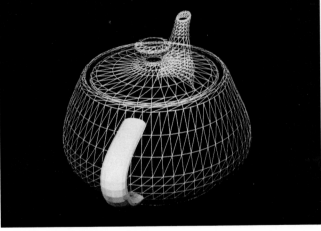

◄ Paolo Uccello's perspective drawing of a chalice, dated 1460, anticipates the initial wireframe stage in the rendering of a faceted computer-aided solid model. Some parts of the design are completely "wireframe," while others have hidden lines removed.

▲ A partially rendered Newell teapot (a well-known benchmark in cad circles), modelled in 1988 using Doré (Dynamic Object Rendering Environment) software from Ardent on a Titan supercomputer. This too has some hidden lines removed.

The story so far

A fanciful design historian might relate the first link between drawing and manufacture to the time when, according to a Greek legend, Dibutades traced round the shadow (a *projection*) of his daughter's lover, which he then cut out and made into a sculpture. Symbolic or schematic drawings have been around since the Bronze Age – there is a plan view of an ox-drawn plough dated 1500 BC at Fontañalba, and equivalent schemes can be seen in Egyptian paintings. Whether these can be considered design drawings is another matter.

The ancient Greeks, as we know, laid down the foundations of western geometry, and the methods of Euclid were taught almost exclusively until the end of the 19th century. Greek astronomers, notably Apollonius of Perga at around 250 BC, were the first to conceive the notion of projections. It is known that the Greeks used and understood both orthographic (also known as parallel) and stereographic (or conical) projections in their flattened maps of the hemispherical heavens. Bearing in mind that a great number of Greek writings have been lost over the centuries, it is almost impossible to believe that they missed completely the theory of perspective, especially when the stereographic projection is considered to be a special form of generalized perspective.

Both the artist Paolo Uccello and the architect Filippo Brunelleschi are credited with inventing the principles of perspective from around 1420 onwards. This is not to say that in drawings the third dimension did not exist at all, for various kinds of non-converging oblique projections can be seen in drawings of all cultures from the earliest times.

In the middle ages, drawings – it seems to our modern eyes – gave more weight to the mechanical features and attributes of a machine than to depicting physical reality. The Abbess Herrad of Landsperg, in her *Hortus Deliciarum* of

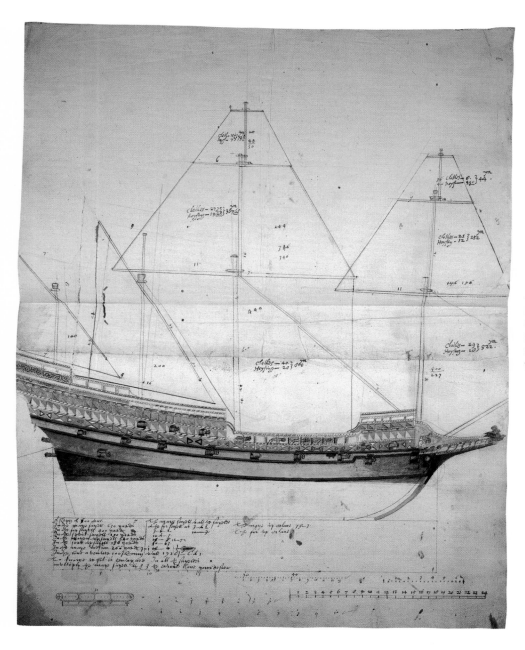

◀ Watercolour drawing of a 16th-century ship, with a schematic layout of the sails and rigging, from Matthew Baker's *Fragments of Ancient English Shipwrightery*. This precursor to the presentation drawing was probably undertaken as a showpiece to record the external details of the as-built ship.

1160, would sacrifice geometrical truths and comparative sizes and positions of components in favour of describing in the conventions of the times how the undershot mill or whatever was being depicted actually worked. Her empirically produced drawings are to this generation of designers as inscrutable and difficult to "read" as an engineer's orthographic (plan and elevation) drawings are to the lay person of today.

The many types of drawing currently used by designers evolved mostly independently of each other in different disciplines during the middle ages in Europe, for the communication and dissemination of ideas were obfuscated by the guilds, who kept control of their trades by surrounding themselves with arcane mysteries. The "one object, one drawing" school of thought can be traced down from the perspectivists; the multi-view (plan and elevations) approach came mainly from the architects.

The earliest documented plan of a building is carved on a statue of Gudea of Ur in the Louvre and is dated 2130 BC. It depicts a ziggurat – a temple with stepped sides – carved on to a drawing board, with accompanying drawing instruments. For many centuries the plan view appeared to be sufficient for builders and master masons to build cathedrals; they must have improvized from the foundations up. In the 16th and 17th centuries, details such as arches were shown co-related to the plan at the same scale so that measurements could be taken off. Amedée François Frézier in 1738 is reputedly the first architect to have shown plans and elevations drawn together, to scale and projectionally linked by means of construction lines.

Architectural practice, being a more mature methodology, crossed over into engineering at the start of the industrial revolution. The late 18th century steam-engine drawings of Boulton and Watt are reminiscent of architectural drawings of the time, finished as they are in watercolour washes, with shading and added shadows to heighten the realism.

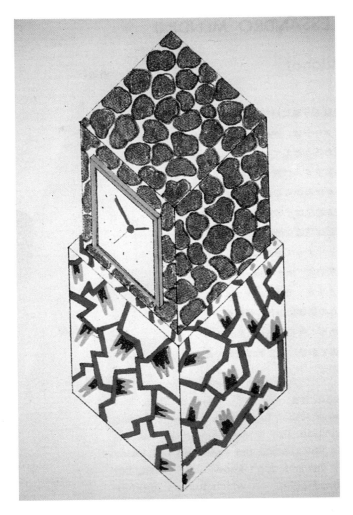

▲ The "Acapulco" clock by George Sowden for Memphis, 1982, uses an axonometric projection (with true plan) rather than perspective, a convention common in architecture but until recently rare in product design presentation drawings.

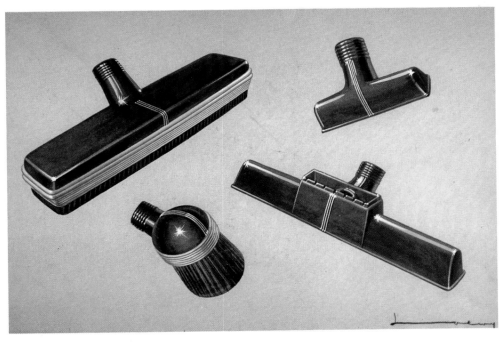

◀ Raymond Loewy was a fashion designer by training: his glossy renderings in gouache for AB Electrolux of Stockholm, dating from the 1940s, betray a straightforward, no-nonsense pictorial approach, still seen in American drawings today.

Introduction

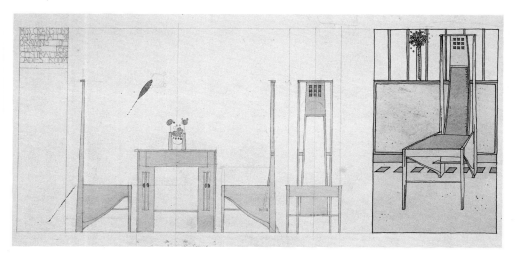

◄ These delicate wash studies of 1903 for chairs by Charles Rennie Mackintosh use a simple elevation for overall dimensions and proportions, supplemented by a more deliberate perspective (right), in which the chair is placed in its contextual environment.

► A rendered elevation drawing of a 19th-century steam engine by L. Poutays, with colour tinting and shadows to heighten the sense of realism.

That engineers were taught the architects' way is apparent in all those Doric and Ionic columns and brackets with leaf embellishments that found their way on to pre-modern machinery. As well as feeling that they were endowing those demonic machines with respectability, the engineers must have also had the understandable attitude that if they had taken the trouble to learn how to draw these details, then why waste the skills?

The history of design drawing goes hand-in-hand with the development of drawing instruments. Euclidean geometry demands only compasses and a straight edge. Protractors and set squares came much later and were derived from master masons' tools, like those of Villard de Honnecourt whose 1220-35 sketchbooks are preserved, containing fanciful drawings of a mobile angel and an articulated eagle.

Gaspard Monge, a fortifications designer and friend of Napoleon, frustrated by the empirical methods of the masons and the impracticality of Euclidean geometry, revolutionized design thinking in 1795 with his theories of "descriptive" geometry. By 1868, an Englishman called A.W. Cunningham was writing pamphlets saying that in continental Europe there were "elegant drawing methods through which all manner of three-dimensional problems could be tackled on paper." Elsewhere, he said, it was still necessary to make a model or shape a piece of material in order to resolve a particular design problem.

He was overstating the case. Craftspeople did undoubtedly make drawings, even though they were probably scratched on slate, chalked on a blackboard or inscribed on the material to be worked on. But Cunningham wanted to see systematic drawing education replace custom and practice. Monge's methods were by this time being applied throughout most of Europe, in the USA, in Egypt and – via a French deserter – in Russia. His geometry was so important to the French that it had been treated by Napoleon as a military secret. As such it was known to British spies as early as 1840. By then work had been allegedly shown to some English academics who dismissed it as dry and unimportant, with no practical value.

Obscurity almost befell the Reverend William Farish – another pioneer of drawing methods – whose 1820 work on isometrics (see Chapter 4 for an explanation of the metric projections) languished for many years in the *Transactions of the Cambridge Philosophical Society*. He also had the insight to work out that the orthographic projection could be considered as a type of perspective – one that was seen at an infinite viewing distance.

Early in the 19th century, almost all design drawings were produced directly by engineers and craftspeople in the manufacturing trades. By the middle of the century, the sheer weight of work meant that increasing numbers of less skilled draftsmen and copiers were involved in the design process. This led a William Binns in 1857 to develop the three-view orthographic or solid geometry drawing method (Monge's geometry demanded only two plane views) so that a highly finished drawing could be created from a designer's rough. It was not an entirely new method, but was based on Dürer's anatomical drawings of heads and feet, shown in several related views in plane gridded "crates," done around 1525.

The methods for representing complex "sculptured" surfaces – often curving simultaneously in two dimensions – derive mainly from shipbuilding. During the late 16th century, ship designs were conventionally drawn in three views: sheerplan (side view), draught (front view) and bodyplan (plan). Ribs were drawn full-size on the lofting floor as templates for the manufacture of the real wooden ribs.

By the end of the 17th century, drawings had become more stylized. Rib sections were simplified by depicting only the outside curves. And because the ribs were symmetrical about a line running down the centre of the ship, only half of each side was drawn: stern to amidships shown on the left of a centreline; bow to amidships to the right. Various waterlines were also drawn, to show how the ship would sit in the water under various load conditions. In the course of time, these were abstracted into imaginary planes that could themselves be used to define the shape of the hull: as curves in the plan view; straight lines in the elevations. A set of these "contours" could henceforth be used as an alternative method to define any solid streamlined body. More usually, however, they would be treated as an additional method, as a series of sections accompanying a conventional three-view set of drawings. Contour *maps*, incidentally, had already been invented, but the secrecy endemic among the guilds of the middle ages prevented the percolation of ideas amongst the trades.

Although there was some mass production in the early-to-mid-19th century – of buttons, pins and needles – most engineering was still crafts based. If something was to be made, a craftsperson was told what was wanted and perhaps supplied with a few rough sketches, and left to proceed according to his own judgement.

In 1815, the US military decided that it would manufacture standard muskets with interchangeable parts in many different armouries up and down the country. A number of "perfect" muskets were made, conforming to a master set of

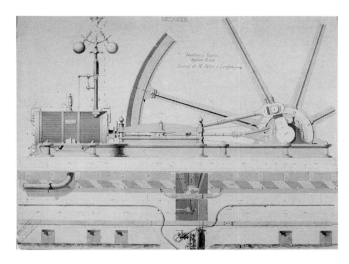

gauges, templates and jigs, and these were sent – with the instruction to "allow no deviation" – to the various armouries, which would be responsible for making their own jigs and gauges. The aim was that muskets would be produced that could be stripped down, the parts thrown in a heap along with parts from other armouries, reassembled randomly and always work first time. The "American method" was very soon adopted throughout Europe.

By 1852, Ferdinand Redtenbacher, a German engineer, had thought of a better method. He wrote that a drawing is an ideal representation of a machine, costing little and easier to handle than iron and steel. He had recognized that the drawing can be considered an instrument for design, imitating real objects on paper so that they can be assessed, any failings judged and incompatibilities smoothed out in changes to the drawing before an expensive prototype is fabricated. Furthermore, the drawing is also a means of communication that would make it possible to distribute the work to be done among a number of workers or subcontractors.

The use of the drawing as a symbolic representation of the product meant that the process of design could be separated from the process of production. It meant that things too big for a single craftsperson could be handled by the division of labour; it also meant that the rate of production could be stepped up, with small, mass-produced and standard component parts of the product being manufactured simultaneously.

This was arguably the beginning of the product design profession as it is recognized today. The new role of the drawing put the designer in the privileged position of becoming what design theorist J. Chris Jones calls a "wholeist" rather than an "atomist." A designer with a drawing was capable of a greater perceptual span than the craftsperson who went before. With the elevated status of the drawing as an analogue for the designed object, designers were no longer prevented by partial knowledge or the high cost of alteration from making fairly drastic changes to a design early in the design-to-production cycle, when the implications of change are at their cheapest.

In the mid-19th century, manufacturing worldwide was carried out in jobbing shops, in which the machine tools were located around the edge, by the windows, and assembly was carried out in the middle; production lines came much later. Drawings then carried basic dimensions, supplemented by descriptive tolerances, such as "running fit," "sliding fit" or "press fit." Most products were one-offs, so they were built to fit by the craftspeople.

Eventually the hand-painted shadows on the drawings gave way to the shorthand of shadowlining – edges vertical to the plane and in shade were made heavier – and colour washes went out when blueprints came in at the beginning of this century. Until then a convention had grown up to indicate the material of manufacture by artists' colours: Payne's grey for cast iron, purple for wrought iron, gamboge (a yellow pigment) for brass and so on. It soon became customary to send a tracing, in ink, rather than the original to the workshop. The First World War and the coming of reprographic methods of copying meant the end of colour codes, which had to be replaced by more legible mechanical tints or forms of cross-hatching.

Since 1927, engineering drawing practice has been the subject of national and international standards. In the UK, the appropriate code is British Standard BS308; the later but more far-reaching US standard is ASA Y14, with the appendages -1, -2 and so on up to -17. These standards govern and police all manner of considerations, including size formats, line types, lettering, dimensioning, the way sectioning should be done, and such details as the symbols for representing screw threads. European countries have their own DIN standards, and there are moves to introduce international ISO standards as soon as all interested parties can agree. In the meantime, designers often take a pragmatic approach in using those conventions they feel comfortable with. The standards issue is exacerbated by large companies having their own internal standards and design practices can be forced under contract to conform to the client's "house style."

As engineering drawings became more mannered and abstract in the quest for the totally unambiguous representation of the designed object, it has become necessary since the end of the Second World War to revive forgotten "artistic" rendering skills to help put over pictorially the designer's intentions to those unable to "read" orthographic drawings.

The presentation drawing is a recent invention, whose development runs parallel with the growth of the design groups and their relationship with industry over the past thirty years. The perspective "realism" of the presentation drawing was challenged by design groups such as the Italian Memphis group who borrowed axonometric and oblique projections from the architects (Italian – and Scandinavian – designers are often trained in schools of architecture) to communicate different truths about a product's form and function. Designers such as Aldo Rossi go further, publishing philosophical "concept" sketches and contextual paintings to help sell the products they design.

From the 1920s until the 1950s, the look of the engineering drawing changed only in the way tolerance information was represented. The ideal then was to allow designers to define on paper their functional intentions and requirements, leaving those responsible for manufacture to interpret them using any production method they thought fit according to the equipment available. Towards the end of the 19th century, books on engineering design (or "machine drawing" as it was called) were beginning to assume a fund of knowledge about the methods of orthographic projection and were concentrating instead on the designer's ability to solve engineering problems, setting exercises intended to instil in the designer/draftsman an intuitive sense of rightness, in terms of shape and proportion. Today, cad (more of which later) promises to return designers to the days in which they carried on their shoulders the responsibility for realizing their original concepts all the way through the design process without compromise or interpretation by others on the factory floor.

Computer-aided design and the changing role of the designer

Computer-aided design is probably as old as Napier's bones. The principles of automatic repeatability and programmability in machines certainly have their origins in the punched-card-operated looms of Falcon (1728) and Jacquard (1800). Most present-day cad systems are derived from a computer program called Sketchpad, developed in 1963 and based on the PhD thesis of Ivan Sutherland at the Massachusetts Institute of Technology. Sketchpad had many of the features expected in modern 2D drafting systems. It was interactive: the designer could communicate instantaneously with the computer using a lightpen and cathode-ray tube (previously, jobs would be processed in batches, sent away to a central computer and the results received perhaps the next day). Sutherland also introduced the concept of data structures so that commonly used elements could be stored in "libraries" and called up when needed in new drawings. It never should be necessary, he insisted, to do the same thing twice.

Designers involved in projects that require a great deal of repetitive work, modification or updating have always been the real beneficiaries of cad. But techniques such as parametric programming can generate families of parts from a single initial geometry at the touch of a button. In the garment industry, for example, the pattern for a size 12 dress can be "graded" into all the other sizes automatically – and that is not a trivial operation, not merely a matter of scaling the drawing up or down.

Cad systems are no longer mysterious black boxes. Vendors now provide languages called macros that enable users to customize frequently used calculations or design sequences to their own ways of working. Drawings can be created full size at a scale of 1:1 and output later at all the different scale factors required by the various contractors and allied trades in a multi-disciplinary project.

The computer is not only good at remembering things and organizing data. Its computational skills at handling complex geometric constructions – drawing a circle through three points, for example – can result in productivity gains even on one-off products.

Cad speeds up the design-to-production cycle, getting better products out to market faster, giving companies that use cad a competitive edge in world markets. It can be used to unify the various stages in the design process, smoothing into a seamless transmission of ideas the once distinct phases from concept design, to visuals, to model, to parts drawings. With the increased capacity and tighter management control, firms can thus take the opportunity to open up new markets and produce more diversified and better targeted products.

With cleaner, legible and more precise drawings – especially if 3D solid modelling is used from the start of a project – cad can eliminate ambiguity (and "draftsman's licence") from designs, and give designers the confidence that the integrity of their concepts will not be compromised as they travel downstream through the design-to-production process. Cad means more communication between engineers, designers, management, sales and clerical staff.

Despite a common apprehension among non-users, cad does not seem to stifle creativity but on the contrary gives the designer time to try alternative "what if?" solutions. Cad can be integrated with analysis, simulation and evaluation programs to test a design for strength and to check that it meets performance expectations, so that potential design failures are caught and eliminated on the screen rather than on the shopfloor. The need for prototypes may not be eliminated, but fewer of them will be required and the ones that have to be made will be nearer to the real thing. And as legislation on product liability becomes increasingly important to manufacturing industry, new methods must be found to help designers avoid errors, predict and circumvent potential pitfalls and control the escalating amount of complex data associated with product reliability and safety.

Designers using cad can offer new services to the client. With cad it is easier to work out exactly how much a product will cost to make, and so the factory can reduce the amount of stock and work-in-progress on the shopfloor in line with current "just-in-time" practice. Materials and machine time can also be saved by using optimization and "nesting" routines

◄ ► **This folding trolley for transporting heavy gear across rough terrain, intended to be folded into two square feet and carried on a fire engine, was modelled by Steven Spenceley at the Dorset Institute, using CGAL software on an Apollo workstation. Several different views can be generated from a single computer model. Every component, even when hidden, exists in the 3D model, and important details can be exposed using transparency effects.**

that, for example, lay out the pieces to be cut from a sheet of steel more efficiently.

Manually produced engineering drawings also take up a great deal of physical space. Storing this information in a computer database not only makes it more accessible and more likely to be consulted (no more re-inventing the wheel) but liberates valuable office space.

Documentation will be up-to-date and there will be more of it. Managers will have a better appreciation of what is going on, and where any potential pitfalls may occur. If the geometry of the product – plus the associated material type, costing and sourcing information – is held in the computer as a database, then everything that needs to be known about making the product – drawings, parts lists, manuals, paper or magnetic tape to drive machine tools – is automatically accessible.

Over the years, developments in computer technology and improvements in software writing have reduced the prices of cad systems. Systems built around personal computers, such as the IBM PC and its compatibles, are now affordable by even one- or two-person companies, making them able to compete with the largest multinationals. A PC–cad system supplemented with a high-quality display can look, feel and perform like the expensive minicomputer-powered system of just a few years ago – with the crucial difference that a PC–cad system suffers no loss of response as other users share the processor. When it is switched on, the system on the desk is for the designer's or engineer's exclusive use – a personal workstation.

There are still many disincentives to the mass take-up of cad. It is expensive when compared with conventional tools. It requires an investment of time in which to learn how to derive the most benefit from the system – and designers may resent being hauled off real projects for training. It may even require designers to change their working methods. But the time is almost here when cad can be regarded as just another resource, to be called upon by the designer as and when it is deemed necessary. Cad does not impose a visual style of its own – drawings from different design practices but generated from the same brand of system can look quite different and reflect the idiosyncrasies of individual designers. It is simply another tool, like a pencil or marker – albeit an immensely powerful and flexible one – that can be applied to streamline the design process and ultimately help produce better designs faster.

This book aims to guide the reader through the various stages of the design process as product design is currently practised. After some introductory chapters examining the nature of design drawing, describing the tools of the trade – both traditional and computer-aided – and explaining the basic skills of drawing and rendering, the progressive stages of concept design, presentation and engineering development are examined in turn. The importance of the appropriate materials and techniques for each of these phases is demonstrated using original drawings from American, British and European designers.

During the preparation of this book, design practices all over the world were asked about their working methods in an attempt to detect and compare any national idiosyncrasies in styles of practice. Not surprisingly, in these days of world products and transnational clients, there seem to be few differences. The only general conclusions that can be drawn result rather from the educational background of the designers. Italian and Scandinavian designers usually have a training in architecture and are thus more likely to use architectural devices such as exotic metric projections in their drawings – Aldo Rossi and the Memphis designers, for example. British designers have a tradition of coming from an engineering background, and are more used to offering the "extra" services of engineering and tooling drawings. The great US designer Raymond Loewy was originally a fashion illustrator. The newer designers in the USA and Germany – and some in the UK – seem to be following the Italian method: they are responsible for the styling, and then hand over the design at the general arrangement stage.

In any case, much depends on the relationship with the client, and the degree of integration and cooperation with the client's own in-house resources. One could imagine a future in which the downstream activities of design are handled almost automatically by a computer system – assuming, of course, that the designer in charge of the project is sufficiently skilled in materials and production methods to take the responsibility of overseeing such a system.

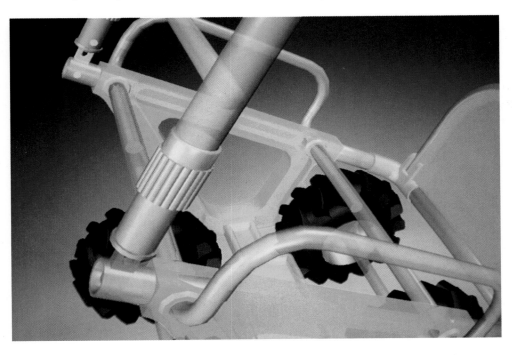

Drawing is a means of finding your way about things, and a way of experiencing, more quickly than sculpture allows, certain tryouts and attempts. The act of converting an idea into lines and other marks on paper often excites the mind and frees the imagination, encouraging the flow of creative thought

Henry Moore, quoted in "Drawing: Technique and Purpose," 1981

1 The Designer's Drawing

What is a drawing? And how does a designer's drawing differ from an artist's drawing? Most designers will agree with the sentiments expressed in the above quotation from sculptor Henry Moore – substitute "model" or "prototype" for the word "sculpture" and it could have come from any practising designer.

In fact, a designer's drawing and an artist's drawing have more in common than might first be supposed. They are both preliminaries to some future work, a preparation for action. And until quite recently, the artist's drawing was kept as secret and mysterious a document as a designer's drawing is today. It is only the increasing demand for works of art and the growing use of media such as pencil and charcoal in the 20th century as a means of expression that have brought the artist's drawing out of the codex and plan chest. Now it is embellished with a frame and hangs on the gallery wall to be appreciated as an art object in its own right.

A drawing, according to Philip Rawson in his book *Drawing*, is "that element in a work of art which is independent of colour or actual 3D space, the underlying conceptual structure which may be indicated by tone alone." Or, by Jean Leymarie in the book *History of an Art: Drawing*, it is defined as "a strange challenge to the powers of mind and hand, this art of representing the coloured mass of objects or recording one's inner visions on a thin flat surface by means of lines which do not exist in nature."

A more conventional dictionary definition might be concerned with delineation, as distinguished from painting, and how arrangements of lines determine form. Arguments about whether a drawing can be coloured or not, and about line versus tone, are not particularly fruitful to the practising designer. But these issues, although seemingly trivial today, have had a profound effect in the past on the way designed objects look.

The "design process" of the Renaissance painter, as described in Jean Leymarie's book, bears a striking similarity to the working methods of a contemporary design consultancy. After receiving a commission and briefing from the patron, the artist puts down the first idea (*primo pensiero*) as a rapid sketch in diagrammatic strokes usually in pen and ink

▶ The "H-Arp" lamp for Anthologie Quartett, West Germany, designed in 1987 by the London-based consultancy of Daniel Weil and Gerard Taylor, aligns a familiar image with up-to-date lighting technology. In Weil's view the bland boxes more normal for lights are a hopelessly inadequate reflection of the marvels they contain. Weil and Taylor usually draw chaotically on to huge rolls of wallpaper liner ("drawing, a neglected art in the age of the slick visual, is a crucial part of the process of discovery"), but here they constrain the object to an outline of a Van Gogh chair.

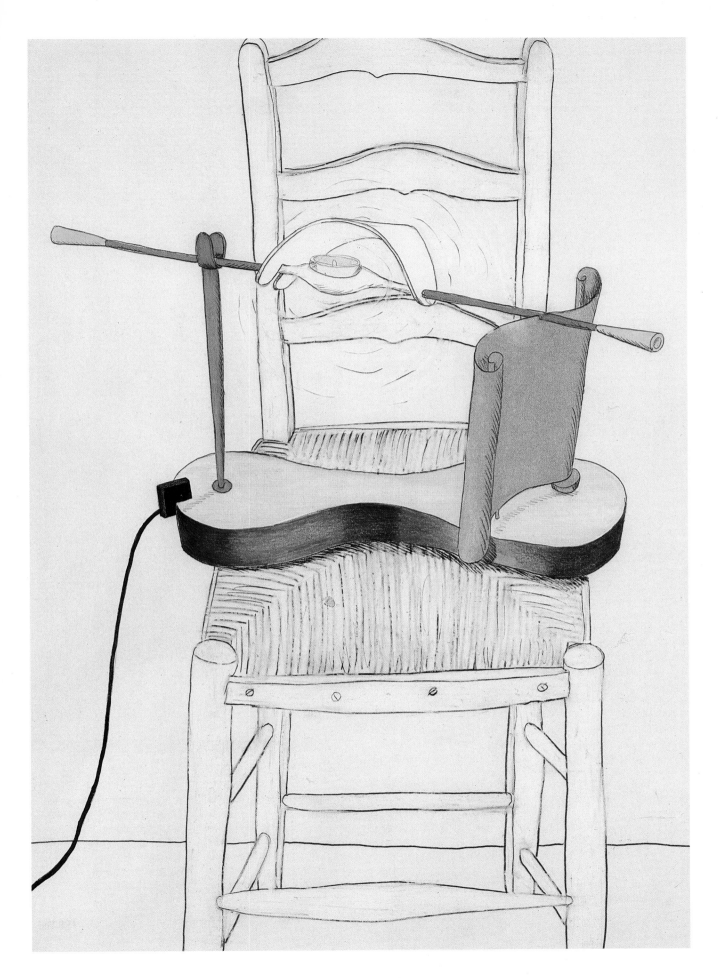

or red chalk (cf. the concept sketch). This is followed by a series of preparatory drawings leading to a single composition (cf. the general arrangement drawing). The artist then studies in detail all the individual parts of the composition (cf. detail drawings). When satisfied with these, the painter produces a full and accurate drawing (the *modello*), a small-scale version of the proposed work executed in media akin to the proposed painting and indicating the tonal values, which is submitted to the patron (client) for approval. The last stage is the cartoon, produced full-size by "squaring-up" the *modello*. Few cartoons survive because they were used on-site as a pattern for the production of the final painting – the lines were pricked out and pounced (transferred) to the wall or canvas using chalk dust.

Artists, such as Michelangelo, would also produce "presentation drawings" which were more analogous to the technical illustrations of this book, in that they were usually made after the painting was finished. These "arrested" drawings were elaborate, finished in a single medium, and signed, and were given to the patron or to a friend to mark the culmination of a project.

There were artists in the 17th century who even separated the act of design (*disegno interno*) from the act of execution (*disegno esterno*) in the way that some product designers content themselves with conceptualizing, and leave the production details to craftsmen in the factory. These would design work in the form of a sketch (*bozzetta*) and leave the execution entirely to their assistants. Such was the primacy, at the time, of the idea over technique.

Not all artists' drawings have had direct utilitarian purpose, however. A doodle may turn out to be the germ of an idea for a major work. An exercise in drawing from nature can generate a form which may be incorporated into a future composition. Delacroix is said to have loosened up his hand before commencing painting by drawing from his imagination. Sketches thus made provided him with a bank of ideas which could be dipped into at a later date.

Artists have always been free to express their ideas in their own ways. This was presumably true of the designer/craftspeople who were responsible for the implementation of their own concepts. The industrial revolution, however, required that designers use new graphic conventions to communicate their ideas to the means of production with unprecedented prescriptive clarity using universally comprehensible codes.

The design process of today's designer thus incorporates all kinds of drawing techniques, each appropriate and necessary to a particular stage in the design-to-production cycle. During the concept stage, the designer is mostly externalizing thoughts – a seemingly solitary process – but must also be able to jot down and encapsulate ideas at briefing meetings with the client, and be able to communicate shapes to colleagues in a multi-disciplinary team.

Presentation drawing must give a convincing impression of the finished object quickly and economically, to people untrained in "reading" conventional engineering drawings. Production people, on the other hand, are sticklers for precision and demand complete and unambiguous drawings that conform to national, international or in-company standards. The role of the drawing in design may remain constant throughout the design process, but its form and degree of accuracy change stage by stage.

▲ ▶ Michelangelo's early sketches (right) for the tomb of Giuliano, Duke of Nemours, in Florence (above) reveal a desire to express three-dimensional form on the flat plane of two-dimensional paper, a concern still representing a challenge to today's product designers. A drawing in this context is a way of experiencing certain attempts at a solution more quickly than the act of sculpture allows.

How drawing is taught

The way drawing has been taught and the importance attached by society to a drawing education has had a fundamental bearing on the way the world looks.

In the mid-15th century, the commentaries of Ghiberti and the systematic treatises of Alberti extended to sculpture and architecture the basic theory and practice of drawing, which thus became the common unifying principle of the three major visual arts. The Venetian sketchbooks of Jacopo Bellini contain studies for architecture, painting, sculpture and ornamentation in a graphical style confident of its means and purposes. For Leonardo da Vinci, drawing became "not only a science but a deity," permitting the precise exploration of areas where language is powerless. He saw painting as a science of knowledge; drawing as a method of enquiry. Drawing, he said, is the tangible form of the idea, the inventive act which produces a work of art. This is echoed by Giorgio Vasari (1511–74) who said, "Drawing is nothing else but a visible expression of the concept we have in our mind."

"Drawing," says Philip Rawson, "embodies a genuine and independent way of thinking. Someone who draws actually sees more and knows more of the world he or she lives in than someone who does not draw." And, says Susan Lambert in the introduction to *Drawing: Technique and Purpose*, "drawn marks provide parallels with experience, suggesting form, space, light and movement without having any true similarity to the subject they describe."

A drawing is thus a means of externalizing a concept, but it is also a very personal statement; it is something much more than just an arrangement of marks on paper. A drawing is an analogue of the real thing: a stylized collection of symbols, assumptions and learned shorthand that can be read, or misinterpreted, just like writing.

David Hockney, in a preface to Jeffrey Camp's book *Draw: How to Master the Art*, says, "In learning to draw (unlike learning to write) you learn to look. It's not the beauty of the marks we like in writing, it's the beauty of the ideas. But in drawing it's a bit of both – it's beauty of ideas, of feelings and of marks. If you can draw, even a little bit, you can express all kinds of ideas that might otherwise be lost – delights, frustrations, whatever torments you or pleases you. Drawing helps you put your thoughts in order. It can make you think in different ways. It naturally gives you a sense of harmony, of order."

"Drawing is a special language," says Camp, "full of suggestion beyond the concrete presence of its lines." This is all well and good, but drawing is a language that has been codified and formalized over the years and the way we draw influences the way we see. Form and harmony are not intuitive absolutes, but are the result of systematic drawing methods.

The codification of drawing began in the treatises of the Renaissance and was perfected in the textbooks of the 19th century, in which axioms were presented to analyse design problems. Most of these textbooks, according to design historian David Brett, taught drawing in a dry linear style. This was true not only for mechanical design, but for the decorative arts as well, for example textile design, in which design was being constrained by the technology of the increasingly mechanized means of production.

An example of the dogmatism can be seen in William Robson's *Grammigraphia* (1799) which states: "Lines are four; perpendicular, horizontal, oblique and curve. All the variety of appearance in nature are presented by a combination of these four lines placed agreeably to proportion and position. A line is the continuation of a point. A point can proceed in four ways only and from these we can derive a mathematical account of all the common figures: angle, square, circle, ellipse, oval, pyramid, serpentine, weaving and spiral. Use line as distinct and as determinate as possible." In 1842, William Dyce was writing: "The purpose of drawing is to study nature and its laws to form abstractions, beauties of form and colour [which] by the very fact that they are abstractions assume, in relation to the whole progress of art, the character of principles or facts, that tend by accumulation to bring it to perfection." Drawing based on empirical observation began to take a back seat.

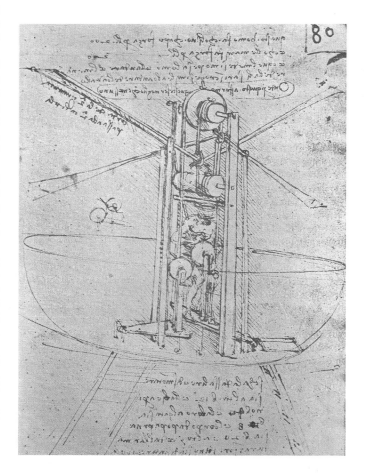

▲ Leonardo da Vinci's drawing of a fanciful *macchina volante* is a pictorial concept sketch with notes. Leonardo often used exploded and cut-away drawings to help explain the inner workings of his inventions. He virtually invented orthographic projection, showing multiple views of the same object, but always with a third dimension added.

In a period of national resurgence following the Napoleonic wars, the German states, especially Prussia, adopted the ideas of the Swiss educationalist Johann Heinrich Pestalozzi (1746–1827) for teaching drawing in kindergarten schools. This *pedagogische Zeichnen* was quite distinct from expressionistic or *Kunstzeichnen* drawing and was based on an "alphabet" of simple geometric figures. After the conservative reaction of 1848, when drawing was taught by copying from prints and plaster casts, geometry came back into favour following the unification of Germany in 1872.

There was a philosophical connection here: Kant argues that space and form are *a priori*. The activity of drawing, according to Pestalozzi and his followers Alois Hirt and J.C. Buss, should begin with exercises specially designed to enlarge and develop the understanding of space and form that already exists in the child's mind. "Angles, parallels and arcs comprise the whole act of drawing," wrote Buss in 1828. "Everything that can possibly be drawn is only a definite application of these three primary forms."

Friedrich Froebel introduced an *a priori* perceptual grid (like the squaring-up of paintings) for developing "form consciousness," also using bricks and blocks to explore spatial and volumetric experience. The architect Frank Lloyd Wright was later to acknowledge a debt to the Froebel education he received. These methods were brought to the USA by Horace Mann, Secretary of the Massachusetts State Board of Education, and introduced at the Massachusetts Normal Art School in 1873.

Engineer and member of the Edinburgh Aesthetic Club, James Nasmyth, writing in 1883, said: "Viewing the abstract forms of the various details of which every machine is composed, we shall find that they consist of certain combinations of six primitive or elementary geometrical figures, namely: the line, the plane, the circle, the cylinder, the cone and the sphere." This was not just a statement of fact and the practical problems of precision machining; it was also a statement of aesthetic intention. He was developing a visual grammar appropriate to the technology.

This pedagogical form of drawing became known as "conventional art" by the mid-19th century. The expected manner of execution was hard, clear, unshaded pencil work. The designer Christopher Dresser wrote in 1858 that drawing for decorative purposes should "coincide with the architect's plans of building a series of drawings . . . which shall convey a perfect knowledge of every part."

Dissent came from art critic John Ruskin who, also in 1858, spoke of the savagery of geometric drawing. His *The Elements of Drawing* in its promotion of tonal and impressionistic drawing was anti-linear and anti-geometric. Pedagogic drawing pointed towards an industrial future and the cult of the machine, so naturalistic drawing pointed towards the handcrafted past and the cult of the vernacular. Despite the protests of Ruskin, pedagogic drawing was adopted by schools of design almost universally. It was factual, positive and modern.

By the end of the 19th century, art was being considered as a spontaneous creative impulse, not a mode of research lending itself to codification. Paul Cézanne argued that "conception cannot precede execution since expressions can never be the translations of clear thought. Drawings and paintings are no longer different factors: as one paints, one draws. The more harmony there is in the colours, the more precise the drawing becomes." And in the world of the artist, drawing is increasingly seen as a discipline separate from but equal to painting, another branch of art.

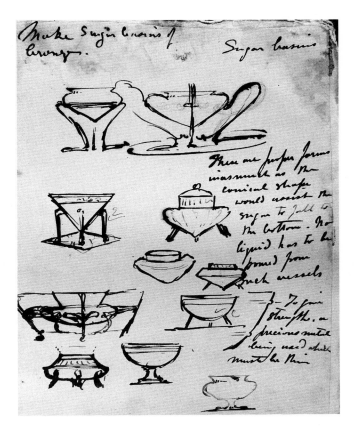

▲ A page from Christopher Dresser's sketchbook, showing designs for sugar basins. Although associated with the Arts and Crafts Movement, Dresser sought geometric forms from nature, anticipating the Bauhaus. The conical shapes shown here are considered "proper" because they "would assist the sugar to fall to the bottom." Horizontal ribs are added to gain strength when fabricating the vessels from thin precious metals.

Form follows drawing method

An attempt to teach art and design together – perhaps the last – was made in the Bauhaus at Weimar. This movement has many sources, which include the "education through art" teachings of the Italian doctor Maria Montessori, a re-examination of the methods of Froebel which were suppressed in 1851 and the German *Jungendstil*, which rejected academic standards, explored literary and musical analogies, and celebrated the vernacular. In its turn, the *Jungendstil* owes much to the work of Ruskin and William Morris.

The Bauhaus was preceded and influenced by the Deutsche Werkbund of 1903, a movement in which Lothar von Kunowski encouraged students to "reveal the essence rather the appearance of nature and materials in order to achieve true expression." Peter Behrens (1868–1940), trained as a painter, taught at Nuremberg before he was appointed "artistic adviser" to the electrical company AEG where he designed light fittings, posters and the world's first modernist building. He wrote in 1907 that "inner laws determine form in architecture, industrial design and craft." His students were encouraged to consider the intellectual principles of all form-creating work and "to attempt to discover and reconcile the laws of art with those of technique and material."

Another important influence on the Bauhaus was the Dutch De Stijl movement. The Theosophical Society, with which members of De Stijl were associated, taught that harmony could be established through a geometry of order and that a systematic approach to design could lead, through rationalization and standardization, to a total unity and harmony of formal expression.

In 1919, Walter Gropius issued the founding manifesto of the Bauhaus. He believed that art could not be taught, but that craftsmanship could, so it stated that six categories of craft training would be offered: sculpture, metalwork, cabinet making, painting and decorating, printing and weaving. Drawing was listed separately and would include landscape, still life, composition, freehand sketching from memory and imagination, and "design of furniture and practical articles."

Drawing was taught by Johannes Itten at Weimar, who encouraged self-expression among the students. He rejected "dead conventions" and also taught that the laws of form and colour could be interpreted and understood both intuitively and objectively. Before drawing a circle, students had to experience a circle eurhythmically by swinging their arms, first simply then together in the same and opposite directions. The three basic forms – the square, triangle and circle – were experienced through gesture, modelled in clay, and then represented graphically on a 2D plane. Students were made to absorb the qualities of materials by touching, handling and drawing from memory, and to create new textures by montage and collage. This would provide a sensuous appreciation of the quality of materials that would lead to an understanding on both an intellectual and emotional level of their potential for design purposes. Drawing in the early Bauhaus years, however, had little to do with designing.

In 1923, Laszlo Moholy-Nagy was instrumental in turning the crafts-based workshops into "laboratories for evolving new type-forms and norms for mass production." The concern, however, was with creating prototypes that would serve as guides to craftsmen and industry, rather than drawings. Wilhelm Wagenfeld's light-fitting, which looked as though it could be manufactured inexpensively by machine, was in fact a costly craft design described by Wagenfeld himself as a "crippled bloodless picture in glass and metal."

▶ The Bauhaus taught that the forms of products could be assembled from simple "primitive" geometrical shapes – the cone, the sphere, the cube and so on – as shown in this 1931 cover of the *Bauhaus* magazine by Herbert Bayer. Computer-aided solid modelling systems use the same principles today.

▶ Peter Behrens was "artistic adviser" to the German electrical company AEG and designed products, buildings and graphics for them. This brochure cover of 1908 is, strictly, a technical illustration, drawn after the fan was designed for the purpose of marketing.

The Designer's Drawing

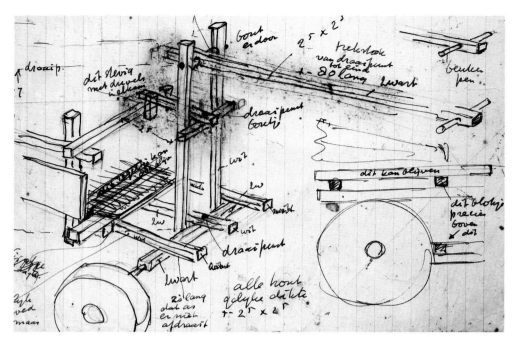

◄ Gerrit Rietveld's 1923 sketches for a baby wagon show a form developed from the same straight, machined lengths of wood used in his famous "Red/Blue Chair." The drawing uses isometric projection, with details in elevation; architectural drawings from the De Stijl movement were rendered mainly in axonometric.

By 1925 the Bauhaus had moved to Dessau, where analytical drawing was taught by the artist Wassily Kandinsky as "an education in looking, precise observation, and the precise representation not of the external appearance of an object, but of constructive elements, the laws that govern the forces (= tensions) that can be discovered in given objects, and of their logical construction. An education in clearly observing and clearly reproducing relationships, where 2D phenomena are an introductory step leading to the three-dimensional." In the Bauhaus, Kandinsky – and Paul Klee – continued to work as painters, their theory rather than their practice contributing to a theory of form.

The painter as a form-giver was fundamental to early 20th-century design theory. In De Stijl, abstract painting demonstrated the universal laws of form. The red and blue chair of Gerrit Rietveld showed that an object of beauty could be made from nothing but straight machined parts.

Gropius had hoped that the skill and vision of the painter could be directly applied to industrial production. But the activities of art and design proved too fundamentally different to mix successfully, as Georg Muche admitted in 1926 when he wrote: "The forms of industrial products, in contrast to the forms of art, are super-individual, in that they come about as a result of an objective investigation into a problem. Functional considerations, and those of technological, economic and organizational feasibility, become factors determining the forms of a concept of beauty that in this matter is unprecedented. The limits of technology are determined by reality, but art can only attain heights if it sets its aims in the realm of the ideal."

The subject of drawing in design has been given scant attention during the 20th century, its role relegated to a necessary but relatively unimportant component of the design process. Modernism and its fundamental tenet of "form ever follows function" (an aphorism attributed not to Le Corbusier nor Ludwig Mies van der Rohe, but to US architect Louis H. Sullivan) led to design being systematized through the 1960s, with an emphasis on word-game problem-solving skills. Drawing seemed just too intuitive and obvious to really help. Designers' drawings became invisible. They were there, but not made public.

Post-modernism, with its sometimes irreverent clash of art and design, again makes a show of the designer's drawing. Drawing is still little discussed in the manifestos of groups such as Memphis, the Milan-based architect-trained designers who were led by Ettore Sottsass Jnr (born 1917), but they are there to be seen, in glorious technicolour, among the product photographs in the group's catalogues and publicity material.

Sottsass, and fellow designers such as Michele de Lucchi and George J. Sowden, were allegedly inspired to set up Memphis in 1981 by a line in a Bob Dylan song entitled *Stuck inside of Mobile (with the Memphis blues again)*: "Your débutante just knows what you need, but I know what you want." Design is never the solution to a problem, says Sottsass, because no problem in the age of fashion and consumerism is a motionless event that can be isolated and grasped. Memphis designs endeavoured not to convince but to seduce, inventing functions and creating demands.

In a way, this echoes the stance made by the US "anti-Modernist" industrial designers of the 1940s, such as Harold van Doren and Walter Dorwin Teague, who, when faced with the difficulty of finding an "honest" or "natural" form for new consumer products like the vacuum cleaner, enclosed them in sleek, streamlined and visually simple shells, deliberately intended to appeal directly to the consumer and hence increase sales.

Sottsass and the other Memphis designers stripped away apparent usefulness – to the horror of the Modernist rearguard – and, with an ambivalent use of the aura of art, produced freestanding objects claimed to be empty of meaning. Of course, Memphis is old enough now to be seen as a style, and one that has already – as Sottsass predicted – gone out of fashion. Beauty, function and utility are not absolute metaphysical values according to Sottsass, but respond to a culture. His success at using design as a vehicle for direct (two-way) communication with the consumer, and improving the potential of design's semantic dynamics as well as updating its contents, has had repercussions throughout the design world and has helped increase the public's awareness of the role of the designer in shaping the world.

At the very least, the achievement of Memphis, and of the other Post-modernist groups, was to reintroduce colour, pattern and ornament into design. Design today is not only solving functional needs, but creating fun, excitement and anticipation. This is nowhere more evident than in the colourful and stylized drawings of the Memphis group and in the "lifestyle" drawings made to accompany the products of designers such as the Italian Aldo Rossi.

These designers have forsaken conventional means of representing three-dimensionality by using unexpected axonometric and oblique projections (which are also an indicator of their architectural training). They often prefer flat, cartoon-like colour to "realistic" rendering in order to stimulate an emotion in the potential user of the products, who has been taught to equate "design" with "good taste."

Elsewhere Sottsass asserts that design should be "a real-time activity." Only the act of drawing, as opposed to model-making or direct craft-like manufacture, can deliver the spontaneity to keep up with such a prolific and fertile creative mind. Sottsass, in his preface to Penny Sparke's 1982 monograph, laments about real life: "The daily grind, the anxiety, the confusion, the excuses of a headache or the radio that would not let you work in peace, the thousands of cards covered in sketches that seemed so brilliant because you never risked finishing them . . ." Despite this (ironic) melancholy, in the hands of designers such as Sottsass, Rossi and the New American designers, the future importance of the design drawing is assured.

► Nathalie Du Pasquier's designs for beds (1981-82) illustrate the Memphis method of drawing with metric projections, a predilection that betrays the architectural background of the designers. Mainstream product designers find the metric projections unnatural, preferring perspectives – a factor that added to the shock value of the Memphis sketches.

The process of design is based on the use of a variety of tools and media in the extensive simulation of design hypotheses. Your ability to use time effectively in visually manifesting your ideas to yourself and others is crucial to your professional operation

Philip Thiel, "Visual Awareness and Design," 1981

2 Tools and Materials

The tools of the trade are vitally important to some designers, who will almost superstitiously cling to a particular brand of pencil or marker, knowing it to come up with the (consistently predictable) goods; others may find a new type of medium exciting, stimulating and dangerous; the choice of medium is irrelevant to others, who put their skills as problem-solvers above mere questions of technique. Designers or not, most people will be familiar with the instruments of writing and drawing. They are effectively the same; they are both used for making marks and communicating ideas. And anyone fascinated by stationers' shops or graphics supply stores will be aware of the amazing variety of the products on sale there.

Each has its place in the designer's toolkit and the purpose of this chapter is to categorize these products, identifying them according to their most appropriate place in the design process. The next chapter is intended to help clarify and perhaps demystify the newer and sometimes more unfamiliar "tools and materials" that make up a computer-aided design system.

▶ Pencil elevation by Sergio Asti for his "Profiterolles" lamp of 1968. The orthogonal cross-hatching adds depth to the glass forms in an otherwise almost flat, Cubist composition.

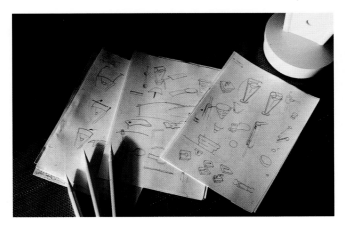

◄ Pages from the sketchbooks of Philip Davies at Moggridge Associates, London, show the development of concepts for his "Nile" low-voltage decorative lighting. He works in soft pencil and coloured pencils.

Pencils

The pencil is the original disposable drawing instrument, economical and efficient. Pencils are controllable and versatile – producing an infinite tonal range which is both permanent and adjustable – and black graphite ones, at least, are easy to erase. Before pencils were invented, thin rods of silver, zinc or lead were used for drawing. These are collectively known as silverpoint.

The term "lead pencil" is a complete misnomer – it contains no lead, and the word *pencillus*, meaning "little tail," refers to the brush used by the Romans to write on papyrus. When graphite (pure black carbon) was first discovered at Borrowdale in Cumbria back in 1564, it was mistakenly called plumbago – that which acts like lead – and the association has stuck ever since.

It is excusable to take the humble pencil for granted, but once it was worth its weight in gold. The Borrowdale mine was the only deposit ever found containing graphite of such purity. It was worked for only six weeks of the year, shipments to London were protected by armed guards, and until 1860 the English Guild of Pencilmakers held the world monopoly on the sale of the thin square sticks.

In the 17th century, the German carpenter Staedtler used sulphur and antimony to bind crushed graphite into usable sticks. Pencil "lead" today is composed of less pure graphite – mostly from Mexico – and Bavarian clay, fired like porcelain in a kiln. The process was devised in 1795 by a man called Conté, an officer in Napoleon's army, when war cut off supplies of the English and German products. And for the first time, pencils could be graded from hard to soft by varying the relative proportions of graphite and clay.

The firm of Faber was established near Nuremberg in 1761, and by 1840 was producing the familiar hexagonal pencil in its standard size and grades of hardness. A classification of the time had HH for engineers, H for architects, F for sketching and B for shading. Pencils were not made in the USA until the 1850s, when Alfred Berol founded the Eagle Pencil Company.

The more clay there is in a pencil lead, the harder it is. The midpoint for hardness (or degree) and the most general-purpose of pencils is HB, standing for hard and black. Softer and blacker pencils of degree B to 6B are favoured by artists and designers, for freehand sketching and rendering (2B is the degree most favoured for general-purpose work around the designer's studio).

On the other side of the scale, pencils of degree H to 9H are used mainly for technical and engineering drafting – the very hard ones being used by stonemasons and steel workers. Odd grades include F (for firm), between HB and H, used by shorthand writers, and the extremely soft EB and EE.

The traditional wooden pencil has the lead, which also now contains some wax for smoothness, bonded into a sandwich of mature Californian incense cedar slats. Despite there being 10 billion pencils produced each year, there is apparently no threat to the environment as the annual logging in the Pacific northwest does not exceed the growth rate.

A good quality pencil has a bonded lead, usually etched with acid, that will not shatter inside the wood if the pencil is dropped, nor slide out in use. The six-sided cross-section of one pencil design is an ingenious way of preventing the pencil from rolling off the drawing board.

Recent developments in pencil technology include Berol's Karisma Aquarelle and Rexel's Derwent Sketching; these are water-soluble graphite pencils in three grades – light (HB), medium (4B) and dark (8B) – for a line and wash effect, monochromatic equivalents of the Swiss-made Caran d'Ache "watercolour" pencils. It should be remembered, however, that water makes paper cockle and it should be stretched beforehand.

Polymer-based leads for drafting on translucent film or Mylar were first introduced in the 1960s by Faber-Castell. The clay binder of the traditional pencil is replaced by a combination of oil and a polymer resin. This produces a lead that is stronger, denser and harder-wearing than conventional lead; a solvent-based eraser is required, however, to correct any mistakes.

Coloured pencils are manufactured in a similar way, from a mixture of white kaolin, waxes, pigments and adhesive binders, but are not fired. The range of colours (most suppliers have 72) can include metallics, and both warm and cool greys. Some types, such as Berol's Verithin, are hard and thin; others, such as the Prismacolor line (called Karisma in the UK) are soft, flat and blendable, with the finish of dry gouache.

Other indispensable pencils include a non-reproduceable blue for "invisibly" marking artwork, and a greasy Chinagraph that will draw on anything, including glossy photographs.

Clutch pencils first appeared in the 1900s, using leads originally produced by Faber for use in compasses. These have spring-loaded jaws, activated by a push button that also houses the sharpener. The lead can be withdrawn into the barrel for protection when the pencil is not in action. In a recent article in the British journal *Design Week* on essential studio equipment, Glen Tutssel, creative director of London practice Michael Peters, said he would never flee from a flame-engulfed studio without his battered 15-year old Faber-Castell clutch pencil.

Push-button mechanical pencils from firms such as Pentel are now replacing the clutch pencil. These come with leads fine enough not to need sharpening, in different lead thicknesses (0.3 – 0.9mm) for consistent weights of line, and look sufficiently hi-tech. They are inexpensive and lightweight, and the round ones can be revolved between the fingers on long stretches of line to achieve an even finish. The removable button usually reveals an eraser and a cleaning wire. Top-of-the-line ones have auto-lead feed for non-stop drawing and adjustable lead protector sleeves. Designed for drafting, mechanical pencils are also useful for carrying around for sketching at briefing meetings.

◄ **Mechanical pencils, such as these from Pentel, require no sharpening and are available with leads of different thicknesses. The range shown here – from 0.5 to 0.9mm – covers the most popular sizes. Plastic lead (shown far left) can be used to give an ink-like weight to engineering drawings on polyester film.**

▲ **Karisma Colour/ Prismacolor pencils from Berol come in 72 colours including metallics and warm/cool greys. They are claimed to be both highly blendable and capable of producing a flat, gouache-like application.**

Pastels

Pastels are used for subtle shading and rendering rather than line drawing. Weakly bound pigment has been used to colour drawings from the 15th century, and was revived by the 19th-century Impressionist Edgar Degas. Soft pastel is used by designers as a quicker substitute for the blending effects best produced by airbrush. The medium is extremely fragile and vulnerable and the drawing needs to be protected with pva fixative as soon as it is completed. The act of fixing the pastels, however, can make the colours darker.

Soft pastels are made from powdered pigment bound in gum tragacanth or methyl cellulose, and usually contain a fungicide. There are over 550 shades, but for most purposes between 50 and 100 will suffice.

A boxed set is a beautiful object in its own right and should last for ever – but designers should ensure that the chosen brand sells single stick replacements for the commonly used colours. Unwrapped pastels with a square cross-section such as Faber-Castell's Polychromos range (72 shades) are more versatile than the round paper-wrapped types – they can be applied quickly using the long edge and do not roll off the drawing board.

Pastels can be used directly, or scraped into powder using a scalpel and applied with cotton wool. They can then be manipulated and blended using the finger or a proprietory rolled-paper stump (known to artists as a tortillon). An eraser can be used to create the effect of highlights. Pastel dust can also be dissolved in solvent and applied in broad "streaky" strokes like a marker.

Oil pastels are more flexible versions of crayons, being made from pigments, hydrocarbon waxes and fats. Heat melts them (hot hands make them harder to control), and white spirit can be used to dissolve them. Effects useful for backgrounds and textures can be achieved by combining oil pastels with water colour or acrylics.

Chalk and so-called conté crayons (in the "traditional" colours of sanguine, sepia and bistre, as well as black and white) used on mid-to-dark toned paper is also a time-honoured method of producing an effective "fully toned" image directly and economically. The white chalk creates highlights of great luminosity.

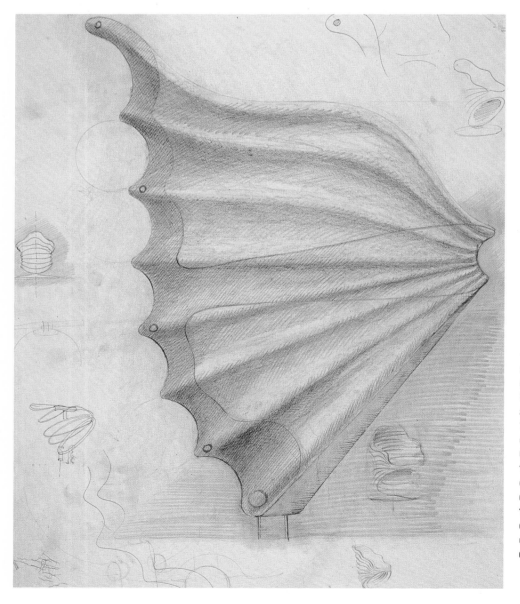

◀ Designers rarely use a single medium to render their drawings. The Italian designer Mario Bellini used ink, pastels and charcoal on paper for this 1970 drawing, with sketches, of his "Teneride" office chair. Charcoal, made in sticks from fired willow, is a fast, expressive and responsive drawing medium, favoured by fine artists for initial sketches or drawings, but usually considered too messy by most designers.

Pens

Pens make more permanent marks. And whilst a cult fountain pen such as a Lamy Safari, Parker Duofold or Mont Blanc Meisterstück Diplomat will be useful for signing autographs, contracts or cheques, fine-lined water-based fibretips from Edding or Nikko are more likely to be found around the designer's studio as general-purpose sketching pens.

A visit to a stationer or graphic arts supplier will unveil a bewildering selection of pens to choose from – and everyone has their own favourite type for writing with. There are ballpoints, rolling-ballpoints, felt-tips, brushtips and fibretips, and the ink they each use varies from water-soluble to indelible and permanent. Each has its place in the designer's studio.

The common ballpoint – invented in 1938 by Hungarian emigré Laszlo Biró, and popularized by Frenchman Marcel Bich – can be used to create crisp edges on presentation drawings. Daring designers like the thrill of not being able to erase ballpoint lines. The nitrogen-powered Fisher ballpoint, developed for NASA, will write at any angle, even pointing upwards, under water and at 50 degrees below freezing point. It has a shelf life of 100 years and will write for three miles before the ink runs out.

For freehand drawing it is difficult to find better than a dip pen tipped with a Gillott 303 or "lithographic" 1950 nib – with which the line width varies responsively according to hand pressure – using non-waterproof indian ink for its flow qualities.

Technical pens for stencilling or drafting consistent lines in indian ink on tracing paper or film have been in use since the 1930s, notably the conventionally nibbed Graphos. Before that, engineers used ruling pens looking like adjustable forceps, the blob of ink being kept in its place by a miracle meniscus of surface tension. The Rotring Rapidograph was introduced in 1952, a tubular fountain pen with a removable cylindrical nib regulated by a wire filament available in different widths from 0.1mm to 2mm. The aim of all developments since has been to ameliorate the big problems of blobbing and of the indian ink's drying and clogging the nib, and to obviate the irritating need to keep stopping and shaking the pen in order to keep the ink flowing evenly.

All manner of inventions have been tried, from damp and hermetically sealed caps, ultrasonic cleaners and standby humidifiers, to disposable capillary cartridges – and completely disposable pens, such as Letraset's Letratech. Pens are available with tungsten carbide (most makes), "synthetic jewel" (Faber-Castell's TG1-J) or ceramic (Pentel's Ceranomatic) tips – all proprietory solutions to the same problem of wear – for drawing on to matt drafting film. If lineboard is being used, it should be cleaned with lighter-fuel and tracing paper dusted with talcum powder to remove grease before a technical pen is used, to prevent smudged or broken lines. Technical pens are also useful for stippling and freehand hatching.

Computer-aided design systems and their output devices make even greater demands on the technical pen for high-speed precision and reliability. Companies such as Staedtler address this market with their Marsplot "system," which also includes plastic-tipped points (for drawing on to glossy film), pressurized ballpoint and rolling-ball cartridges.

Erasers

Of course in theory a good craftsperson never needs an eraser. But the person who never made a mistake never made anything – and an eraser can be a creative tool, too. The grubby rubber that was only good for smearing meticulously prepared artwork is now a thing of the past, thanks to modern-day plastic erasers. These can be cut and shaped to make a sharp clean edge. Putty or kneadable rubbers that can be moulded to a point are useful for picking out highlights on presentation drawings.

Inks and polymer-based pencils need their own solvent-based non-abrasive vinyl erasers which can be used in conjunction with a stainless steel erasing shield to restrict the eraser to the area where it is needed.

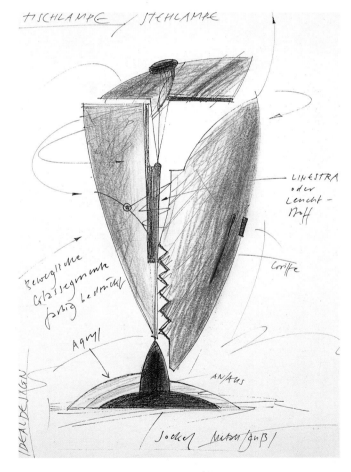

▲ The West German designer Peter Engelhardt made this expressive crayon drawing of a table lamp directly on a photocopy enlargement of a concept sketch. He uses the medium to convey more about "lifestyle" than a dry engineering drawing could ever do.

Markers

The stock in trade of the graffiti artist and the scourge of the subway manager, the ubiquitous marker has all but replaced the airbrush as the *de rigueur* medium for design presentations. The spirit-based felt-tipped markers are quick and convenient to use, although the result is often ephemeral – marker colours can be very fugitive and fade fast under the influence of ultraviolet light – and marker rendering, which is akin to watercolour painting as a technique, has been the subject of a proliferating number of books in recent years.

Since their introduction in the 1960s, markers have become available in a bewildering range of package shapes and sizes, point sizes from 0.1mm to 40mm, and with an ever increasing range of colours – Letraset's Pantone broad-nib range, for example, has 203 colours, including 11 warm and 11 cool greys. Acrylic fibre and polyester are now used in place of felt (so the term felt-tip pen no longer applies), with polyacetal for fine points. Healthier xylene-free inks are also being introduced – the smell of the old-style inks can be quite addictive.

There are markers with interchangeable points, refillable ones, and ones with replacement nibs (for example the Graphic Marker range), some that are double-ended, and others that can be adapted as an inexpensive airbrush device (Letraset's Letrajet). Neutral blender pens can be used to mix colours, effectively increasing the range of colours available, and increase the versatility of the medium.

The original marker is the Magic Marker, with its stumpy body (so that it stands upright) and chisel-edged nib. These spirit-based markers come in 130 colours, including nine cool greys tending towards blueish-black and nine warm greys to brownish-black. For those who prefer it, a limited selection of colours come in a Slim Grip version. Some within the range are linked to the Coates 50/50 colour system (which in turn conforms to the Colourtech Imaging System) – which, like Pantone, coordinates with other graphics products, such as papers and boards, and aids colour specification when working with printers, for example.

Chartpak's AD range is a market leader in the USA with a range of 200 colours. A xylene-free alcohol-based range called Spectrum is available with 140 colours. They have slim tapered barrels that can stand upright, and have a removable wedge tip, which can be replaced by a bullet point, a fine point or an arrow-head brush tip.

Other suppliers include Mecanorma with their aluminium-bodied Art Marker range of 116 colours (the company also markets metallic markers and a valve-based opaque gouache range); Edding's Grafik Art – the 606 Twin Point has a chisel at one end and an ultra-fine point at the other (and is marketed as a less messy alternative to changing the nibs); Schwan-Stabilo's water-based Stabilayout range, shaped like

Paint and ink

the highlighters; Staedtler's Marsgraphic 3000 series with the flexible brush tip (and its straight-edge adaptor); and the Benday markers, which come in different strengths of the four process colours, to generate an almost endless number of colours for a relatively small outlay. Most other graphics suppliers sell ranges of markers, but their limited selections of colours make them of little interest to designers.

Designers will have their own preferences, in terms of marker shape, and may supplement one range with the colours from another.

Before the advent of markers, designers coloured their drawings using washes of watercolour (aquarelle), the more opaque gouache (body colour), or a combination of both. These traditional media have been joined lately by acrylic and pva-based paints which can be used thick or thin and hence have the characteristics of both watercolour and gouache (and of impasto oil paint, for that matter – a technique which is not often used by designers). They have strong adhesion to all kinds of surface and are waterproof when dry.

Gouache and specialist paints such as process white are still used by designers for adding highlights to marker drawings, and for brushing-in fine details and lettering. It is still considered good advice to buy the finest quality sable brushes (a good selection comprises sizes 00, 1 and 3) and to look after them – they should be washed and rinsed straight after use and stored with the points upwards.

Drawing inks come in beautiful bottles, but usually contain shellac for water-resistance when dry, so brushes should always be cleaned with methylated spirit or proprietory solvent. Rotring's ArtistColor is a lightfast, finely pigmented transparent colour, waterproof when dry, that can be applied by airbrush and technical pens, as well as steel nibs and brushes – even a palette knife when mixed with acrylic binding paste. It is said to stick to any grease-free surface, including paper, board, plastic or glass, and 340 colours can be mixed and repeated from 12 basic bottles.

◀ **Steve Mattin of the Mercedes Benz automotive company uses markers boldly and expressively to convey a real sense of motion in these concepts of 1988.**

▼ **Presentation drawings and models are often used together to communicate design ideas to a client. This designer at Brand New, a London-based consultancy, has used a limited number of Pantone markers to illustrate the colour scheme and detailing on the "Keeler Pulsair Tonometer" (a device for detecting glaucoma), while the full-size model gives a feel for the overall shape.**

Airbrush

There is evidence that 3,500 years ago, Aurignacians used air painting – blowing pigments through the hollow leg-bone of a deer – to decorate their caves. The airbrush as used by designers and illustrators today was invented in 1893 by Charles Burdick as a quick and efficient way of applying paint to a surface. It was taken up first mainly by photographic retouchers and championed by Herbert Bayer at the Bauhaus (where it was used to produce the geometric shapes on the famous 1928 Bauhaus journal cover illustration, for example) who was attracted by its combination of art and technology.

Airbrush is used mostly in technical illustration because of its capacity to make soft gradations of tone which subtly model 3D form and give a smoother finish than ordinary brushwork. Its mechanical "untouched by human hand" finish is also ideal for the technological nature of many subjects.

The airbrush has no peer for generating slick, seamless, technical illustrations, but as a technique it is labour-intensive in the extreme. Designers, dogged by tight deadlines and ever-shortening leadtimes, shrug and wish they had more time to produce the highly rendered visuals that only an airbrush is capable of achieving.

The main drawback is that the instrument must be cleaned thoroughly every time the colour is changed, and there is a great deal of methodical structuring of the execution needed before all the stencils and masks are cut. Most designers will use an airbrush at some time or other, however, even if they do not use it exclusively – to put reflections or extra shine on a marker drawing of a car body, for example, or for spraying models to make them look more "solid."

The basic principle underlying the operation of an airbrush is that when a stream of gas, for example compressed air, is forced through a narrow orifice, its pressure drops. If a tube feeding from a reservoir of liquid, for example paint, is positioned where the gas flow is at its fastest, then the pressure drop will cause the liquid to be drawn into the stream of gas and atomized into a uniform fine spray.

The cheaper airbrushes used by modelmakers work by external atomization, with the gas blown across the liquid feed at the very tip of the airbrush. This results in an incomplete mix and a less than perfect spray. Most professional airbrushes intended for design applications use internal atomization to mix the liquid and gas under more controlled conditions. The quantity of paint, ink or dye mixing with the gas is controlled by the position of a tapered needle which fits snugly into the nozzle through which the spray emerges.

There are three basic types of airbrush: the single-action, the fixed double-action, and the independent double-action.

The single-action airbrush has a control button which is pressed to allow gas to flow. The ratio of paint to gas cannot be controlled, nor can the spray pattern. All the designer can do is to move the airbrush closer or further from the paper. Some simple airbrushes have a control ring, by means of which the ratio of paint to gas can be preset. The Badger 200 is an example of a single-action airbrush.

A fixed double-action airbrush, such as the Conopois F, has a lever that controls the flow of both the paint and the gas but not the ratio of one to the other. The first fraction of travel opens the gas valve, the rest retracts the needle allowing paint to flow into the gas stream. Thus a designer can begin spraying gradually and finish off by reducing the paint flow to nothing.

An independent double-action airbrush, such as the Badger 100LG, the DeVilbiss Super 63, the Thayer and Chandler A or the Olympos SP-B, gives the designer the greatest amount of control. The lever is pressed down for the gas flow; pulled back to vary the paint supply. Thus a designer is able to spray pure air at full speed and then feed in the paint in small controllable quantities, to achieve delicate effects. This type of airbrush is easier to keep clean, as an occasional blast of air can be used to clear any obstructions in the nozzle. Some models are fitted with a cam ring or screw that fixes the lever at some desirable point to maintain the paint-to-gas ratio without tiring the finger.

The Paasche Turbo uses an unconventional technology which is said to give the designer an even greater degree of control. It can also be used as an air eraser to "sandblast" away areas of colour using a stream of abrasive particles.

The paint feed also varies from model to model. To cover large areas it is best to use a suction feed connected to a jar underneath the airbrush. Most designers will use a gravity feed – from a bowl, cup or recess on the top of the airbrush. This takes a smaller quantity of paint, which has to be topped up now and again, but this arrangement makes the airbrush lighter and more manoeuvrable. Proprietory liquid inks and watercolours for airbrushes come in bottles with droppers in their caps for filling the cup or recess.

The gas supply can be from cans of butane or freon gas, from carbon dioxide cylinders (as used for beer pumps), or from air compressors. Most compressors are powered by electric motor. Diaphragm types, in which the air is sucked in and then sent to the airbrush via a flap valve, are the cheapest but are prone to pulsing. More sophisticated models have a storage tank which acts as a reservoir to smooth out the fluctuations in pressure.

The most expensive types are the automatic piston-type compressors that cut out when the pressure in the reservoir reaches a preset value and cut in again as the pressure drops. Designers have been known to use car tyres coupled to a regulator to delay the fall-off in pressure.

The media used in airbrushes should be bleedproof, quick drying and finely ground. Watercolour should be diluted with distilled water; gouache and acrylics should be the consistency of milk. Some inks can leave deposits inside the airbrush which are difficult to clean; and if acrylics are left to dry inside the airbrush, special solvents will have to be used to remove the water-resistant plastic coating. Some pigments, such as cadmium yellow, are toxic when the vaporized paint is inhaled. If using these substances, a face mask and goggles should be worn. In any case, an airbrush should always be used near an extractor fan.

The technique of airbrushing revolves around the application and arrangement of stencils and masks to shield the areas of the drawing that the designer is not currently concerned with. The simplest form of mask is a ruler or french curve. Loose masks of paper or clear acetate film cut into shapes used with weights or coins give a slightly blurred edge, which may be desirable under certain circumstances. Softer blurs can be achieved using cotton wool. Liquid masks, using a rubber compound which is painted on and peeled off when the paint is dry, can pull away the paint.

Most designers use a combination of masking film and tape. Low-tack self-adhesive film, such as Frisk film, is cut in position on the drawing using a scalpel. The two sets of masks thus produced (one a negative of the other) are thus guaranteed to fit together exactly. For large areas it can be more economical to mask most of the area with plain paper, reserving the film for the critical edges. Masking tape is used for straight edges and smooth sweeping curves.

The so-called computer airbrush, as found on a 2D "paint" system such as Quantel's Paintbox, never has trouble matching colours for retouching, however, and can do things that a conventional airbrush artist would find impossible to do mechanically – make cut-and-paste stencils with a soft vignetted edge, for example.

For spatter effects, an inexpensive and disposable alternative is an old toothbrush, dipped in paint and flicked with the back of a ruler. For more predictable results, a "spray-marker" such as the Letrajet blows air across the point of an ordinary fineline marker. For finer sprays, another recent development is the electrostatic Spraypen which has the advantages of no external air source, compatibility with marker colours, and no cleaning necessary.

◄ **The Aztek airbrush rendered, in airbrush, by Ray Mumford. Designers with tight lead-times cannot often afford to use this hyper-realistic technique during the presentation phase of the design process. It is associated more with technical illustration, done later to aid in the marketing of the product (see chapter 8).**

► **Airbrush is ideally suited for rendering the smooth, shiny lines of highly polished automobile bodies. This example comes from the Italian Bertone automotive design studio.**

Drawing instruments

Most designers will be familiar with the traditional geometry set of compasses (for drawing arcs and circles), dividers (for marking off distances and comparing measurements), rulers, protractors and set squares. In the past, fascinating devices were invented for generating ellipses and variable curves, for enlarging and reducing, and for aiding the production of perspectives – all collectors' items now and commanding high prices at auction. Designers now make do with sets of templates for ellipses, and french curves for more complex shapes – or will rely on drawing freehand "by hand and eye." Computer-generated curves, however, are more accurate and controllable.

Conventional drawing boards now include built-in straight edges with parallel motion, and combination protractor/set square devices (called drafting machines) with convenient clickstops at the most commonly used angles: 15, 30, 60 and 90 degrees, for example.

Papers and boards

Paper is a gloriously organic product, just natural plant fibres (and perhaps some unnatural ones) held together by their own molecular forces. The surface texture and absorbency of the paper are a function of the amount of filler, usually clay, added and the degree of pressing through rollers. HP (hot pressed) is the smoothest and best for line work. Rough and the so-called Not (meaning not hot pressed, i.e. cold pressed) are more suited to watercolour painting.

Paper that is to take watercolour or gouache should be stretched first by immersing it in water and attaching it to a slightly absorbent surface like an unprimed wooden drawing board using gummed paper tape.

Most designers find it easier to use ready-made card-board-backed paper which does not cockle. Traditional boards, such as Bristol board, have been superseded by the lighter-weight polystyrene foam-based boards, for example Fome-Cor which is available in three different thicknesses: 3mm, 5mm and 10mm.

The weight of paper is measured in gsm (grams per square metre) although some paper is still graded in pounds weight per ream (500 sheets of the specified size): layout paper is graded at around 50 – 70 gsm; cartridge paper for sketching at 96 – 150 gsm; watercolour paper at 285 – 535 gsm. The sizes of paper have been standardized and the quaintly named octavo, foolscap, imperial and double-elephant sizes replaced by the DIN standards A0, A1, A2 and so on, each having half the area of the preceding size. Designers will mostly encounter A4 (210×297mm) for sketching and the larger A1 and A0 for production drawings.

Layout paper is used a great deal by designers at the concept stage. This comes in metric A-size pads and its translucency helps in developing successive designs from embryonic ones. This quality of layout paper also allows underlay drawings to be used when building up perspectives. Bleed-resistant and bleedproof layout pads are also available.

Coloured cover paper, sugar paper, black art paper or Ingres (with ingrained fibres of contrasting colours) can be used with pastels for presentation-quality drawings. Only the most expensive papers are pigmented at the pulp stage with lightfast pigments; most use dyes that eventually fade.

Letraset sell Pantone coloured papers with a graduated tone across the sheet. These are useful for quick backgrounds that look airbrushed. They come in 24 colours with two different degrees of graduation: either a "slow curve," from 100 per cent to 5 per cent, or a "fast/medium curve," from 100 per cent to 5 per cent and back to 100 per cent.

Other equipment

The **drawing board** has become synonymous with the iterative nature of the design process. The plain rectangular drawing board with tee-square has been around since the 1700s, though the forerunner of today's model was introduced by the elder Brunel and developed by Stanley in about 1870. Even in practices with cad, drawing boards are still seen – they are good places at which to sit and think, and are ideal for spreading around lots of scraps of paper. The latest development of the cad vendors is the electronic drawing board, a large-format screen that can double as a digitizer to input dimensions to the cad system.

A surgical **scalpel** and a heavier duty **craft knife** are useful for cutting masks, paper and board. And to stick things back together and for mounting paper on to board, **rubber solution**, such as Cow gum, can be spread thinly with an applicator or spatula. Surplus gum can be removed cleanly when dry using a home-made "rubber" of dried-up gum. Some designers prefer **aerosol adhesive**, such as Scotch Spray Mount, for wrinkle-free mounting. Adequate ventilation is essential before using spray glue, and more makes are now using CFC-free propellants, labelled as being "ozone-friendly." Many graphics designers now use **hot wax coaters**, such as Letraset's Waxcoater, for sticking paper to board – they also keep the studio warm in the winter!

Other essential accessories include an electric pencil sharpener, low-tack masking tape and matt frosted "magic" tape for mending, a large soft brush for removing debris from the work in progress, talcum powder for de-greasing and "lubricating" surfaces, a cutting mat with a "self-healing" surface and lighter-fuel to stop it getting sticky, plus rolls and rolls of soft toilet tissue or kitchen roll to mop up accidents and generally keep things clean and tidy.

▶ Standardized paper and board sizes are based on a sheet, A0, which is nominally one square metre in area, with sides in the ratio 1:√2. Each successive smaller size has half the area, with the longer side equal to the shorter side of the bigger size – the longer side of A4, for example, is equal to the shorter side of A3.

◀ This designer at BIB, London, is using ellipse templates to develop drawings of a central heating thermostat for Trane. Later it will be rendered, using Magic Markers (see pages 140-43).

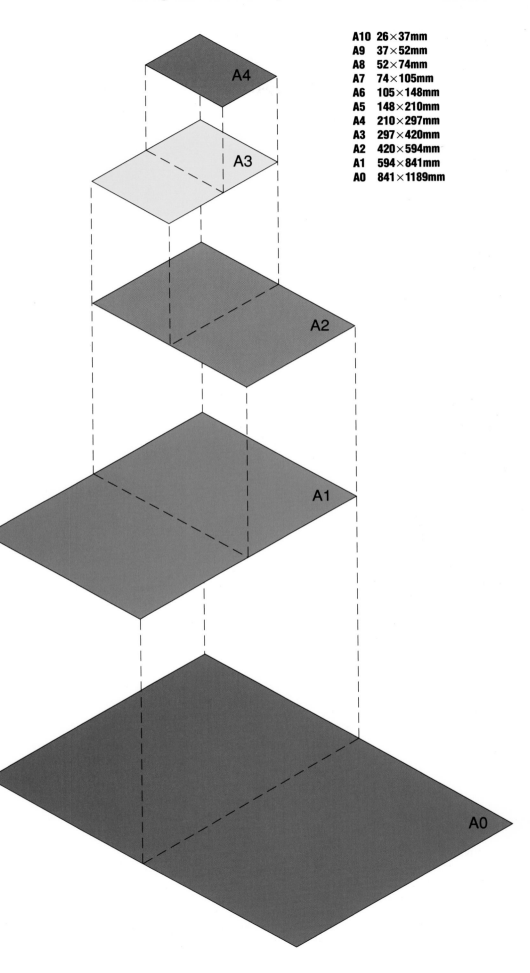

A10 26×37mm
A9   37×52mm
A8   52×74mm
A7   74×105mm
A6   105×148mm
A5   148×210mm
A4   210×297mm
A3   297×420mm
A2   420×594mm
A1   594×841mm
A0   841×1189mm

► **Drawing rendered in coloured pencil, made to assist at the modelmaking stage.**

► **"Varius" chairs for Casas, Spain, designed by Oscar Tusquets Blanca. The range was launched in 1984 and has been enormously successful.**

Case study: **Oscar Tusquets Blanca, Barcelona**

A designer with an architectural background, Oscar Tusquets Blanca is in the Italian tradition. But, ironically, according to Alessandro Mendini of *Domus* magazine, he became one of the eleven best-known architects in the world for making a tea set. The tea set in question was the Juego de Té Orando designed between 1980 and 1983 for Alessi as part of the Tea Coffee Piazza, which also introduced architects Aldo Rossi, Richard Sapper, Michael Graves and Robert Venturi as designers of tableware. But as with Alvar Aalto, Oscar Tusquets Blanca's objects are not merely scaled-down versions of his buildings.

Another similarity with the Italian tradition lies in Oscar Tusquets Blanca's close cooperation with the manufacturers of products and with their technicians. It is very rare for a Spanish or Italian designer to produce working drawings from their designs. Concept sketches serve only to convince the designer himself and his assistants within the studio that a design proposal is possible. Discussions with those responsible for manufacture are made face to face, and designs may be modified many times before the shape and form of the product is finalized. "There are two types of technician," says Oscar Tusquets Blanca. "Those who only see difficulties; and the usually older craftsmen who say, 'This may seem impossible but if I make it *this* way, perhaps it is possible.' If a designer does not propose silly things, the technician will respect him. It is not possible to improvise in design". This process is obviously time-consuming – and expensive – and relies on a very personal level of collaboration between designer and craftsman. Oscar Tusquets Blanca is an insistent supervisor, however. "If the design is a failure, it is completely my fault."

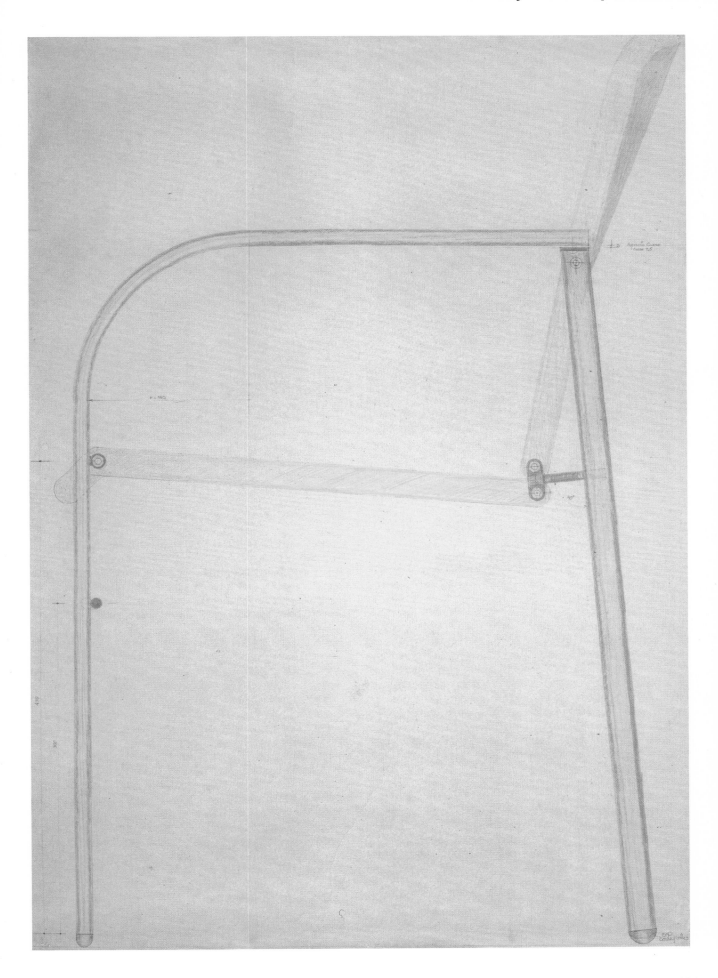

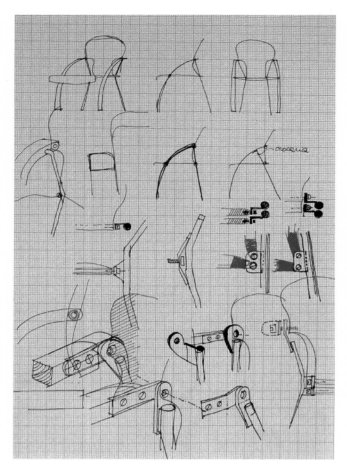

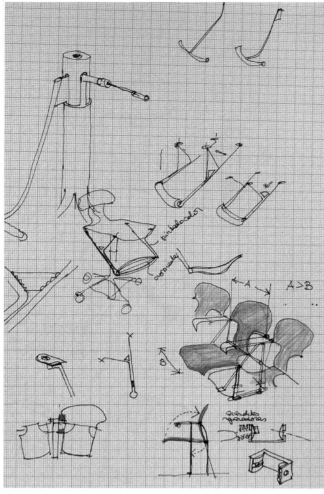

He works at present with just four or five factories, owned by personal friends, whose technicians "are clever and full of suggestions, rather than coercive." A disagreement with the furniture manufacturers, Knoll International, was over the suggestion that he submit three separate design solutions for a chair. "It is so difficult to arrive at one solution," he says, "that it would be impossible to come up with three."

It goes without saying that it is unheard of for Oscar Tusquets Blanca to generate slick presentation drawings for the scrutiny and approval of clients. "Design is like film making: there has to be a good working relationship between the producer, director (designer) and all the technicians. Like cinema, design is an expensive art – one mistake and you lose a lot of money." To illustrate the point he cites Vico Magistretti's career: "His best period was when Cesare Cassina was alive. In the history of Italian design, suppliers like Cassina and Alessi rank with the designers Sottsass and Castiglioni."

Oscar Tusquets Blanca was born in Barcelona and studied at the Escuela Técnica Superior de Arquitectura. After working in the studio of Federico Correa and Alfonso Milà, he set up Studio PER with other graduates from his year at college: Pep Bonet, Cristian Cirici and, his collaborator on many projects, Lluís Clotet. His group also created a small manufacturing company, BD Ediciones de diseño, when nobody in Spain was interested in producing their ideas. He still works with Studio PER, which has a new partner, Carlos Diaz, but now has his own design studio with a young Austrian designer from Linz and a modelmaker and draftsman from Spain.

▲ **Two of Tusquets Blanca's finely worked pages of concept sketches, made on A4 millimetred paper, so that measurements could easily be taken off. Using soft Derwent pencil (B or 3B) or a Rotring 0.2mm technical pen, he covered almost 100 pages with these detailed concepts, occasionally rendering with Prismacolor pencils.**

Oscar Tusquets Blanca traces his career from architecture to interior design, then to furniture and to industrial design. He has yet to design a high-tech product ("Spain has no electronics industry, but if Giorgio Armani can design a telephone then so can I!"), but has diversified recently by designing porcelain for the restaurant he owns with his wife Victoria Roqué, and a set of three or four golf putters for Felipe Artola. He still spends 50 per cent of his time designing buildings: "I do not like to be too specialized. It is stimulating to be designing a 30,000 square metre building at a scale of 1:1000 at the same time as a putter at 1:1." Oscar Tusquets Blanca also paints, but that to him is a deliciously solitary activity.

His first venture into product design was an expandable TV trolley, designed originally for his parents' new house. Carrito Versátil encompassed a general solution, the rights were bought by the Italian company Zanotta in 1985, and it has been a bestseller ever since. Oscar Tusquets Blanca is perhaps best known for his chairs, however: the Gaulino (the name is a hybrid of its two inspirers, Gaudi and Mollino) for Carlos Jané, and the Varius range (described by Magistretti as "Gaudiesque and not too serious") for Casas.

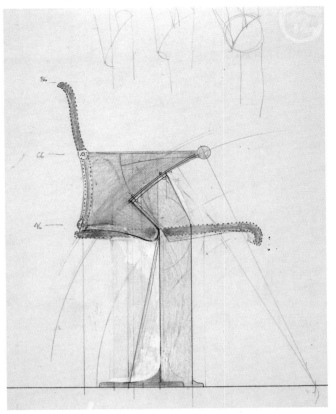

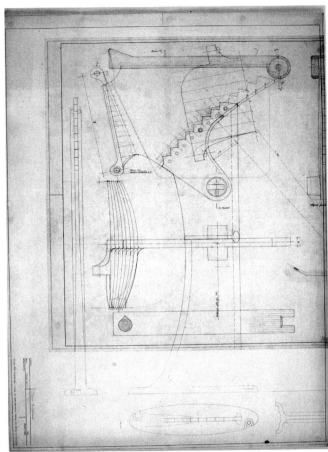

Since the Alessi tea set, Spain has entered the European Community, and the industry around Barcelona and Valencia has begun to change. As import tariffs are dropped, it is no longer cost-effective for manufacturers merely to copy Italian and Swedish designs – Spanish consumers can now afford the real thing. So the Spanish suppliers are actively looking for new designers to make their wares competitive.

The Varius chairs changed Casas; now, with local support, Oscar Tusquets Blanca can try inventions he would not have the courage to try with Italian producers. The range was begun in 1984 and comprises seven different chairs. The latest was designed for the refurbishment of Domènech i Montaner's 1903 Palau de le Música in Barcelona, which Oscar Tusquets Blanca has spent six years enlarging, restoring and air-conditioning. It is described as an auditorium chair and much study has been applied to the acoustical problems – "a good chair for a cinema is a bad chair for a conference hall." Some 60 to 70 sheets of his finely worked concept sketches were exhibited at the launch of the Varius range in Madrid and Belgium. Further drawings at full size were made for the modelmaking.

His studio uses balsa and papier maché for modelmaking. For the Alessi tea set he had a wooden model made professionally, because of his distance from Italy, but still no production drawings. Gaulino, he says, would have been difficult to design for an Italian manufacturer, as there were far too many corrections; it took two days, for example, to change the feet.

Choosing an appropriate supplier is also an important component of a successful end product. His Sofanco park bench, inspired by the American television programme, *The Flintstones*, was described as being indestructible and vandalproof (but cold to sit on in winter); it was made from artificial stone and weighs 600 kg. It was produced by the Catalan firm Escofet who saw no problems in handling such a heavy product. The same company produces Oscar Tusquets Blanca's Valla Rampante enclosing wall units.

Oscar Tusquets Blanca's drawings are small and personal explorations of design ideas and inventions. They may be used to communicate intentions around his studio or, in the case of the Alessi tea set, be used in "letters" to distant producers enquiring whether this or that detail is possible. He has no need of presentation drawings, as used by practices in the UK and USA; and all working drawings are by tradition executed by the suppliers' technicians who collaborate closely with the designer. Despite being a painter, he has never been tempted to produce artworks of his products to help in their marketing.

Vico Magistretti has said, "A good design can be transmitted by telephone. It doesn't need drawings." Oscar Tusquets Blanca does not hold such extreme views, but does believe that good design is simple and derives from close collaboration with craftsmen. The most important thing is the idea – and that could be on the back of an envelope or a restaurant napkin.

We're using computers today just like we use a pencil. We're just making marks and looking at marks. Most of the content is just paper content, even with the fancy windows and other kinds of embellishments

Alan Kay, "Personal Computer World," December, 1987

3 Drawing with Computers – Cad

Of course, none of the tools and materials described in the last chapter will be needed if a cad (computer-aided design) system is opted for – or at least that is what the systems suppliers' literature would have potential users believe. There are some architects who say they have completely dispensed with drawing boards, drawing pins and set squares; but relatively few product designers are using cad exclusively yet, for reasons that will become apparent later.

Cad systems, unlike their manual counterparts, have two main components, each equally important: hardware and software. This chapter will deal with the stuff you can see and feel – the hardware. Software, the unseen factor of a system which supplements the brainpower and experience of the designer and makes the hardware come alive, will be addressed as it is encountered in the chapters that follow.

First some basic definitions and a warning – the language of cad is riddled with arcane jargon. The word "system," for example, is used quite a lot in computing. It does not have any great mystical significance nor can it really be exactly quantified or qualified. It is a catch-all term, like "unit," "centre" or "module." It usually means the whole thing together, although a piece of software on its own can be referred to as a program (always spelt the American way), a package or – again – a *system*. The adjective "powerful" is a word to be suspicious about, too. If a vendor says the system or the processor or the software he wants to sell to you is powerful, ask for the word to be quantified: powerful compared with what?

▼ A photoplotter in the setting of a marble hall: the entire image was modelled, rendered, lit and textured using Intergraph ray tracing software.

Drawing with Computers – Cad

No trade or profession is without its jargon; practitioners will forget they are even using it, until they are abruptly asked to explain themselves to someone from another world of endeavour. Jargon can be offputting to the uninitiated and can be responsible for perpetuating ignorance. People in the pseudo-sciences who borrow terms originally with strict definitions and bend them to suit their own purposes and to add an air of respectability to their often obscure and partially thought-out ideas are the real culprits. Jargon can be wonderfully expressive and succinct. The term "frame grabbing," for example, is evocative and explains itself exactly. A textbook description could take a page of dry words and still leave most readers bewildered. Jargon is unintelligible only when it is misused.

Computing, because it is having to make sense of technology and concepts unfamiliar to most people over the age of 14, has spawned a whole language of its own. It is becoming more comfortable as words cross over into day-to-day speech, but it is generally impossible to talk about computers without using some jargon. The aim of this chapter is to demystify some of the terminology used by the computer trade. Designers need to be equipped with the language skills necessary to explain to the computer suppliers exactly what their requirements are, without being "blinded by science" in return.

Textbooks on computing usually start off by devolving a system into its component parts and classifying them into things like cpus (central processing units), memory and i/o (input/output) devices – rather like teaching music by first defining scales, crotchets and quavers. A cpu is defined as being "a device that manipulates data for you plus a means to enter variable data and a means to extract answers." All very well, but that is a little abstract, and it doesn't take the learner very far.

Most designers will know a computer from the name it has on the front: IBM PC or Apple Macintosh if it is a microcomputer, Apollo or Sun if it is a standalone so-called "engineering workstation," or DEC Vax or Prime if it is a shared-resource supermini. More about the important differences between these later.

A turnkey system is what most designers are likely to use when they first encounter cad – this is a packaged and integrated assembly of all the hardware, software and support needed to get going. You turn the theoretical key and off you go. Turnkey suppliers buy in kit from third parties and re-package or "badge engineer" the components, perhaps adding some proprietory go-faster boards as well as their own software, before passing on the thoroughly tested value-added *system* to the end user.

Turnkey suppliers have been around since the late 1960s, and include names like Computervision, Intergraph and McDonnell-Douglas. Since the fashion these days is for "open systems architecture" – with different makes of system being capable of communicating and sharing data – these companies are making a positive selling point of using only "industry standard" (i.e. well known) suppliers of hardware, and playing down the proprietory aspects of their systems.

There has also been a move in recent years for turnkey vendors to "unbundle" their software to make it available on a choice of hardware "platforms." Ask a consultant how to go about choosing the right system for your particular needs and he will usually say: select the software for the application first, *then* and only then the hardware. Until now, that option has not always been available to a prospective cad user.

As well as general-purpose turnkeys, there are also some that are dedicated to particular applications or tasks. These are found in the peripheral areas of design but the product designer may come across them, and their idiosyncrasies, when having to cooperate, say, with a graphics designer on a project.

"Paint" systems, such as Quantel's Paintbox, use a TV camera to "grab" drawings or other images from paper or frames direct from video, and re-colour or cut-and-paste them into electronic collages. Highly precise "vector" systems such as the Dutch-designed Aesthedes can output precise colour separations for print and packaging applications.

Since the earliest days of cad, software writers have been waiting around for hardware fast, powerful and cheap enough to realize their dream systems. In the past couple of years, however, this has become a tortoise and hare scenario, as hardware makers have taken on the pacemaking, putting applications like solid modelling and ray tracing that previously could only be tackled by huge expensive supercomputers on to the designer's desktop, and are now challenging the surprised program developers to catch up.

The engineering workstation was first introduced by new companies Apollo and Sun in the early 1980s – it was a hint of things to come. Workstations are a familiar enough sight these days and have done much to usurp the traditional-style configuration of several "dumb" terminals sharing a central minicomputer that once dominated the drawing office. The major suppliers of workstations are forever leapfrogging each other with cheaper and faster products, and it would be pointless to quote a typical specification here. Most vendors have followed IBM and for speed have opted for RISC (reduced instruction set computer) architecture for their processor chips. Sun's version is called SPARC (for "scalable processor architecture"). Raw speed in computer terms is measured in MIPS (million instructions per second): a DEC Vax 11/780 is rated at 1 MIPS; a Sun 3 at 10 MIPS; a "personal supercomputer" like Ardent's Titan runs at 64 MIPS; a top-end supercomputer Cray YMP at 928 MIPS. This is *pure* speed, like the top figure on an automobile's speedometer and, as such, is an abstract quantity; how quickly a designer actually completes a given job is dependent both on the efficacy of the software and the proficiency of the operator. One last word on terminology: PC vendors like Compaq are now calling their products personal workstations; workstation vendors are preferring the term "single-user supercomputer."

Engineering workstation, "smart" terminal or turbo-charged PC, the message for the cad user is "ever more for even less." As the hardware suppliers make available more MIPS for the money, the old truism that you get what you pay for (i.e. they'll charge as much as they think the market will stand) just does not ring true anymore. In a users' market, designers should expect cheaper systems that are more responsive, more reliable and easier to operate.

► A personal computer-based cad system from display vendor Westward: this model, 4420, has a resolution of 1280 × 1024 pixels, much higher than most. A joystick for drawing and multiple windows on the screen displaying both graphics and text are useful features.

► A workstation-based cad system: the hardware is by Apollo (with the processor under the desk), and the surface design software shown on the screen is Deltacam's Duct. Workstations can be used alone or networked with other workstations so that data and resources — plotters, disc drives and so on — can be shared.

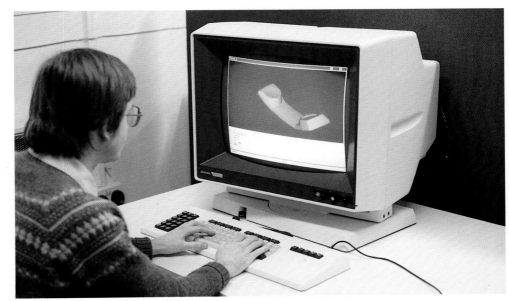

► The Interact from Intergraph has two screens so that a model can be viewed in its entirety on one, while details are worked on using the other. Although it has some inbuilt intelligence for manipulating the image on-screen, this "workstation" has to be connected to a host computer, usually a Vax supermini, which handles the majority of the processing. The whole worksurface acts as a digitizing tablet (notice the puck and the menu), while commands can also be made using the function buttons on the keyboard.

The processor

Of course, the computer can be treated as a black box with trust in a higher authority that it will always do what it is supposed to do – in much the same way that a car will always start first time on a cold wet morning. But curious designers will want to know what goes on inside, or at least have an inkling of what all the parameters that specify a given system mean.

A computer is a cocktail of solid-state physics, micro-electronics technology, mathematical concepts alien to anyone born before 1975 and software engineering. Their strong points are speed (millions of operations per second) and programmability – the same box of tricks can balance your accounts, rotate 3D images on a colour screen, or control the tunes on a chiming doorbell.

The brain of a computer is the cpu (central processing unit) or processor. This can be a single silicon chip (silicon is refined sand, not silicone, which is for furniture polish), a chipset, a pcb (printed circuit board) full of chips, or several boards (or cards) connected together.

Computers nowadays have lots of brains working together, each dedicated to a specific task: input/output, communications with other cpus over a network, controlling the image on the screen, and so on. Some vendors buy-in processor chips from companies such as Motorola (their chips are numbered in a series beginning with 68000, then 68020, and so on) and Intel (series 80286, 80386, and so on), with "second source" suppliers in the Far East; some manufacture their own. Other vendors buy-in complete computers and "badge engineer" them – integrating them with other components, adding software and selling them on to the end user.

There are many levels of software inside the computer, apart from the applications software, that are invisible to the user. At the lowest level, you need a program to load (or boot, as in "pull yourself up by the bootstraps") all the other programs. This and other utilities reside on a rom (read-only memory) chip ever available to the cpu.

The system software is the next level. The operating system looks after the housekeeping, particularly the operation of the disc memory, and is peculiar to the make of computer: PCs use MS/DOS, while workstations mostly standardize on the more sophisticated Unix which comes in several versions. The top level is the applications software. This converts the general-purpose computer into the kind of system the user wants: for a designer this will be draw or paint software. On PCs, this arrives on floppy discs with an enormous manual, and unless you have a supplementary hard disc unit where these discs can reside permanently, they have to be loaded each time you sit down to use the system.

Software is written in a programming language. The computer's own language is called machine code, which is incomprehensible to all but the most hardened hacker. One step up is assembler, which substitutes mnemonics, one for one, for the hexadecimal numbers the computer prefers. Easiest to use are the so-called high-level languages such as Basic (beginners all-purpose symbolic instruction code), Fortran (formula translator), or the newer less prescriptive ones like Pascal, C, or Prolog. There is a trade-off in using them, however. High-level languages are not as efficient at run-time as assembler: they take up more memory and slow the processor down translating the English-type instructions to machine code. So proprietory systems, like arcade games, are usually written in assembler with higher-level languages sometimes available for the user to write customizing "macros" of routines.

Local memory, containing the immediate job in hand, is in the form of ram (random access memory) chips which are wiped clean each time the computer is switched off. The amount of ram a computer has available is measured in bytes, each equal to 8 bits (or binary digits): a k or kilobyte is not a thousand but 1,024 of them; a Mbyte is more than a million.

Saved data is sent to the disc drive: either individual floppy discs containing, say, 800 kbyte chunks of information, or bigger (and noisier) hard Winchester discs that can hold 20 or more Mbytes. Back-up is advised to streamer tape drives, which use cartridges like audio cassettes, but these units are very expensive. Data travels round the computer on buses, and the "width" of the bus determines how much data can be processed each clock cycle (measured in MHz) and how much local memory can be managed.

A computer does not have ten fingers, it has two states: on or off, 0 or 1 – it uses binary arithmetic. An old-style home micro with an 8-bit processor and a 16-bit memory bus can only address 2 to the power of 16 permutations of 0s and 1s, or 64k possible memory locations. A 32-bit processor can handle several Mbytes. Some computers have cache memory that holds ready the most recently used data, thus increasing the apparent capacity.

Computers for interactive graphics applications have special requirements and the cpu is augmented with various speed-increasing subsystems – such as floating-point coprocessors to handle the repetitive transforms involved in manipulating images in 3D, pcbs (printed circuit boards) to control the colour graphics on the screen (although on bigger systems with "intelligent" terminals these functions are handled by the device itself), and dma (direct memory access) to expedite the movement of data from the disc to the screen.

There is also a short-term memory store between the cpu and the screen called a frame buffer. This contains the current image in pixel (picture element) form and comprises several layers or planes – with one bit (a 1 or 0) stored for each pixel on each plane. The number of planes and hence the number of bits allocated to each pixel determines how many colours or "greyscale" shades the displayed pixel can be. Thus an 8-plane system can handle 2 to the power 8 (i.e. 256) different colours or greyscales; a 24-plane system can conjure up a staggering 16.8 million, a number considered suffficient by most to produce the kind of realistic-looking images demanded by designers.

▶ **Software for computer-assisted drawing and design comes in many guises – from packages to aid in the production of 2D orthographic drawings to 3D solids modellers that can be shaded to generate realistic renderings. Some of them may be linked with other programs of use to the designer, as this diagram illustrates.**

Computer-assisted design:
the software

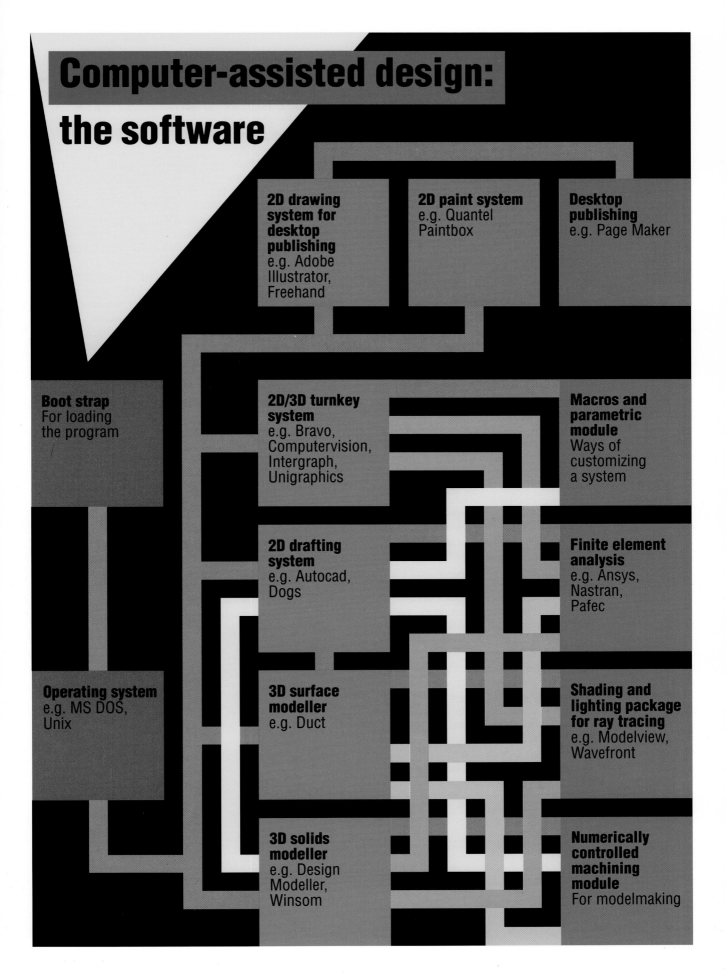

2D drawing system for desktop publishing
e.g. Adobe Illustrator, Freehand

2D paint system
e.g. Quantel Paintbox

Desktop publishing
e.g. Page Maker

Boot strap
For loading the program

2D/3D turnkey system
e.g. Bravo, Computervision, Intergraph, Unigraphics

Macros and parametric module
Ways of customizing a system

2D drafting system
e.g. Autocad, Dogs

Finite element analysis
e.g. Ansys, Nastran, Pafec

Operating system
e.g. MS DOS, Unix

3D surface modeller
e.g. Duct

Shading and lighting package for ray tracing
e.g. Modelview, Wavefront

3D solids modeller
e.g. Design Modeller, Winsom

Numerically controlled machining module
For modelmaking

Input devices

The input device is probably the most important component of a cad system, as it is the means with which the designer communicates with the machine and is an integral part of the so-called "user interface." With many turnkey systems, the designer is offered no choice. Systems such as IBM's Cadam and McDonnell Douglas's Unigraphics have been designed to make use of a proprietory box of function buttons, for example. All Apple Macintosh applications are mouse-driven and utilize pull-down menus, icons and windows – methods of interaction that are migrating to other systems.

Computer graphics users have long abandoned the computer keyboard in favour of other methods for manipulating on-screen cursors and entering shape descriptions. There have been light pens and touch screens, rolling balls, joysticks, thumbwheels, digitizing tablets (which come with a pen-like stylus or a puck with buttons depending on preference), and of course the mouse. Also included in the category of input device are the "frame-grabbing" video cameras and scanners that can be used to input existing pictures or small 3D objects ready for computer processing.

Until there are methods of direct brain-to-computer communications (military aircraft already use weapon-pointing systems that rely on the movement of the pilot's eyes), the input devices that will be used are the ones that combine functionality with ergonomic design and personal preference – users are willing to learn less conventional methods of data entry if it can be demonstrated that their performance or accuracy is enhanced.

The digitizing tablet is currently the most popular way of interacting with the system. It performs a dual role: it can be used to point and pick software commands from a menu (either a piece of paper or film literally taped to the tablet's surface or one that appears on the screen); or it can be used to create pictures (or more exactly, to input positional information). Larger-format models can also be used to digitize (or trace) existing drawings or, more usually, maps. Most, like the Summagraphics Bitpad, are electromagnetic devices containing a grid of fine wires embedded into the work surface, others use sonic techniques to detect the position of the stylus or puck.

The mechanical mouse suffers from friction or the lack of it (a mouse pad is advised) and they work in relative co-ordinates rather than absolute ones (they get lost in space). This is fine for menu picking, but no use for direct input of shape information, which is best done in terms of numerical dimensions from the keyboard. Turn the mouse upside down and you have the **rolling ball** – a device that has been used in air-traffic control applications for decades. These are intrinsically variable devices and are much more sensitive than **joysticks**. They are rugged, do not trap dirt and have a small "footprint."

In the automotive industry **3D coordinate measuring devices** are used to input three-dimensional information from clay models, to be smoothed and rationalized by a cad system. It is likely that these will eventually become cheaper and may be of use to the generalist product designer.

Frame grabbers and **scanners** allow the designer to input already existing images – commissioned photographs, stills from videos or images plagiarized from magazines – or the silhouettes of small 3D objects into the cad system. In this way, a paint system can be used to generate electronic collages, useful to the product designer for presentation drawing backgrounds or for mapping textures such as wood grain on to a surface.

Scanners are often thought of as a fast and convenient way of inputting existing drawings into a cad system for updating or amendment. But beware – scanned data, whether it comes from a CCD camera, a regular TV camera, a laser scanner or direct from satellite, is in its raw form a bit-mapped image. A **bit-map** is an array of memory corresponding one-to-one to the pixels on the screen, so what you see is what you get. Most higher-resolution cad systems store the image symbolically, as a display list of lines, arcs and formulae. A bit-map is good enough for a paint system to get to grips with, but a 2D drawing package will need some raster-to-vector conversion software.

This is not a trivial process, and it relies on the latest pattern recognition algorithms. The computer has no idea, for example, that a collection of dots or pixels scattered in a vague ring shape is, geometrically and topologically speaking, a circle. It may be broken, it may be intersected by a line, there may be a huge coffee stain on the old engineering drawing that you would dearly like to digitize. There is still a lot of human interaction required to interpret a bit-map "snapshot" of a drawing into the display-list format of lines, arcs, text and formulae necessary to fuel the average cad system. And, it should not be forgotten, the old manually produced drawing may not be that accurate – subject perhaps to a little draftsman's licence – in the first place.

▶ **At the heart of the cad system is the processor, whether this is a personal or a larger computer. Around the computer are shown the array of input and output devices that help the designer in the creation and visualization of the designed object.**

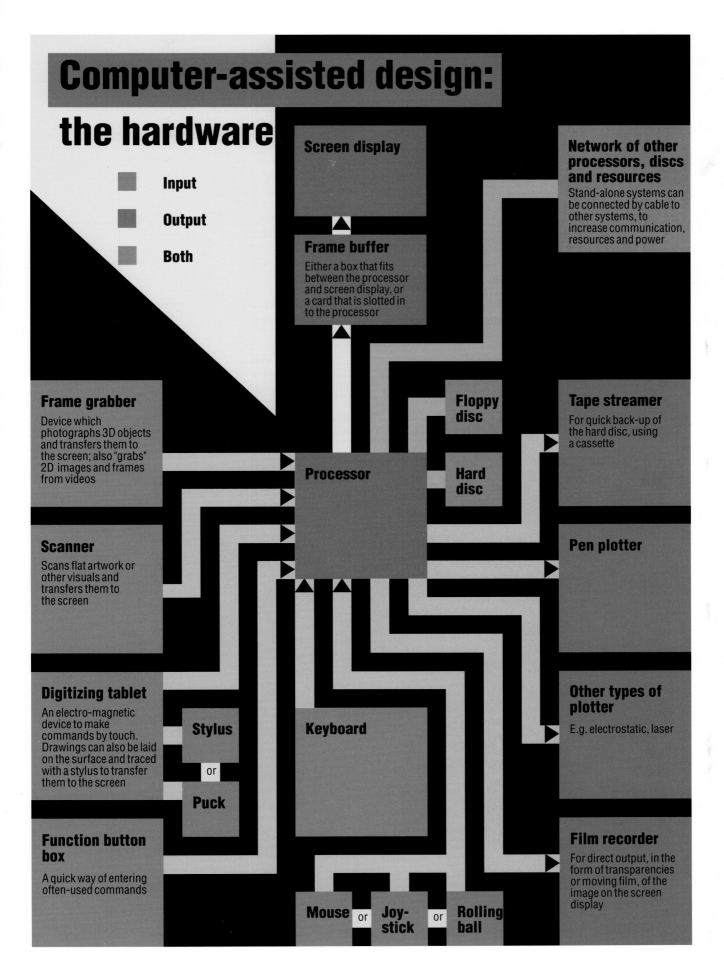

Computer-assisted design:
the hardware

■ Input

■ Output

■ Both

Screen display

Network of other processors, discs and resources
Stand-alone systems can be connected by cable to other systems, to increase communication, resources and power

Frame buffer
Either a box that fits between the processor and screen display, or a card that is slotted in to the processor

Frame grabber
Device which photographs 3D objects and transfers them to the screen; also "grabs" 2D images and frames from videos

Floppy disc

Tape streamer
For quick back-up of the hard disc, using a cassette

Processor

Hard disc

Scanner
Scans flat artwork or other visuals and transfers them to the screen

Pen plotter

Digitizing tablet
An electro-magnetic device to make commands by touch. Drawings can also be laid on the surface and traced with a stylus to transfer them to the screen

Stylus

or

Puck

Keyboard

Other types of plotter
E.g. electrostatic, laser

Function button box

A quick way of entering often-used commands

Film recorder
For direct output, in the form of transparencies or moving film, of the image on the screen display

Mouse or **Joy-stick** or **Rolling ball**

Displays

The computer's display is the window into the system. Cad can be done without a screen – the very first systems had no screen and output the results direct to a pen plotter – but nowadays a screen is considered to be essential. It is important to remember, however, that the image on the screen is more often than not a crude representation of the model that exists inside the computer's database. Nevertheless, picture quality is continually improving and in some instances – showing clients a visualization of a proposed product design, for example – the display will prove to be an invaluable output device in its own right.

The majority of computer displays are based on the crt (cathode ray tube), the same type of object that takes up all the space in a TV set. What makes the crt work are substances called phosphors, electrically active materials that luminesce when bombarded by electrons, first discovered in 1603 by an anonymous Italian shoemaker who heated together coal and barite hoping to transmute them into gold.

The first computer displays appeared in the 1950s. These were called vector refresh or calligraphic displays because the electron beam drew the picture on to the phosphor in random vectors, lines and arcs, in the same way that a pen plotter scurries in all directions across the paper. Although the image was superbly crisp, they were expensive and, as the frequency with which the phosphor was refreshed was directly related to the number of vectors on the screen, they were prone to flicker as the drawing became progressively more complicated. Shaded colour was impossible, but depth cueing – brightening the lines nearer the viewer – could make sense of 3D models.

Displays became affordable when Tektronix invented the direct view storage tube towards the end of the 1960s. This type of screen did not require continuous refreshing, an' electron gun wrote the picture on to the screen in a similar way to the vector refresh display and a low-voltage flood gun kept it there until the altered drawing became so cluttered it had to be repainted. Tektronix needed a phosphor that was bright, had long persistence and that could hold a stored charge. The only one that would fit the bill happened to be green. The popularity of the green-screened 4014 display all through the 1970s gave the colour a new meaning – green is the colour associated with high technology.

The storage tube is all but extinct now. It too had high screen resolution, was flicker-free, but was painfully slow to repaint. Designers would build up a picture, literally crossing out any mistakes and only when they could no longer stand the mess on the screen, go and make coffee while the latest amended version of the drawing emerged, line by line, on the screen.

The raster display (from *rastrum*, the Latin for rake) is predominant today. It works like a domestic TV, with the electron gun scanning the whole screen in horizontal lines, top to bottom, usually 60 times a second (60Hz). If a display is described as being non-interlaced, this means that each line is scanned on each refresh cycle – unlike a TV set, in which only

every other line is scanned each time, resulting in two "fields" per cycle. Non-interlaced screens flicker less.

Each scan line is chopped into pixels and the resolution of a raster display is measured by the number of pixels horizontally by the number of scan lines vertically, e.g. 1280×1024. The early raster screens had low resolutions of, say, 512×512 compared with the equivalent 4000×4000 of a vector refresh screen, but their big advantage was that changes to the picture could be made instantly, and at last there was the possibility of images in full colour.

Raster displays became cost-effective with the emergence of cheap memory on semiconductor chips. You need 1 Mbyte to keep tabs on a 1024×1024 screen with 8 bits of colour or greyscale per pixel.

The first commercial raster screens were introduced by Ramtek in 1971. The highest display resolution is held by the US company Metheus: a 20-inch Sony screen delivering 2048×2048 pixels. It is not cheap, and takers so far include the FAA for air-traffic control applications. UK-based Westward (who sell in the US through Ramtek) has a monochromatic display delivering 2048×1568 on a 19-inch screen refreshing at 57Hz non-interlaced. Industry experts consider that the limits of resolution have been reached. Any improvements await the mainly Japanese tube manufacturers, such as Sony and Hitachi. As resolutions increase further, there are problems in reading the memory fast enough to colour each pixel, and in powering up the electron beam to switch the pixels on and off every 3 nanoseconds or so (a nanosecond is one thousand-millionth of a second).

New technologies, such as gas plasma and liquid crystal, all have size, speed and quality trade-offs. Liquid-crystal shutters that control cathode ray tubes are being used in oscilloscopes, and the technology has also been utilized in prototype "electronic drawing boards" and large-screen preview displays, to control a laser writing to a drawing-board-sized combined digitizer/screen.

Meanwhile, vendors use hardware techniques such as "pixel phasing" or optical illusions such as "anti-aliasing" to improve the perceived resolution of their screens. Anti-aliasing ameliorates the staircase effect seen on near horizontal lines by colouring the pixels around the ones that actually define the line or edge in subtle shades of the current foreground and background colours. This and various shading algorithms (more of which later) are now ever available and instantly accessible, on chips, inside the display.

◀ ▼ **A designer at Volkswagen at work using a top-of-the-range Evans and Sutherland picture system. A wireframe representation of the car is shown on one screen, initial rendering of a model on the other. The stylus is being used to choose commands from a menu placed on a digitizing tablet. The box of dials to the right enables the designer to pan, zoom and rotate the model in 3D space. The fully rendered model is shown below.**

Hardcopy

In the "paperless" design office of the future, there will in theory be no need for hardcopy. A designer will be able to visualize a concept on-screen, work up the detailed production data and generate the information required by the machine tools to make the product, without leaving his or her seat. But in reality, computers have created an unprecedented demand for paper. The designer still wants something in the hand and on the desk every so often to scribble on and modify; clients prefer to spread out the different options so they can be compared and contrasted with one another; production engineers, despite the availability of less sensitive "ruggedized" terminals designed for factory-floor use, still crave the reassurance of fully dimensioned orthographic drawings.

A hardcopy device, such as a pen plotter, can be the highest priced component of a cad system, but surprisingly perhaps it is still often bought as an afterthought. First-time users tend to go for pen plotters because they feel comfortable seeing an imitation hand scurrying around, building up a drawing line by line, arc by arc, as a designer would do if he were using manual methods. But this is a red herring – a drawing may be developed that way when the designer is working on the screen, but how it is printed out is irrelevant.

How big do you need the plot to be? When it comes to paper hardcopy, there is quite a lot of technology choice, and the main buying decision will depend on size. A user who must have large plots (A1 size or larger) will have to choose between a pen plotter and an electrostatic plotter. For smaller formats (A4 and A3), these options are joined by laser, inkjet and thermal-transfer plotters or dot-matrix printers with graphics facilities.

Pen plotters come in all shapes and sizes: from free-roving robots, through small-format flatbeds and mid-format pinchwheel drum plotters, to the large-scale high-precision models bedded in vibration-proof concrete and used by the aerospace and automotive industries to provide highly accurate full-size templates.

Most flatbed plotters have the pen moving in both the x and y directions on a stationary piece of paper, usually held in place by a suction pump; the more popular A1 and A0 size drum plotters have the pen moving in one direction and the paper in the other. The best-selling Hewlett-Packard 7580 was the first to use abrasive pinch rollers to grip the edges of the paper, eliminating the necessity for expensive sprocketted media. This method has now been adopted by most mid-range plotter manufacturers, including CalComp, Océ Graphics and Houston Instrument.

Hewlett-Packard entered the market in 1984 with an A1 single-sheet plotter and created its own market. Today there are over 20 firms supplying the market, mostly Japanese. What is certain is that plotters, with their mechanical parts, are not getting a lot cheaper – in 1980 an A0-size plotter would have cost around $16,000, in 1988 that was down only to just below $10,000.

There has also been a shift in the type of system being sold. In 1984, only 9 per cent of cad systems were PC-powered, compared with 73 per cent that were minicomputer-based. By 1991, PCs will account for 17 per cent of the market, the lion's share of these (47 per cent) being built around workstations. So plotter customers have changed: from technical end-users (who could program) in the 1970s buying direct from the plotter manufacturers, to turnkey suppliers such as Computervision and Intergraph supplying large companies in the early 1980s. Today plotters are sold through dealers to almost anyone needing a drawing.

Requirements have changed and users today, according to Océ Graphics, are interested more in reliability and ease of use than speed and throughput. Their 18 Series, destined to replace the lower end models in the 16 range (17 is apparently an unlucky number in Italy) has been designed accordingly to appeal to the new breed of convenience-seeking PC system users.

The plotter arrives from the local dealer in two boxes that can fit in the back of a van (and upright in a lift) – and can be assembled by two people in a few minutes with no engineer necessary. It has paper and pen storage in the pedestals, holding four rolls of paper. A starter kit includes cabling for common configurations such as Autocad running on an IBM PC.

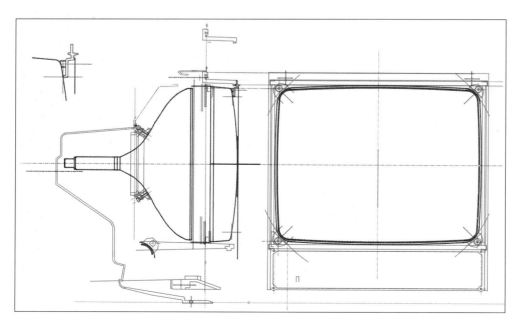

► ▲ Despite often being the most expensive components in any cad system, pen plotters are frequently bought as an afterthought. The 18 Series from Océ Graphics is designed for a new type of PC user, who is likely to be buying an off-the-shelf system.

◄ Coloured pen plot drawings of Bang & Olufsen's MX3000 television, designed at Brand New in London on their Apollo-based Dogs drafting system, and output at A0 size on a CalComp 1043 using ballpoint pens. Pen plotters use coloured ballpoint, tungsten or fibretip pens to indicate different attributes.

Today's pen plotters also incorporate chip-based "intelligence." As well as the 16's "pen manager" that watches for ink running out, an "area manager" minimizes the number of pen changes (a different pen is used for each line thickness) and optimizes the pen's path. A soft-landing feature slows the pen speed before it touches down, preventing bounce and prolonging the pen life.

Plot speed on this particular model is 85cm/s (with the pen down, in contact with the paper) and 120cm/s (pen up). The acceleration, an important factor if a pen is ever to get up to top speed, is very high. A "curve manager" inside the plotter draws arcs in a smooth movement rather than lots of short straight lines and prevents ink spots.

There is a 512k "smart buffer" so that the PC is only tied up for a few minutes each plot and the designer can continue working as the drawing is plotted, and dual ports so the plotter can be shared by two different computer systems in turn. Having the buffer also means that drawings can be replotted in different colours, and segments of the whole drawing can be blown up without having to bother the computer. Some designers find it cost-effective to buy a PC that is just dedicated to operating the plotter, so that the main PC can be used continually for designing.

These mid-range pen plotters usually come in either single-sheet or dual mode. A dual-mode plotter can handle rolls of paper so that many drawings can be plotted one after the other.

At the low end of the market, Japanese manufacturers are making a big impact on the cad community. Firms such as Graphtec, formerly Watanabe, Epson, Hitachi, Rikadenki and Panasonic dominate the A4/A3 size market.

Electrostatic plotters were first introduced by Versatec but are now also on offer from other manufacturers. Unlike pen plotters, which draw vectors from point-to-point, these plot raster-fashion in horizontal lines. Dots of electrostatic charge are deposited a line at a time on specially treated paper. Toner is attracted to the charged bits and clings there. The image is then sealed by applying heat.

This means that electrostatic plotters draw fast regardless of the image complexity. They can also plot shaded images, and colour is possible but very expensive. The vendors claim that they can have a lower cost of ownership taken over the long term, compared with pen plotters. Accuracy is not an issue: at 400 dots per inch electrostatic plotters can produce drawings of as good a quality as pen plotters, especially if they are to be reprographically copied anyway.

Dot-matrix printers may be good enough if the quality of output is not important or if a quick-look plot is needed. They are cheap and can double-up with a word processor. With a cyan, magenta, yellow and black ribbon, 14 colours can be created. Newer 24-wire printheads can produce a dot of around 0.25mm, but colour fill can be messy.

Non-impact technologies such as thermal-transfer, inkjet and laser are also finding application as smaller-format colour hardcopy devices.

Thermal-transfer plotters use an inked-roll cartridge sandwiched between the mechanism and the drawing, acting like carbon paper, to "iron" the image on to clay-coated paper. Thermal-transfer plotters currently produce the best quality output for shaded colour visualizations: black and white versions are sold as well as colour.

Inkjet plotters spray microscopic electrically charged droplets of ink which are deflected by electromagnets – like the beam in a TV tube – to build up the drawing on to a moving roll of paper. A variation is the **thermo-jet plotter** which sprays melted plastic on to the paper.

Laser plotters work like photocopiers. A raster-scanning helium-neon laser is deflected by a rotating mirror on to a photo-receptor plate and the image transferred to the paper by xerography. Laser plotters, developed mainly for typesetting but capable of graphics, are used mainly in desktop publishing applications. Versatec has a large-format (A0 size) laser plotter which has a resolution of 400 dots per inch and produces an A0 size plot in 70 seconds. Colour is on the way – a spin-off from high-tech photocopier technology.

None of these newer technologies is completely satisfactory at present: electrostatics need messy toner, inkjets clog up, thermal transfers need disposable donor rolls, lasers do not have the power to cover large areas. But only a fool would be surprised if, with the current pace of technological advance, a completely revolutionary hardcopy device comes along to eclipse the lot of them.

For presentation-quality renderings, the designer will often want to take a 35mm or larger format transparency off the cad system. Most users can make do with a photograph shot straight from the screen, using a blanket draped over the proceedings, or a proprietory hood. This method can result in "pin cushion" or "barrel" shaped distortions and it is better to use a **film recorder**, from a company such as Matrix, which captures the image on a small flat TV tube built in to the device, making three consecutive exposures through red, green and blue filters. Hitachi has a colour video printer that uses thermal die transfer to produce 77×97mm prints or transparencies at a resolution of 560×620. Selected frames or animated sequences can be output to video and it is now possible to produce **holograms** from a computer model. Some specialized turnkey systems aimed at packaging design are able to output four-colour separations direct to film, same size.

A numerically controlled **machine tool** can also be considered as an output device. Low-cost milling machines are available that can be wired up to a designer's cad system to produce wax or polystyrene models direct from a computer database. An experimental kind of intermediate device is the **stereolithography machine** which deposits 3D objects layer-by-layer by solidifying cross-sectional "slices" of ultraviolet-curable polymer.

Increasing use of cad

Computer hardware is only so much silicon and steel without the applications software packages required to bring it to life, and these will be discussed as they are encountered in subsequent chapters. Cad software has entered the designer's studio via the backdoor, initially as an aid to drafting and engineering design.

Surreptitiously, however, cad is being used earlier and earlier in the design-to-production cycle. Computers are already being used in designers' offices for word processing, general administration and project management. It is only a small step to buy the software and peripherals and have a rudimentary cad system up and running. Cad is becoming cheaper and more powerful by the month, but it is tempting to forget the human component of the system.

As in the implementation of all new technology, care taken at the outset will be repaid many times over later. Training, for example, can make or break an installation, and it is the way designers are paid that usually militates against a successful implementation. Top designers are often thought too busy to be taken off fee-earning projects to learn how to operate a cad system. Yet it is a system which, if properly used, could be giving them even more earning power and the time to explore more potential solutions. Cad is an investment in both money and time. The temptation is to train only junior

designers, or technician-like operators. The result is that the juniors get headhunted by other more enlightened consultancies and the company using dedicated operators loses many of the potential benefits of cad.

Health and safety aspects of the installation must also be taken seriously. It is not enough to plonk a system on a designer's desk without first considering environmental factors such as lighting, ergonomic seating and noise levels. Anyone envisaging using a cad system should have an eye test and it is advised that pregnant women should keep away from cathode ray screens. A cad manager should be appointed to look after the maintenance of the system (plotters especially need constant attention), order stocks of media, manage eventual upgrades of the installation, and allocate work.

Used and managed properly, a cad system can do more than pay for its keep. It can allow a design consultancy to take on more work and handle larger projects, as well as reducing leadtimes and, hopefully, increasing the quality of the work produced. Misused and carelessly implemented, cad could alienate a consultancy's design staff and bankrupt its principals. Cad is a neutral technology: it is not an end in itself nor something to impress the clients with, but just another tool – albeit a potentially powerful means of assisting the designer through each and every stage of the design process.

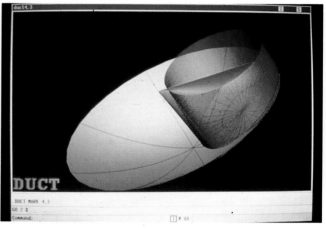

◄ ▲ **From concept sketches drawn manually with a marker, designers at Brand New used cad to design, develop and test this European direct broadcast satellite dish for GE Plastics. The screen images here are the surface modelling package Duct, which defines and verifies the cutting paths for direct machining of the patterns for toolmaking. The design is functional, economic to manufacture in thermoplastics, fast and easy to install, and has an aesthetic edge on its competitors.**

► **The design process is inevitably iterative and recursive, requiring a great deal of cooperation and liaison with the client. Here the design-to-production cycle is outlined schematically, showing how 3D solid modelling software can be used to streamline and unify the various stages, and perhaps help to get a better product to market faster.**

The design process using a 3D solids modeller

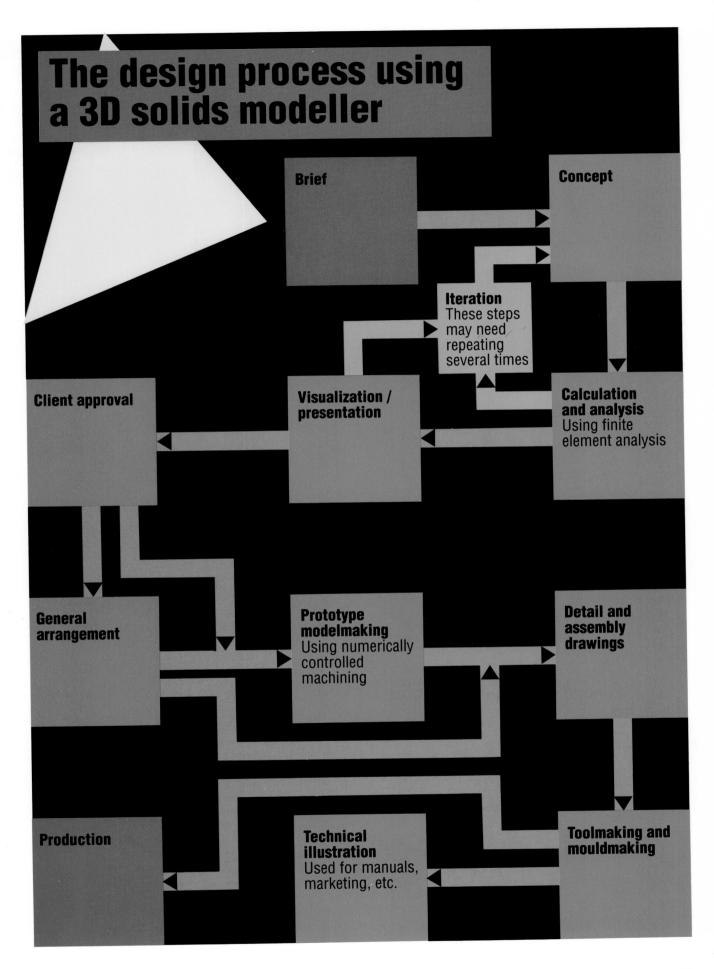

Brief

Concept

Iteration
These steps may need repeating several times

Client approval

Visualization / presentation

Calculation and analysis
Using finite element analysis

General arrangement

Prototype modelmaking
Using numerically controlled machining

Detail and assembly drawings

Production

Technical illustration
Used for manuals, marketing, etc.

Toolmaking and mouldmaking

◀ The Dancall 5000 portable telephone, designed by the Moggridge team: John Stoddard, Nick Dormen and Charles Ash. The project began in November 1985 with a schematic drawing done after a week of brainstorming following the first brief with the clients.

Case study: **Moggridge Associates, London**

Bill Moggridge set up Moggridge Associates in 1969, working from home in London. In 1979 he opened a San Francisco office, ID Two, and has lived and worked in the USA ever since. His first project was the matt black Grid Compass computer in 1980, now a permanent exhibit at the Museum of Modern Art in New York. He has specialized in designing and engineering "Silicon Valley" products ever since, with a particular expertise in working with people who concentrate on "user interface and interaction" design. The local start-up companies in high technology needed design to give them visibility in new markets.

The manager of the London office is John Stoddard and Hedda Beese recently moved to Germany to head the German office, Design Drei. Their recent projects include the BP solar lantern by Hedda Beese and the Dancall cordless telephone by John Stoddard.

The three offices collaborate on "cross-cultural" work, such as Ford's in-car radios for the US and European markets, designing a coherent range of products to different national safety standards which appeal to subtle differences in consumer taste. The opening of the German office heralds an expansion in consumer-oriented products, such as furniture, photograph frames and toothbrushes.

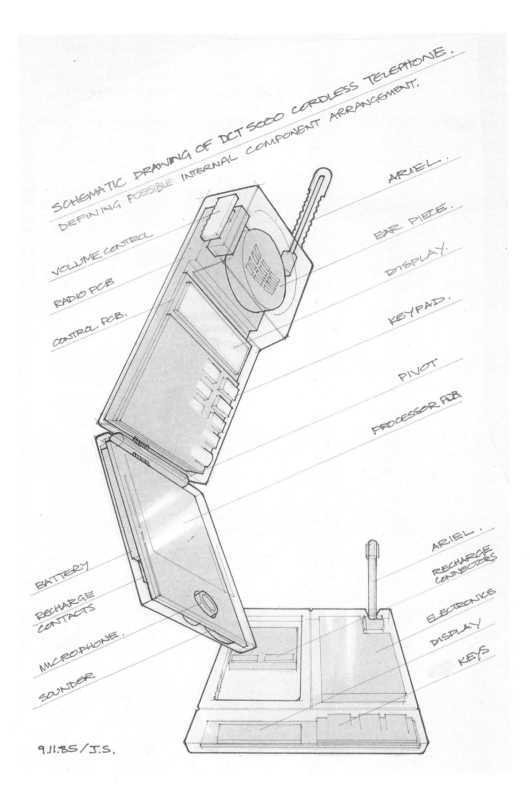

SCHEMATIC DRAWING OF DCT 5000 CORDLESS TELEPHONE.
DEFINING POSSIBLE INTERNAL COMPONENT ARRANGEMENT.

ARIEL.

EAR PIECE.

VOLUME CONTROL

DISPLAY.

RADIO PCB

KEYPAD.

CONTROL PCB.

PIVOT

PROCESSOR PCB.

ARIEL.

RECHARGE CONNECTORS

BATTERY

ELECTRONICS

RECHARGE CONTACTS

DISPLAY

MICROPHONE.

KEYS

SOUNDER

9.11.85 / J.S.

► An early schematic drawing, made with Rotring or Faber technical pens and partly rendered with watercolour fibretip pens. Though it is kept simple, a considerable amount of detail is shown.

Case study: Moggridge Associates

▼ Sketches of three different concept stages, again accompanied by details of how the apparatus would function. The concepts were rationalized to six choices, with a couple of drawings to describe each one: a 3D view or elevation, plus an exploded diagram or cross-section. At

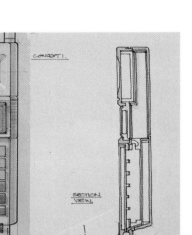

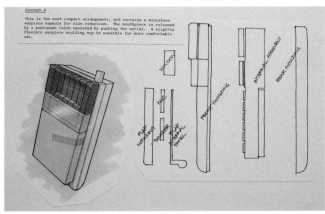

Moggridge was one of the first product design consultancies to use cad. ID Two used the McAuto system belonging to their toolmakers Ronningen in Kalamazoo, Michigan, on the peripheral modules for the Grid Compass, and on a telephone for Telenova. The design details on the telephone – fine vertical grooves along its tapered base – prompted Clive Gringer of the London office to claim that cad could bring new levels of sculpture to product design. Since then, Moggridge have used cad bureaux, but have not yet purchased a system of their own.

Moggridge identifies three stages in design: concept, design development and specification. At the concept stage he enjoys drawing manually, but agrees that if cad is used for initial layouts it gives an opportunity to check fits, and lift data out to compile a parts specification. He has no difficulty in visualizing and reading from 2D orthographic drawings, so a 3D system is not important for him.

After answering all the important questions, he then offers the client several ordered and analysed choices – from three to 20 – in sketches, elevations and models showing size and form, but not detail at this stage. He identifies three kinds of sketch communication: designer to self; designer to peer; and designer to customer.

In the first kind it does not matter if the sketch is a back-of-the-envelope scribble or a beautiful rendering: the drawing is merely a tool for the development of a personal idea. The second kind is a way of expressing ideas to help have a conversation about the project: it can be rough, but must be stylized. The third type of sketch is more explicit, and usually rendered full size in marker. The choice of material depends on the individual designer: it can be chalk, marker, pencil or mixed media, but never airbrush, which is too time-consuming. The style should be current and appropriate, always evolving but right for the time.

At stage two, design development, the team selects a particular direction and brings it to a point at which a commitment can be made to invest in tooling and components. They are saying – to the satisfaction of the accountants, toolmakers and suppliers – that this is what the product is going to look like. At this stage Moggridge uses a 6H pencil on many layers of Mylar film, with dimensions in sufficient detail to make a model. Any details that are not obvious are described on separate drawings.

At the final stage, specification, one to three drawings are produced per part, each comprising up to 20 sheets or layers. This is where cad proves very useful, cutting the time it takes to get to the tooling stage by half, and making the drawings far more coordinated. The practice does not undertake technical illustration, preferring to use photographs, perhaps with a drawing overlaid, for the best of both worlds.

Not all Moggridge projects make use of cad. On the Dancall 5000 telephone project, John Stoddard used manual methods. The work was started in October 1985, the engineering development completed by summer 1986 and the product was launched in October 1987. The task was to design a cordless telephone that was pocket-sized and genuinely portable, rechargeable, with a professional image. The Danish clients wanted all aspects of the design – styling, mechanical engineering, electronics and software – done in parallel. At a technical and marketing briefing, the clients and designers discussed the importance of the design from the user's point of view, and decided on details such as the components, size and volume, radiation shielding, and other statutory requirements. Should it be short and stubby, or long and thin? Because it is traditional in Denmark for the installation engineer to offer the customer a choice of colour, mouldings were to be designed to snap or slide on in situ.

this stage, the drawings are precise, but the style is deliberately quite loose and the sketches hand-drawn so that the design does not look

too "finished" and unchangeable. They are accurate, but look spontaneous, with construction lines visible.

Coloured pencils are used for tints and graded pastel for effects such as diffuse reflections.

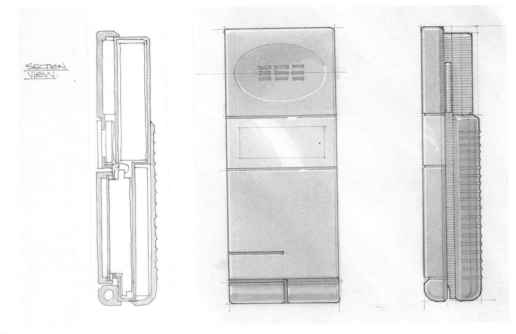

SECTION VIEW.

▼ Schematic arrangements of the technical details. The two lower presentation sketches were made with technical pens and Pantone markers on bleedproof A3 or A4 layout paper. The designers were restricted in parts of the design by the clients' requirements, and so worked using diagrams as underlays.

Design and engineering were considered together from the start. Stoddard worked on the styling, Nick Dormen decided how the aerial would fold away, and Charles Ash test-rigged the friction-damped hinge on the flip top and the wiring management. Dancall handled the electronics, providing a diagram for Stoddard to use as an underlay when he worked on the ear-to-mouth cross-section. The concepts were rationalized to six choices, with a couple of drawings describing each one – a 3D view or elevation, plus an exploded diagram or cross-section.

Once a concept was chosen, a further presentation drawing was done to confirm the decision, made at the completion of the first stage. A4-sized detail sketches followed, with exploded diagrams to visualize how assembly would be achieved. Production drawings were done in pencil on polyester film in third-angle projection to BS308, but with vertical dimensions turned 90 degrees for speed of execution. The toolmakers then made their own drawings, showing allowances for expansion and contraction of the plastic in the moulds.

In all perhaps 100 pages of sketch drawings were produced, with another 40 developing details. Each product had a four-to-six sheet general arrangement drawing and about 100 individual component drawings. The aim all along was to produce drawings that enabled decisions to be made and that clearly communicated the designers' intentions to all concerned. Each stage should be a pleasant surprise to the client, claims Stoddard, never a disappointment.

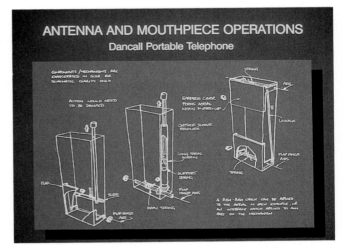

ANTENNA AND MOUTHPIECE OPERATIONS
Dancall Portable Telephone

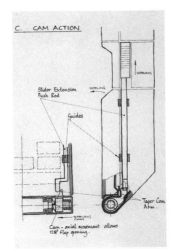

C. CAM ACTION

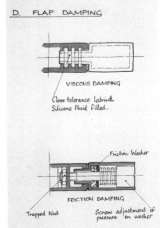

D. FLAP DAMPING

Oh! che dolce cosa è questa prospettiva!
Oh! what a sweet thing perspective is!

Paolo Uccello

4 Basic Drawing Skills

The main aim of the product designer's drawing is to make a representation in marks on 2D paper of a real or imagined 3D object. If the designer's intentions are to be communicated faithfully to others in the design team and to those responsible for manufacture, this drawing must be a complete and unambiguous representation of the designed object, and various conventions have grown up over the years to expedite this process. While a pictorial sketch may be adequate at the earlier stages of design development, the 2D orthographic projection – a plan and two elevations – is the conventional way of communicating the form and geometry of the product from design to production, and that is where we begin.

But a set of orthographic drawings may not be sufficient to explain a complex 3D detail, and auxiliary views may be necessary. Orthographic drawings are also difficult for the layperson to visualize, to "read." So when a designer presents proposals to a client or manager it is now expected to be in the form of a 3D pictorial representation, usually a perspective drawing. Perspectives are now so ingrained in the collective consciousness that most designers can draw them "by eye." However, for the sake of completeness, a formal but simplified method has been included. Other non-perspective projections, though currently used mainly by designers with an architectural background – the "metric" projections of isometric, axonometric, and so on – are also described.

▶ Shipwright's office of 1586, from Matthew Baker's *Fragments of Ancient English Shipwrightery,* showing designers at work on a plan of a ship. The item being drawn is shown as a plan in this "naïve" watercolour and is therefore not in keeping with the rest of the picture, which is in perspective.

▶ Julian Brown of Lovegrove & Brown in London has used a set of orthographic drawings plus a section in this presentation of a sofa/daybed, rendered in watercolour on transparent film. His approach is highly reminiscent of Victorian engineering drawings.

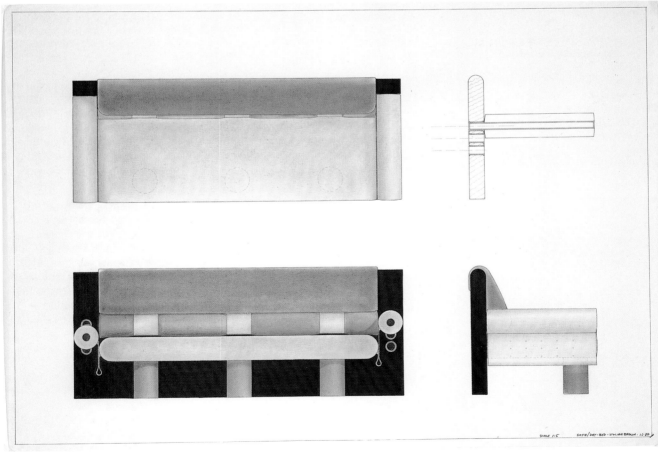

Orthographic projections

Of all the many ways of representing on paper a three-dimensional object, the orthographic projection of a plan, elevations and sections is the most abstract and the most commonplace. Its rigidity has probably been responsible for the way many products look today – boxy and in effect only two-and-a-half dimensional, like the simple extrusion of a profile with maybe a few rounded edges and details added as a finishing touch. More "organic" shapes such as the designs of Luigi Colani, as in the Canon T-90 camera, are almost impossible to communicate orthographically; and traditional designers of doubly curved surfaces, such as turbine blades and automobile bodies, have the tortuous task of drawing series of sections, with the interpolation between them left to the toolmaker.

The method of orthographic projection, perfected by William Binns in 1857 and based on Dürer's method of 1525, is notoriously ambiguous, and hundreds of conventions have grown up to try to make sense of it – describing what should be seen, and what is hidden but must be indicated, say, by a dotted line. BS308 now runs to three volumes. Thus it needs expertise to read these drawings, a privilege not accessible to the layperson, the client or the ultimate end user.

A designer might, for example, have a shape in mind that could be described parametrically – e.g. as a cylinder of a certain height and diameter manufactured in brass – but the production department would still expect to receive, with the instruction to manufacture, a fully dimensioned "engineering" drawing. Except for the simplest shape, it is necessary to accompany the set of orthographics with an "auxiliary" isometric or perspective sketch to complete the description. Unfortunately, the orthographic projection is entrenched in design and engineering culture, despite its limitations, as the "blueprint" and symbol of the design process. It is the domain of the non-designing draftsman and its survival serves only to perpetuate the élitist, arcane mysteries of design and inhibit any form of accountable participation.

The principle of orthographic projection is to float the designed object inside an imaginary box comprising planes at right angles – i.e. orthogonally – to one another. If the sides of this box are thought of as being windows and are peered through in turn, then the silhouette or projection of the designed object on to the bottom horizontal window is called the plan view, the projection of the same object on to the front vertical window is called elevation 1; and on to an adjacent side vertical window, end elevation 2. Now imagine the box to be hinged. The horizontal plane (the plan) is swung down through 90 degrees and end elevation 2 is also swung round through 90 degrees, so that all three projections now lie on the same plane. Remove the object, and an orthographic projection of a plan and two elevations remains.

First-angle projection is when the plan is drawn first, then the elevation of the front face drawn immediately above it and the end elevation to the right. They are all lined up and in scale so that common dimensions can be taken off.

Third-angle projection has the views arranged so that elevation 1 is placed below the plan, with end elevation 2 to the left of elevation 1. This has the advantage of placing the features of adjacent views in juxtaposition, making it easier to project one view from another when drawing, and to associate these features when dimensioning or reading the drawing.

Mixed projection is a combination of the two systems, with the plan placed below the elevation.

The position of salient features on the object will often determine the type or hybrid of arrangement used, although UK and European practice favours first-angle and US practice favours third-angle projections. The European penchant for the first-angle projection is said to derive from the conventions embodied in Monge's descriptive geometry of 1795. US practice broke the tradition towards the end of the 19th century – American draftsmen tended to be college-trained and hence more influenced by educationalists who postulated the idea of drawing as a graphics language. By 1953, the UK drafting standard BS308 had put both first- and third-angle projections on to equal footing. The third-angle projection is now commonly used both in the USA and the UK, although first-angle projection is still the preferred method in continental Europe. Designers tend to use the form of projection most

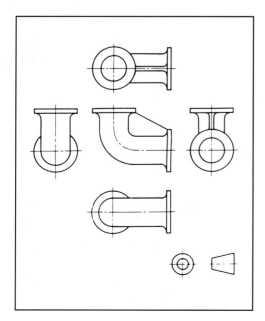
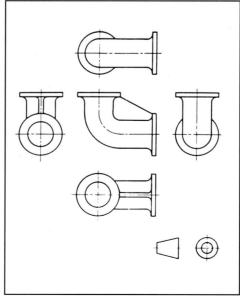

◄ The projection used in a drawing, whether first- or third-angle, is indicated by a conventional symbol laid down in a standard such as BS308. The far left shows third-angle; the near left first-angle. The symbol is in the bottom right-hand corner.

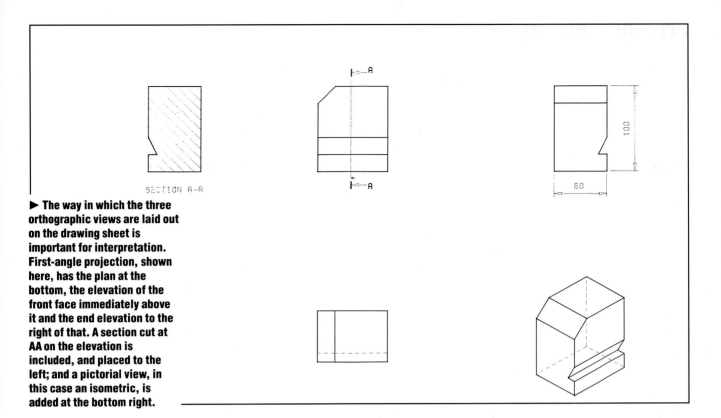

SECTION A-A

100

60

► The way in which the three orthographic views are laid out on the drawing sheet is important for interpretation. First-angle projection, shown here, has the plan at the bottom, the elevation of the front face immediately above it and the end elevation to the right of that. A section cut at AA on the elevation is included, and placed to the left; and a pictorial view, in this case an isometric, is added at the bottom right.

► Orthographic projection imagines a three-dimensional object suspended inside a transparent box with orthogonal faces, i.e. faces at right angles to one another. Views of the object are projected on to three adjacent sides of the box. When these are "flattened out" they should comprise a complete and unambiguous representation in 2D. On the left is the method of first-angle projection; on the right is the third-angle projection.

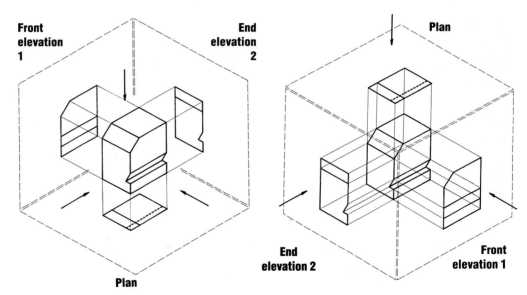

Front elevation 1   End elevation 2   Plan

Plan   End elevation 2   Front elevation 1

appropriate to the application. For drawing a long thin object, such as a train, a third-angle projection would be easier to read: the front elevation, for example, would be placed on the sheet of paper to the left of the side elevation and adjacent to it.

A section is a slice through the object, projected orthogonally, to show internal details or changes in profile for complex shapes. The cut solid is shown cross-hatched and the point at which the section is taken indicated on one of the views according to the chosen national or international standard. Unlike a real section, sections on an orthographic drawing will often show, by convention, details it would not be possible to see with the naked eye.

An auxiliary projection is a view taken from an odd angle, not at right angles to the object, and hence not orthogonal to it, that may be added to the set of orthogonal projections to make an understanding of the form a little clearer.

A scrap view is an enlarged portion of the object, perhaps drawn from a slightly different viewpoint, to highlight an important detail or possible problem area.

Surface or flat pattern developments are used when it is necessary for manufacture to "unfold" an object – if it is to be made from sheet metal, for example. The techniques for opening out a surface graphically on to one plane are similar to those used in orthographic projection.

Metric projections

The metric projections – isometric, axonometric and so on – are simple pictorial methods of drawing objects so as to give an impression of three-dimensionality. They are often dismissed by designers as being cheap substitutes for "true" perspectives, although they were used successfully by the De Stijl group in the 1920s and have seen vogue recently in the work of the Memphis designers among others. They can be set up from orthographic projections and drawn to various scales on proprietory pads preprinted with grids, and are thus a useful addition to the designer's toolkit. Unlike perspectives, they retain length, breadth and height dimensions in measurable form.

Axonometric

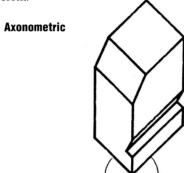

Axonometric projections contain a true plan and are the simplest to set up from existing drawings. As a means of representation, they are most often associated with interior design and architecture. Drawings are usually made with the aid of a T-square and a 45-degree set square, although as long as the plan remains true, the angle at which it is tilted to the horizontal can be varied to produce the best effect. Circles on plan remain true circles in an axonometric projection, but circles in elevation become ellipses. There is some contention between architects and engineers over this term. Axonometric is a word that has been used by architects for hundreds of years for what engineers now often call **planometric**. Engineers use the word axonometric as a generic term to include isometric, dimetric and trimetric drawings. A compromise being considered is that a new word be coined, **axometric**, to help stamp out the confusion.

Isometric

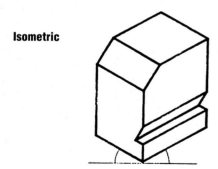

Isometric projections were developed by Sir William Farish in 1820 as a form and derivative of orthographic projection. They produce a less extreme and "unrealistic" drawing than the axonometric projection. Elevations are constructed using a 30-degree set square and as a result the "plan" is distorted. Circles appear as ellipses in both plan and elevational views. Verticals have true depth; measurements along the isometric axes can be taken off the drawing using an isometric scale – they are 0.816 of true size.

Two "pictorial" systems popular during the Second World War, based on isometrics, are the more generalized **trimetric** and **dimetric** projections. Trimetric projections need scales or templates for each axis; the dimetric is a special case in which the scales of two of the axes are the same. Dimetric projections use "idealized" angles of 7 degrees and 41 degrees 30 minutes to the horizontal for the x and y axes. Conventional approximations are used for manual drafting; but precise angles and scales can be built into a cad system.

To recap in general terms: the types of pictorial projection – isometric, dimetric and trimetric – cover the application of one, two and three scales respectively. Exploded views are almost always executed in isometric or perspective.

Oblique projections are used where the front elevation of the object is of particular importance, in furniture design for example; the side and top views of an object are tacked on to the edges of the front face. To make the side and top faces join, they are distorted and the line representing the common edges runs at an oblique angle across the picture surface. The lines representing the top and side faces are usually parallel, though they can diverge – giving an inverted perspective effect – or converge, for normal perspective. Oblique projections are the precursors of perspective and, despite being logically impossible, are found on Greek vase decorations of the 4th century BC and were used in Chinese paintings until the 18th century AD.

Cavalier　　　　　　　　Cabinet

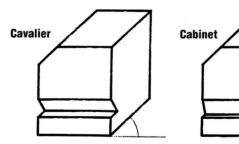

The oblique lines emerging from the elevation can be any length: in a **cavalier** projection they are true lengths; in a **cabinet** projection they are half the true length.

The oblique angle is usually 45 degrees. The horizontal oblique projection, in which only the front and side of the object are visible, and the vertical oblique projection, in which only the front and top are visible, are special cases where this angle is 0 degrees and 90 degrees respectively. In oblique projection, upright cylindrical objects always look distorted.

Any shadow projected on to a flat plane is an oblique projection. Incorporating shadows on to a drawing, as was common practice in the 19th century to add realism (it was called sciagraphy in architecture), is effectively superimposing an oblique projection on to an orthographic projection.

Other projections

Exotic spherical projections, more recognizable in maps of the world, are sometimes encountered by designers. They are an aid to designers of truck or bus cabs subject to safety regulations. European Community regulations, for example, stipulate the driver's ground plan visibility from the windscreen and through rear-view mirrors. In Australia, the cab's B post must not be within 130 degrees of the driver's field of view (the pieces of metal that hold up the roof of the cab are called posts: the one at the front is designated the A post, the next one back is the B post, and so on).

A **Mercator projection**, in which a 360-degree spherical field of vision is mapped on to a cylinder and then opened out flat, can verify that legislation is being conformed to, but would be tedious to perform manually. Ergonomic modelling programs such as Prime Computer's Sammie can – once a 3D scene has been input – generate views in different projections through the "eyes" of a driver direct through the windscreen and windows or via convex, concave or plane mirrors in minutes, and visualize any distracting internal reflections.

Aitoff projections, which are elliptical, are often necessary for aircraft cockpit visibility analysis.

VETRINETTA DI FAMIGLIA 1979

◀ **Ettore Sottsass used an oblique projection, with a true elevation and converging sides, in this drawing of a display cabinet for Studio Alchymia of 1979. It is an appropriate choice, since it is the front of the object that requires emphasis.**

▶ **Isometric projections are particularly suitable for square objects such as furniture, as in this drawing of a modular construction kit for children, designed at BIB in Londqn for Belgian manufacturer Cogebi. The flat colours are produced using Panfoil film on Pantone coloured paper.**

Perspectives

Practical perspective is a way of introducing systematic distortions into drawings to *symbolize* reality. Objects appear to diminish and converge as their distance from the viewer increases. Lines drawn between the object and the observer will intersect the picture plane (the sheet of drawing paper, which is assumed to be held vertically in front of the viewer, normal to the line of sight) at various points. A perspective drawing is made by plotting these points and connecting them together. The horizon is assumed to be infinitely distant – so that parallel lines meet at *vanishing points*. A perspective, it should always be remembered, is a simulation of reality – in real life there will be many changing vanishing points as the designer's (two) eyes and head move and wander around the scene.

It is difficult to believe that perspective had to be invented. The technique has become so embedded in the consciousness of designers these days that nearly all "perspectives" are now drawn freehand, by eye, rather than being constructed according to conventional methods. Designers have been programmed to think automatically of an ellipse when observing a circle in perspective.

Perspective drawing has obsessed artists and architects since the time of Filippo Brunelleschi (1377-1446), a Florentine goldsmith turned architect, who discovered that geometrical mathematics could be used to establish the laws of visual perception in perspective. His theories were used from 1420 by Piero della Francesca and Massaccio, working from plan and elevation with the added effect of a vanishing point. The painter Paolo Uccello (1397-1475) is also credited with establishing the first principles of perspective. Both Alberti and Dürer published treatises on perspective circa 1540 and these were followed by a spate of learned works on the subject.

Perspective aids (the descendants of the camera obscura) began to appear in the 18th century, notably James Watt's perspective apparatus, Cornelius Varley's graphic telescope, William Hyde Wollaston's camera lucida (similar prism-based models are still available today), and Peter Nicholson's perspective delineator (an instrument for drawing lines to inaccessible vanishing points). Most 3D computer modelling programs contain interactive perspective routines, in which correction can be applied to maintain parallel vertical lines.

Perspective drawings convey more or less the actual physical appearance of an object, so they have considerable value in enabling the layperson, client or end user to appreciate the designer's intentions. The underlying theories of perspective are complex, and second-hand shops are full of books ancient and modern outlining systems and methods for setting up perspectives, usually from orthographic projections which – from a design point of view – is putting the cart before the horse. A designer will more often than not be generating an "accurate" and more finished perspective from a rough freehand sketch. The only time a designer might be working from 2D drawings would be in the case where a series of design proposals are constrained to enclose pre-sourced components.

Choice of viewpoint is crucial to the art of constructing a credible perspective: it determines the position of the horizon and the vanishing points. A well chosen viewpoint will give an impression of size and scale, willl show off the object to the best advantage, and bring to the fore its most important features. Small objects, for example, such as telephones, are usually viewed from above. A long thin object, such as a letter sorting machine, might need an accentuated amount of perspective to give it length as it recedes. The vanishing point will be near to the object. A short squat object, such as a washing machine, will be closer to the isometric, with almost parallel edges and almost infinitely distant vanishing points. Consider, too, the composition of the drawing, and the positioning of the object on the paper. In most industrial design applications it is an advantage to render perspectives at or near full size. This is obviously not always possible for furniture and large-scale machinery, and automobile designers are usually content with a full-size elevation.

One-point perspective is ideal for drawing railway lines or long straight roads with telegraph poles either side. The height of the pole can be deduced by the proportion of it between the horizon and the ground, which corresponds to the height of the viewer's eye above sea level. With one vanishing point towards which all lines (except those normal to the viewer's sight line) will recede and converge, it is only appropriate to interiors or vistas, though it can be used to show the layout of components *inside* a computer or piece of hi-fi equipment.

Two-point

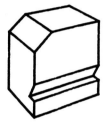

Two-point perspective has two vanishing points, placed on the horizon at the left and right of the object. The traditional systems for setting up such a perspective include: projecting two elevations (top and side) through two picture planes to two observers; using a plan and two vanishing points; and the so-called measuring point system. These methods can be inaccurate, complicated and time-consuming – but more importantly, the methods are prescriptive, in that you need the plan and elevations before you can construct the perspective.

Jay Doblin's system of 1956 is a simplified method tuned to the needs of designers. It uses a cube as a basic perspective unit to measure height, depth and width concurrently. If you can construct a cube in perspective, it can then be multiplied and subdivided to build up a framework for describing any shape of object.

Briefly, Doblin's system imagines the viewer standing on an infinite tiled floor, consisting of perfectly square tiles. If the line of sight is 45 degrees to the sides of the tiles, along a diagonal, it will meet the horizon at the *diagonal vanishing point* (dvp). Lines projecting from the sides of the tiles will meet the horizon at the left and right vanishing points, which will be equidistant from the dvp. The side-to-side diagonal will be horizontal and parallel to the horizon. It will experience no convergence and so provides a constant unit of measurement. Using this grid, a cube of any rotation can be constructed which, with the provisos that it be placed in a position between the centre and around half-way to the vanishing points and that its nearest angle be greater than 90 degrees, will look suitably undistorted.

The cube can be subdivided by first intersecting the diagonals to find the midpoint. A circle within a true square will have its centre at the intersection of the diagonals and will be tangent at the midpoints of the sides of the square. A circle in perspective is in fact an ellipse, although it appears to be asymmetrical – the half nearer the viewer is obviously less foreshortened and looks fatter. This is not an anomaly, because the major axis of the ellipse (the widest distance across the ellipse) is tilted from the vertical. Concentric circles in perspective, as you would find when drawing an automobile wheel, would have displaced major axes. The minor axis (the shortest distance across the ellipse), however, will coincide with a line drawn perpendicular to the perspective circle, i.e. the axle of the wheel. An ellipse guide or template can be used to draw a circle in perspective if it is tangent at the midpoints of all four sides of a perspective square and if its minor axis coincides with the perspective perpendicular.

From the cube and the circle/ellipse, it is possible to construct other "primitive" shapes: cylinders, cones and spheres (the sphere is unique in perspective – in outline it always remains a circle!).

This 45-degree oblique view is useful for drawing objects with two interesting sides but could look dull and monotonous it the sides are of similar dimensions, as in a refrigerator, for example. A similar set-up using a 30/60-degree orientation (and with one vanishing point twice as far from the dvp than the other) would result in a more pleasing composition.

Two-point perspective is a special case of **three-point perspective** in which the vertical lines are parallel to the picture plane. A better representation would have the vertical lines of a small object (situated below eye level) converging towards some third vanishing point directly below the object (and the sides of a large object such as a tower would similarly converge upwards to a vanishing point in the sky).

Three-point

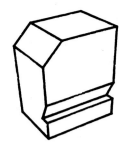

Three-point perspective assumes three horizons, forming the sides of an acute triangle. Simplifications to the construction can be contrived when the cube is symmetrical with the front and rear corners coinciding with the line of sight, and for a less monotonous composition with the faces inclined 45 degrees to one horizon, 30/60 degrees to the others. Most designers will use their judgement to introduce convergence to vertical lines. The foreshortening of vertical distance for small objects near eye level is roughly proportional to the amount of convergence.

Older books on perspective insist that three-point perspective is unnecessary as the drawing is subject to the same laws of optics as the object. If a tall object is drawn with parallel verticals and viewed from the same station point as the original object, the lines on the drawing representing the verticals on the object should converge in the same manner and by the same degree. Remember, perspective is not necessarily the whole truth – it is a convention with many assumptions and not an explicit means of representing the way a person perceives the real world.

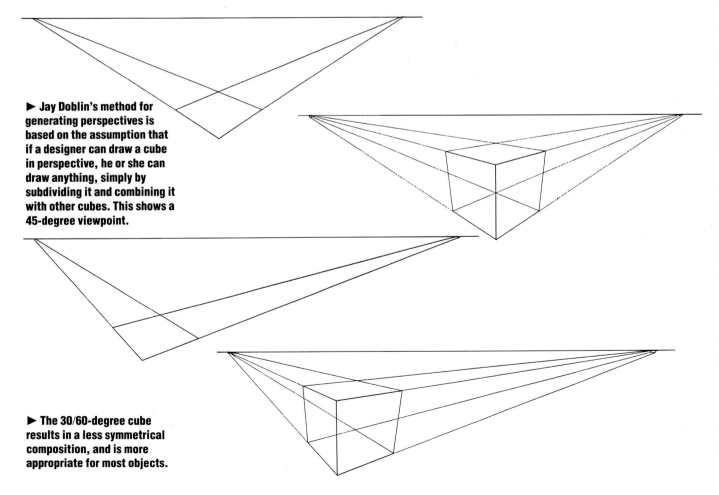

► Jay Doblin's method for generating perspectives is based on the assumption that if a designer can draw a cube in perspective, he or she can draw anything, simply by subdividing it and combining it with other cubes. This shows a 45-degree viewpoint.

► The 30/60-degree cube results in a less symmetrical composition, and is more appropriate for most objects.

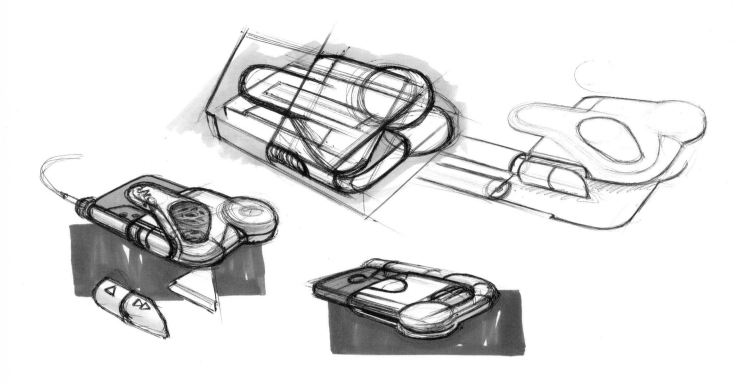

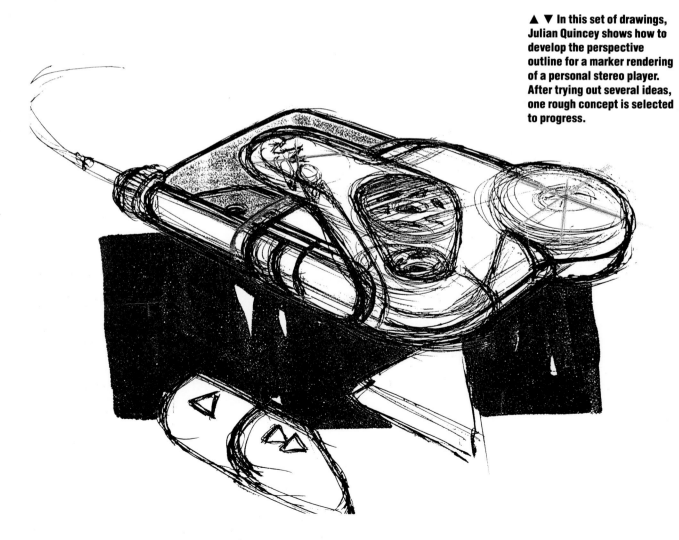

▲ ▼ In this set of drawings, Julian Quincey shows how to develop the perspective outline for a marker rendering of a personal stereo player. After trying out several ideas, one rough concept is selected to progress.

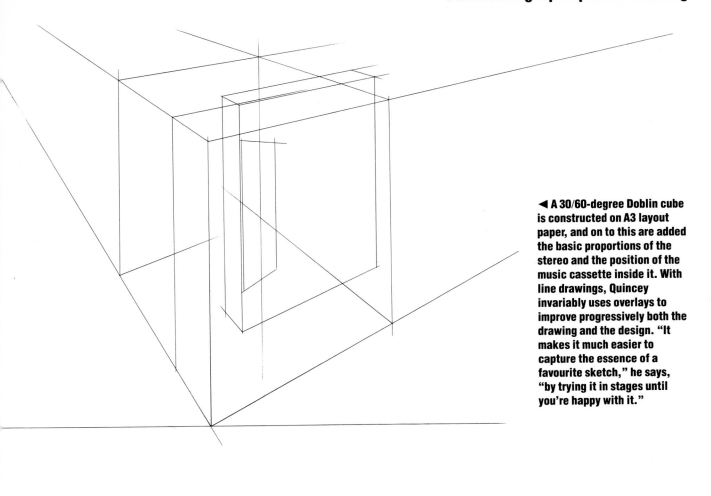

◄ A 30/60-degree Doblin cube is constructed on A3 layout paper, and on to this are added the basic proportions of the stereo and the position of the music cassette inside it. With line drawings, Quincey invariably uses overlays to improve progressively both the drawing and the design. "It makes it much easier to capture the essence of a favourite sketch," he says, "by trying it in stages until you're happy with it."

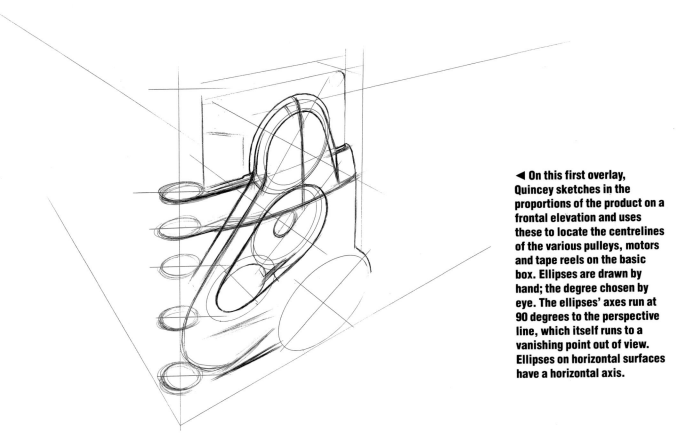

◄ On this first overlay, Quincey sketches in the proportions of the product on a frontal elevation and uses these to locate the centrelines of the various pulleys, motors and tape reels on the basic box. Ellipses are drawn by hand; the degree chosen by eye. The ellipses' axes run at 90 degrees to the perspective line, which itself runs to a vanishing point out of view. Ellipses on horizontal surfaces have a horizontal axis.

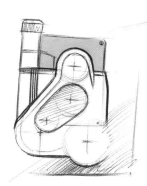

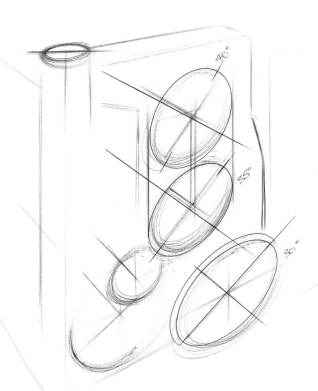

▲ Now the hard points are joined. By referring to the frontal elevation on the previous drawing it is possible to select a particular feature and work from there — in this case, the semicircular motif that covers the upper cassette reel. The transparent window, which allows the user to see the tape revolving, was added next, enabling the diagonal lines running parallel to its edge to be constructed. "If you're not sure what happens when one feature or surface meets another," says Quincey, "it is often useful to draw contour lines around the object. These can help you decide where intersections take place and, in this case, find out which way a straight line lies on a gently bowed surface." Lastly, the hand-drawn ellipses from the previous drawing are corrected using ellipse guides.

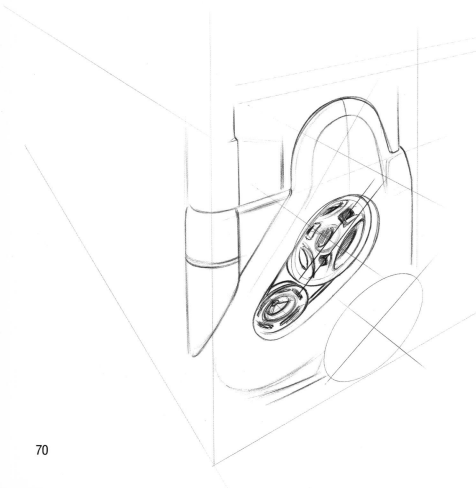

◄ Now the drawing is refined to look more like the initial concept sketch. More detail is added to the pulley/window area.

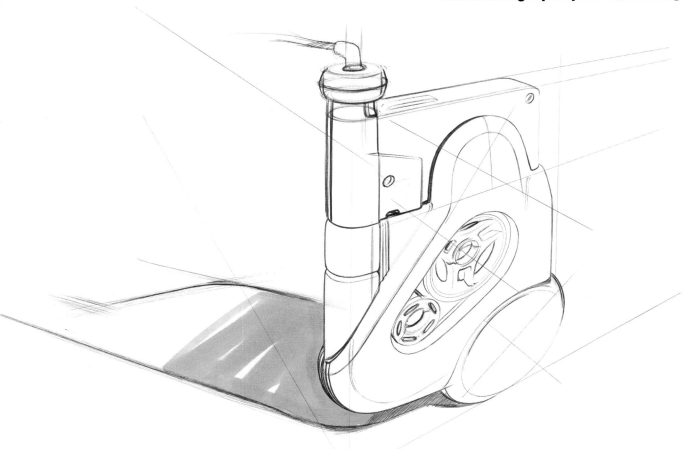

▲ This is the last chance to correct any mistakes, add detail, work out the shape of the shadow, and complete the outline.

▶ The final drawing is a neat tracing of the previous stage, with a greater emphasis on line quality and accuracy. Marker is added, imagining cast shadows on a matt surface and blocking in the drawing ready for full rendering.

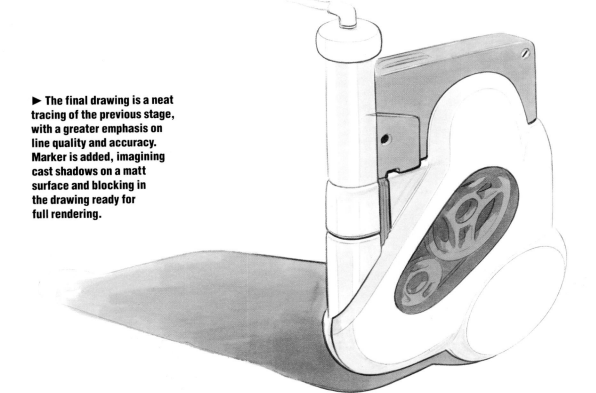

Solid modelling

In a solid and three-dimensional world, it is the natural right of designers or engineers to work in 3D. It is only the limitations of pen on paper that have led them to believe they should think in terms of 2D orthographic projections, an imprecise convention perfected when the industrial revolution demanded the division of labour and a need was established for a method to communicate a designer's intentions to those responsible for implementing them.

It is ludicrous to suppose that designers of products containing complex doubly curved shapes, as found in car bodies, turbine blades or telephone handsets, could even hope – without assuming some degree of telepathy – to retain control of their designs from concept through to production with just a plan, an elevation, a couple of sections and perhaps a sketched isometric to define the part completely and unambiguously. It is no exaggeration to say that most cars, before the days of computer-aided design and manufacture (cadcam), were "designed" by the patternmakers.

With computer aids, however, there is no excuse. But tried and tested methods die hard and despite there having been 3D systems around since the earliest days of cadcam, the engineering drawing still rules. 2D drafting systems which simply emulate the traditional methods retain a dominant position in the market. A solid modelling system does require more power and memory to drive it (though there are PC modellers around and engineering workstation versions are now commonplace) and they have been notoriously difficult to understand and operate. The biggest obstacle, however, is a fundamental one – being able to put aside hundreds of years of irrelevant "tradition" and get back to basics by learning to carve and sculpt "real", albeit computer-simulated, solid models.

There are three distinct kinds of 3D modeller in cadcam: the wireframe modeller, the surface modeller and the true solids modeller (also known as the volumetric or geometric modeller). Although the solids modeller is the highest form of computer modeller, the different kinds of modeller around commercially did not necessarily evolve in that order – Pafec's 3D wireframe extension of their Dogs 2D drafter, for example, was released long after their solids modeller Boxer, as a lower-cost alternative for simpler jobs.

Surface modellers, specifically developed to satisfy the needs of the aerospace and automotive industries with their freeform "fair" shapes, have always been treated separately, although there have been moves recently to integrate all three types of modeller. It has always been the avowed aspiration of vendors to introduce the functionality of the surface modellers and their ability to drive numerically controlled machine tools into their more generalized solids modellers. The suppliers are getting there with differing amounts of success. Most modellers can "sweep" a complex 2D profile through space, either extruded or rotated about an axis. SDRC's Geomod and Cadcentre's Diad, for example, can both project a doubly curved surface on to a plane and the resulting solid can be further manipulated using the Boolean operations of union, intersection and difference. Computervision and Intergraph adopt a common mathematical representation, the nurbs (see Chapter 7), for all three types of modeller.

The most rudimentary type of 3D representation is the 2D (x,y) profile extruded simply and linearly into the z-axis, the kind of shape that can be manufactured by a router or milling machine with a straight up-and-down motion and no undercuts. This is usually referred to as a 2½D model. It is also possible for a skilled draftsperson to construct cavalier and isometric projections of 3D appearance on a supposedly 2D-only system, such as IBM's Cadam.

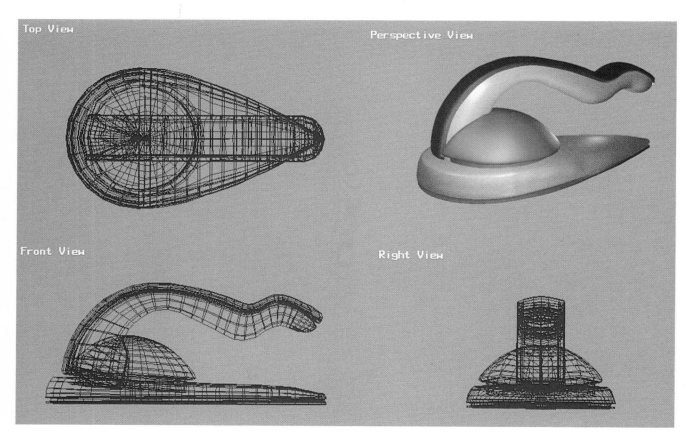

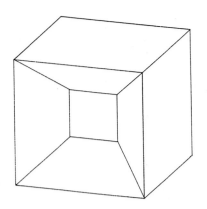

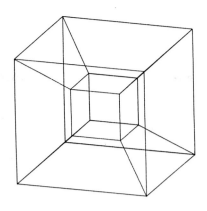

◄ A wireframe drawing is generally difficult to read, despite techniques such as depth cueing. It can be quite inscrutable. This drawing of a cube within a cube can be interpreted in many different ways – the picture on the far left with the hidden lines removed is just one of the possibilities.

The 3D wireframe model is a model composed of edges and vertices. It is as if the shape were constructed from pipe-cleaners, except that they have zero thickness. Although each vertex and line exists in 3D space, a wireframe picture can be confusing and ambiguous to the viewer. Depth cueing – making the parts of the picture closest to the user brighter and thicker – can help, but for hidden-line images to be generated, the designer has to "attach" faces to those polygons where they would be expected to be.

One of the best known surface modellers, and one that has found a niche for itself in the design and manufacture of telephone handsets, is Deltacam's Duct, originally developed at the Cambridge Wolfson Laboratories. It uses a method of interpolating sections perpendicular to a central line (called a "spine"). Other modellers use combinations of patches and surfaces to construct complex shapes and intersections (see Chapter 7). A surface model can be shaded (and hence look solid enough) and can be used to generate toolpaths for numerically controlled machine tools.

A true solids modeller has an in-built sense of identity. The model knows its inside from its outside; what is solid and what is not. Solid modelling promises the designer a simulation that thinks it is a real prototype. The model can be viewed from any angle in photographically real shaded colour, the outside can be rendered transparent so that complicated innards are revealed, assemblies can be exploded, sections cut and, like science fiction, the object can be dematerialized and turned inside out – making holes, voids, risers and feeders (in plastic mouldmaking applications, for example) visibly solid, while the material they were milled and bored from is rendered empty space.

A solid model can be weighed, knows its volume, centre of gravity and moments of inertia, and can detect clashes and interference with other components, clamps or machine tools. It is also the only representation that can form the database at the core of a totally integrated cadcam system, a use that has been championed by firms like Ferranti Infographics for many years. The model can be used to produce the meshes needed

◄ An office stapler, designed using Alias software, showing three "orthographic" views in wireframe and a fully rendered shaded pictorial representation. The 3D model is often built up by manipulation of one or more of the conventional 2D views.

When working on a plan, for example, the computer will automatically update the two elevations. Rendering takes some time and is done at a later stage.

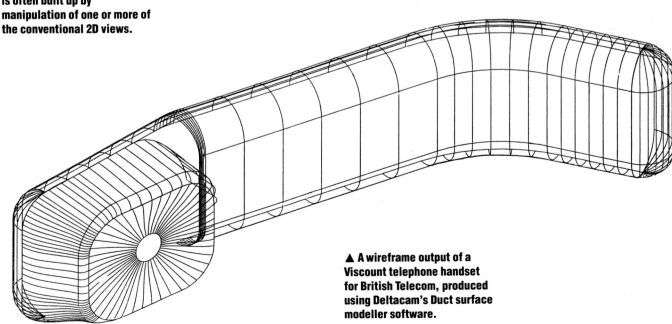

▲ A wireframe output of a Viscount telephone handset for British Telecom, produced using Deltacam's Duct surface modeller software.

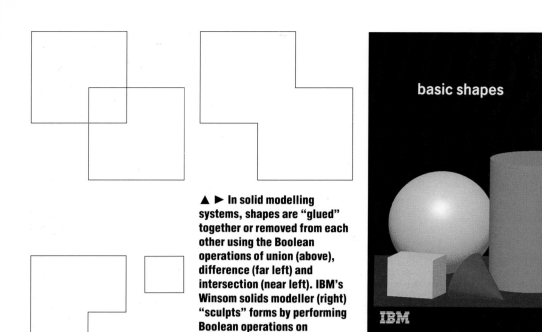

▲ ▶ In solid modelling systems, shapes are "glued" together or removed from each other using the Boolean operations of union (above), difference (far left) and intersection (near left). IBM's Winsom solids modeller (right) "sculpts" forms by performing Boolean operations on primitive shapes.

for stress analysis, to verify toolpaths before machining and to provide diagrams for technical manuals. It can come up with the data for process planning and for automated computer-aided inspection, testing and quality control.

Most solids modellers date back to one of two research efforts in the mid-1960s: the Build system at Cambridge University in the UK which spawned the commercial offshoot Romulus; and the Padl project at Rochester University in the USA, an ancestor of McDonnell-Douglas's Unisolids and – indirectly, via Leeds University's Noname – of Pafec's Boxer. Another early modeller – Magi's Synthavision – is a spin-off from ballistics research and forms the basis of Schlumberger's Bravo 3 modeller and IBM's ISD modeller for Cadam users (IBM supports three commercial solids modellers as well as its own Winsom: ISD, the faceted modeller Catia developed by the French aerospace company Dassault, and the Geomod-lookalike Object Modeller module of Caeds).

Classification of solids modellers is usually by the way they store the description of the shape's geometry. In a CSG (constructive solid geometry) system, the final shape is described and maintained internally by a tree structure of the building-block primitives (simple shapes such as cubes, cylinders and spheres) plus the Boolean operations (union, difference and intersection) that must be used on them to arrive at the model – a step-by-step history of the design process. After construction, individual faces can be selected and "tweaked," but edge-modifying features such as fillets and chamfers are difficult to effect.

A B-rep (boundary representation) modeller keeps a list of all the faces, edges and vertices of the model, together with the topological and adjacency relationships between them (so as to prevent any Escher-like impossible objects from being created). B-rep models are constructed either by converting existing wireframe or surface models by adding faces, or by sweeping 2D outlines along linear or circular paths to enclose a solid object. These can then be further combined or subtracted with other intermediate shapes using Boolean operations. B-rep modellers are also useful for flat-pattern development, in sheet-metalwork.

Most CSG modellers derive from Padl and Synthavision; most B-rep modellers owe a lot to Build/Romulus. Many modellers use a hybrid approach, converting a CSG working model to a B-rep definition and storing both. The CSG model might then be used for mass-property calculations, such as moment of inertia and surface area, and the B-rep file's edge data downloaded to another program to produce 2D drawings. Schlumberger has a two-stage modeller, with a fast interactive faceted modeller used for concepts and a more precise but slower CSG modeller used later when the design is more settled. Faceted modellers, like Medusa and Catia, approximate and replace all the difficult-to-compute curved surfaces by small planar facets like the surface of a gemstone.

The larger the facets, the faster the processing; the smaller the facets, the closer the approximation is to smooth reality. Apart from speed, another attraction is that faceted modellers can reproduce complex surfaces, e.g. the "lobster-pot" facility in Medusa. Euclid from Matra Datavision and Geomod from SDRC are both CSG/B-rep hybrids that make use of planar facet approximations of curved surfaces.

PC-based 3D modellers have proliferated recently. The first (and a true solids modeller) was MicroSolid from Perspective Design, a new company staffed by ex-Shape Data programmers. It links to many popular 2D drafters and can generate tapes for driving numerically controlled machine tools. Robocom's Robosolid is the same modeller with a different user interface.

John Frazer's Design Modeller (described in Chapter 5) is a B-rep solids modeller aimed at educational applications, running on a PC. A designer starts with a solid block which can be "drilled" or "cut" using a mouse-operated cursor which looks on-screen like an x,y,z coordinate symbol. It uses plain words that a designer might be familiar with, such as mitre, rebate and slot, rather than Boolean abstractions, and the modeller keeps track of how the geometry fits together. It has a "rethink" button to rerun and undo the design, and includes such commands as "round off all edges." Tapes for numerically controlled machine tools and 2D drawings are output automatically and the system can be used as a front-end to more

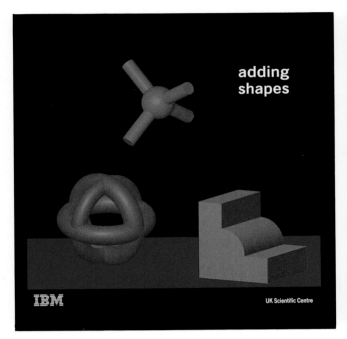

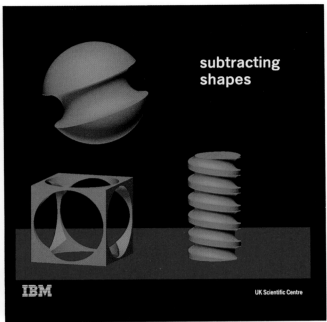

staid modellers. PC modellers do have their limitations: they are slow, lack the many shortcut commands that bigger computers have the capacity to handle, and can only manipulate relatively simple shapes.

Meanwhile, work continues to improve the mainstream modellers. Solids modellers have problems with geometric accuracy: they are generally good enough to produce visualizations, but not to drive a machine tool. And developers have yet to find a way to attach tolerance information to each component part. Tolerances are vital to production engineering and have crucial cost implications on manufacture. Solids modellers are not very good at recognizing and discriminating between surface features such as holes, bosses and pockets. These too have a bearing on economic manufacture – a hole, for example, can be drilled, bored or reamed.

Automated manufacture, with no manual intervention, is the most tantalizing promise of solids modelling, but so far it restricts choice and could make parts more expensive to produce, because the tolerancing information is so restricted. Nevertheless, there are rays of hope. Machining on blanks, on screen, by subtracting the volume swept out by the cutter tool will verify the efficacy of the toolpath and check interference with clamps and fixtures. And new software techniques, such as object-oriented programming, will bring so-called expert systems for "easy" applications, such as sheet-metal development and plastics injection mould design, a few steps closer to practical reality.

The creation of photoreal rendering and lighting effects (described in Chapter 6) and the automatic generation of perspectives (or any other kind of metric projection) from solids modellers can produce "models" that to the viewer's eye and brain are indistinguishable from a real physical prototype. If a perspective drawing is only a *visual* simulation of reality, a computer solid model is a drawing that exists in three dimensions (and hence can be rotated and translated in 3D space) and also possesses almost as many physically measurable attributes as the real thing.

▼ **The solids modeller Geomod was used by Roberto Fraquelli at the Royal College of Art's industrial design department to design and visualize this hand-held anemometer, a device for measuring the speed and direction of wind.**

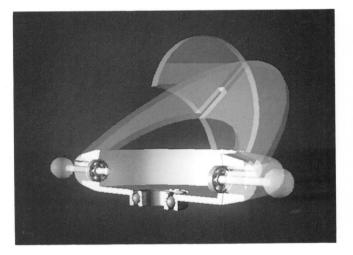

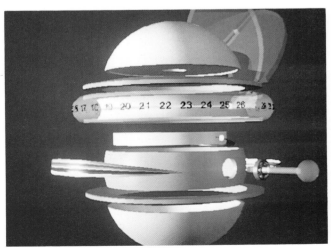

Designers need to draw in order to externalise their thoughts and make them concrete. It could even be argued that, if an artifact has not undergone this process of externalisation, it cannot claim to have been designed at all

John Lansdown, "Computer-aided Architectural Design Futures," 1988

5 The Concept Sketch

What is design? Is it simply "preparing for action"? Or: "a search process in a space of alternative solutions, seeking one or more that satisfy certain design criteria"? Or: "a process of recursive conjecture-analysis operating within the framework of abduction, deduction and induction, proceeding on the basis of a series of paradigm shifts to more detailed levels as the proposal becomes more specific"? Or is design simply what a designer does?

It is not the intention of this book to explore or review current thought on design methods and theories, There are several books on these topics (see Further Reading). This book is constructed on the assumption that the design process as practised proceeds along the lines that follow.

The designer or design practice first receives a commission from a client, in the form of a design brief. A team is then set up, comprising perhaps a project leader and various professionals: a stylist, a design engineer, and so on. They meet the client and sort out a timescale with deadlines, talk about fees and maybe negotiate a more detailed brief or specification. The designers go away to think, scribble on to the backs of envelopes, and eventually – according to the agreed schedule – submit to the client a series of proposals, usually accompanied by presentation drawings and models.

The client deliberates, evaluates these proposals, and accepts one of the variations or a composite constructed from portions of two or more of them. The designers then receive the go-ahead to get down to detail – producing first a general arrangement drawing and later the detailed dimensioned drawings for production and assembly.

▶ **Alvar Aalto used the fine art conventions of his day (mixed media and collage) to investigate the crafting of free-flowing, painterly shapes in three-dimensional form. These 1937 concept sketches of glass vases for the Iittala Glassworks, Finland, are the precursors of his Savoy vases, still in production.**

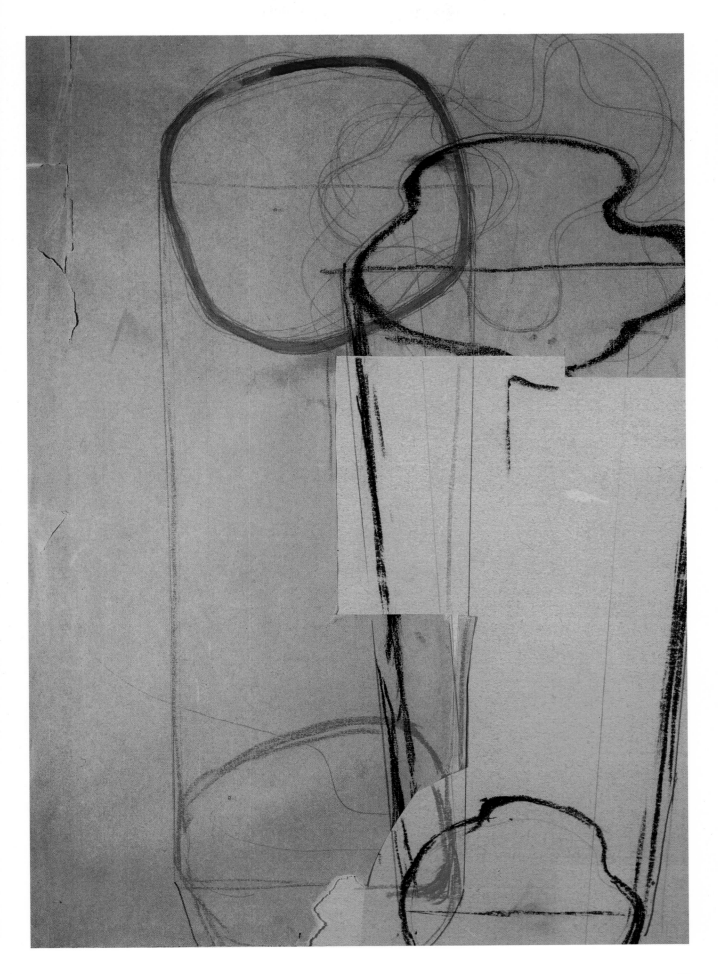

The Concept Sketch

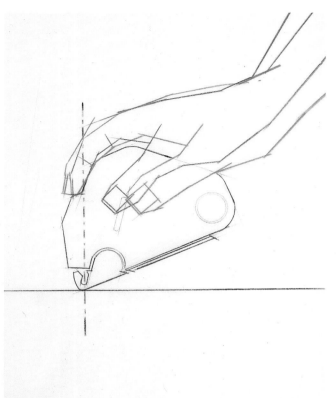

The designers will liaise with technical people, who may be subcontracted to be responsible for special requirements such as stress analysis or the use of new materials. They may even be expected to generate all the tooling and fixture drawings that will be required to manufacture the object. Some design consultancies will produce a working prototype, and after the product has been manufactured they may have to produce technical illustrations to help sell the product and explain to the end user how it is to work or be serviced.

In a one-person practice, all these activities may be undertaken by one person; in a multi-disciplinary practice, the job will be distributed to several specialists. The designers' involvement may end with the styling model, or the designers may be brought in effectively after the object has been designed, to do a "packaging" job. All practices are different, and individual designers within a practice may work in different ways (see the Case Studies for a more detailed look at the day-to-day operation of several different practices).

Design can be top-down: starting with a clean sheet of layout paper and producing a free-ranging solution that could be any shape as long as it satisfies certain functional criteria. Or design can be bottom-up: to design a new car or television set, for example, the designer is given a collection of already engineered pre-sourced components, such as a motor or cathode ray tube, with a printed circuit board or two, and given the task of combining them and containing them into a unified aesthetic whole.

An average product, if there is such a thing, will be a synthesis of proprietory items bought-in from catalogues, such

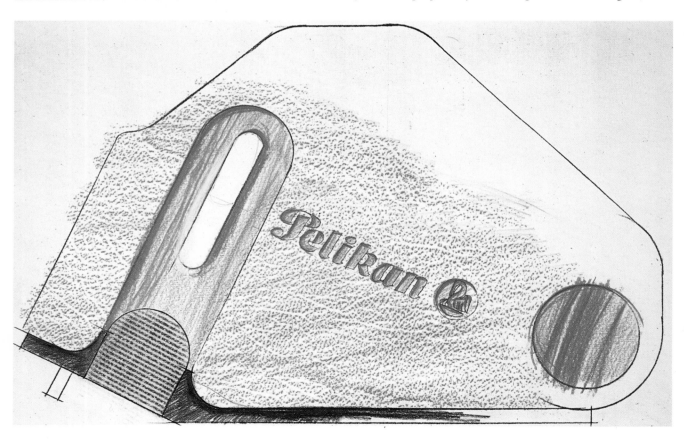

▲ An ergonomic study and a colour-rendered sketch by the Italian designer Michele De Lucchi for the Klebroller (Roll-Fix) glue dispenser for the West German company Pelikan. The designer used coloured pencil on transparent paper, with frottage techniques to create texture. Note that while the linework is quite precise, the colour rendering is remarkably free.

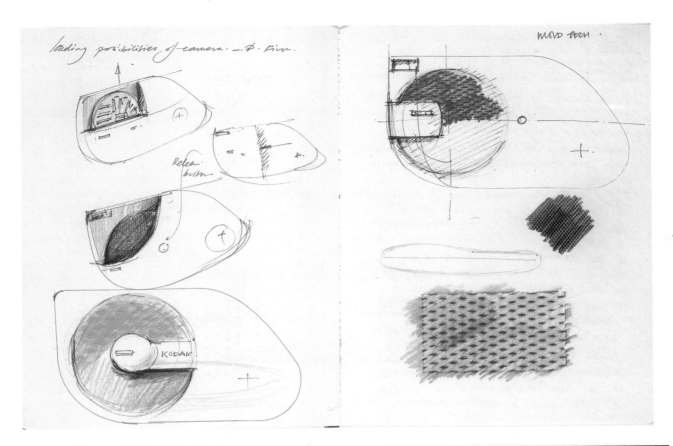

▲ Lovegrove & Brown also used frottage on these coloured pencil studies for a camera for Kodak.

as electric motors, springs, nuts and bolts, with known parts, available parts and parts that have to be specifically tailored to the particular product being designed. The design will be constrained by the suitability and properties of the raw materials (sheet steel, for example, comes in standard thicknesses) and by the manufacturing techniques to be employed (plastic objects will need a taper if they are to be released easily from the mould). Batch size, too, has implications for the design. For capital goods, produced in, say, batches of ten, it may not be economic to invest in the tooling necessary for mass-produced consumer goods.

So according to this model, the first identifiable portion of the design-to-production cycle (for there will be *some* recursion) is called concept design.

The concept sketch is the designer thinking aloud with a pencil: what Aldo Rossi calls "private visions." The designer may be putting on paper – usually on a translucent layout pad – an *aide memoire* of a totally thought-out 3D idea to be worked up later into production drawings; alternatively, and more likely, the very act of drawing is a means of crystallizing a vague inkling that may or may not be worth pursuing. Frequently, the making of a simple sketch to express a concept can in itself suggest further conceptual ideas. Sketches, according to Bryan Lawson, act as a kind of additional memory to freeze and store spatial ideas which can then be evaluated and manipulated. The designer is wrestling with future possibilities, attempting to give form to uncertainty.

Concept sketches might look inexpensive to produce, but the designer must be conscious that it is here that the cost implications of the project are at their most sensitive. It is here that the overall look of the product – as defined by the 3D spatial and proportional relationships – is decided. Concept sketches also focus in on various perceived problem areas or challenges associated with the as-yet-nonexistent product. Unless the designer has specific instructions to fit all the various components into a specific shape or size – the space envelope – prescribed by the client, there are no exact measurements yet.

The initial sketches may be of the overall form of the product, of certain difficult details, or may be a system schematic – a collection of interconnected boxes labelled "motor", "keyboard", "display" and so on. The designer may include a few rough calculations to estimate the final size and proportions of the product. Concept sketches do not have to be to scale, need not be neat nor clean – they are a hardcopy record of the ideas taking shape in the designer's mind. Ideally they should all be retained, bound together in a sketchbook. Even those judged no-hopers at the time might be useful in future projects or when the designer is sent "back to the drawing board" by a difficult client or by a change in the brief.

The medium used is that preferred by the individual designer – concept drawings are rarely shown to the client, or to other designers in the team. The Spanish designer Oscar Tusquets Blanca, for example, uses soft Derwent pencils (B or 3B) in A4 squared notebooks; New York designer Michael Cousins expresses a preference for an Eberhard Faber Ebony pencil (jet black extra smooth/6325) and a Winsor and Newton A4 bound sketchbook. Other designers say the

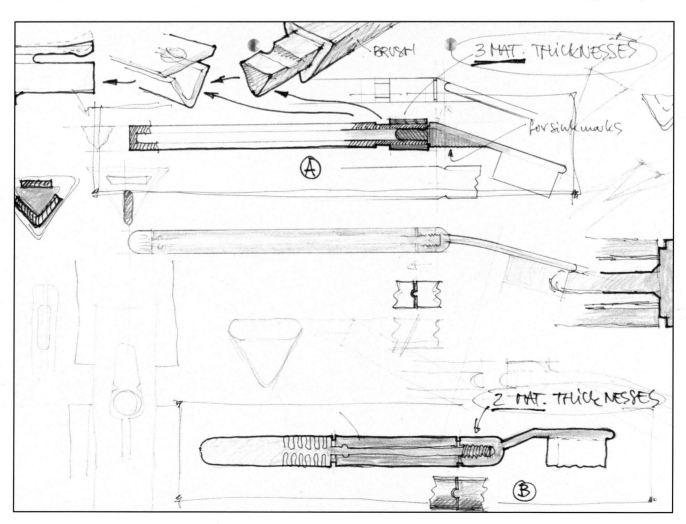

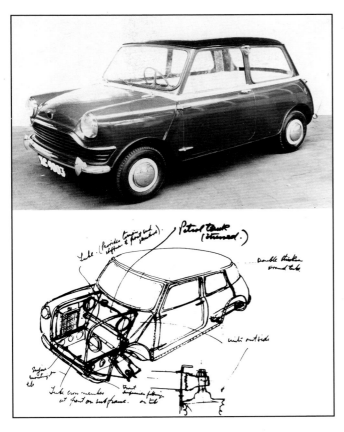

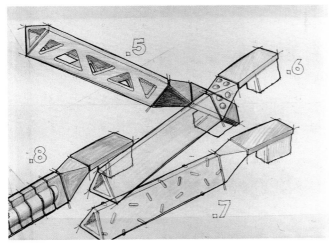

medium does not matter. As Tucker Viemeister of New York's Smart Design puts it: "I do not have a favourite pen or pencil. I do not have special lucky socks that I wear on opening nights either. Ballpoints on napkins work just as well as mechanical pencils on Mylar."

Concept sketches are usually incomplete descriptions of the object being designed. The rest of the information remains locked inside the designer's head or has yet to be thought out. Direct-communication sketches for the benefit of another designer or the client, done on the spur of the moment following a statement such as, "Here, let me show you what I mean . . ." need a commentary from the designer to be fully understood. More committed sketches often begin with an overall light outline, then the designer darkens selected lines, fills in details, and adds notes and perhaps key dimensions. If a sketch is to be copied, paper with feint blue lines or squares that will not reproduce should be used, unless of course the grid is to be made a feature of the drawing.

As the project progresses, the concept drawings will be modified and reshaped in line with any new information, and the results of analyses of performance, durability, cost, reliability and ease of manufacture. And as the concepts develop, so more accurate drawings will be needed to confirm to the designer that the original loose concepts will in fact work. Using the initial concept sketches, plus information from calculations, codes of practice, standards, additional information from the client and catalogues of proprietory items, the designer will then attempt a scale layout drawing to see if and how everything will fit together. This will establish

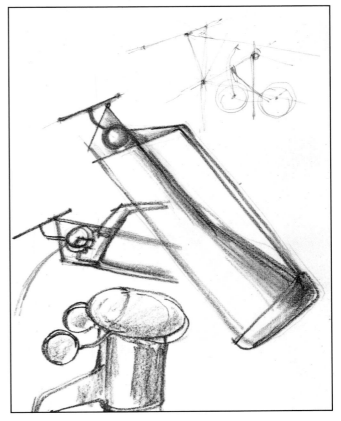

◄ ▲ **Winfried Scheuer at Moggridge Associates designed these toothbrushes for a Forma Finlandia competition in 1987. The pencil and watercolour concept sketches are augmented by elevations and sections that define the forms geometrically and show how they are to be assembled.**

▲ **The Austin Mini of 1959 ▲ revolutionized small car design: cheap to run and easy to park, it became a symbol for the Swinging Sixties. This 1957 concept sketch by Sir Alec Issigonis gives an insight into his method of working: his fluid drawings were simply meant to communicate engineering details to his assistants.**

▲ **Achille Castiglioni, in his oil and vinegar set designed for Alessi in 1984, used a restricted palette of coloured pencils on rough watercolour** **paper. His sketches show not only the form of the product but also how it is meant to work.**

The Concept Sketch

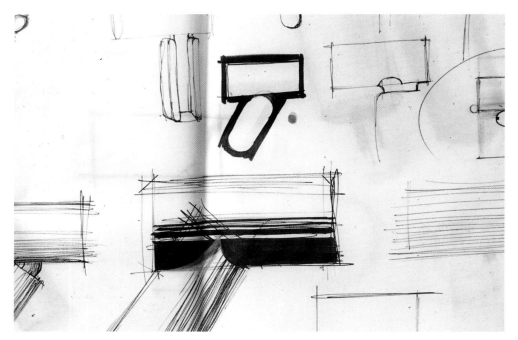

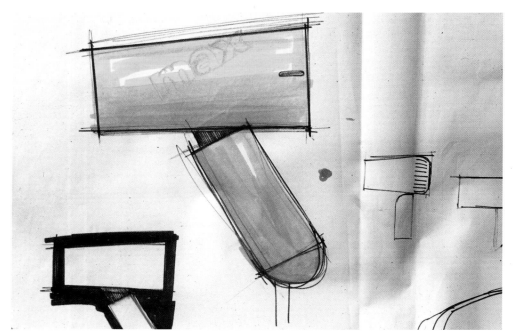

◄ Pen and marker sketches of the Gillette Max 1000 hairdryer, drawn by Michael Cousins of New York consultancy Cousins Design. This is an economical technique to show a product with simple forms.

◄ The prototype of the Gillette Max 1000 hairdryer.

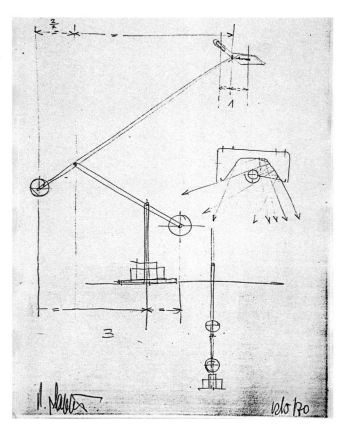

the key dimensions and will probably be drawn, still freehand, in orthographic projection, as a rough first try at a general arrangement drawing (see Chapter 7).

Overlays on Mylar film can be used to experiment with the placement of components to check they do not clash with one another, and to evaluate the parameters of any movement-envelopes. If the layout is drawn in orthographic projection, all three views must be drawn together – the components may fit nicely in one view, but clash badly in another. Sections, auxiliary views (the axes easiest to draw may not be the easiest to use in manufacture) and scrap views (close-ups) may be included with the orthographic to help clarify the proposed solution.

Once the concept has been tested, the contented designer is now ready to move on to the presentation drawings (to convince the client that the solution proposed is the right one), and to the general arrangement drawing – the key to the working drawings required for manufacture.

◄ **Richard Sapper's drawing of his "Tizio" lamp for Artemide, 1970, represents a freehand first try at a general arrangement drawing. A transitional stage between a concept sketch and a fully dimensioned engineering drawing, this is often referred to as a layout drawing.**

▼ **Anthony Dunne's monumental concepts for a central heating controller, drawn while he was a student at the Royal College of Art, London, are rendered in coloured pencils.**

▲ ► Robert Venturi's marker concept on yellow tracing paper of the "Sheraton" chair for Knoll International, USA, is cleaned up, dimensioned and decorated with a collage of coloured paper on a transparent overlay (right).

The computer-aided concept designer

The use of computers to aid in concept design is a highly charged and controversial area. To many, it is synonymous with computer-*automated* design, promoting the idea that computers can *think*. But if there is such a thing as systematic design, and if all that designers are doing when they design is problem-solving – that is, matching a set of manufacturing parameters to a perceived set of performance criteria set out in a specification that has been laid down by marketing people and is constrained by cost considerations and the technological state of the art – then surely all jug kettles would look exactly the same, there would be an *ideal* and optimum shape at any given time.

Designers are in the fast-change fashion business, and computers – even expert systems – do not yet have the kind of mind that can take in and recycle all the diverse ideas that will influence a designer from the world of fine art, popular culture and everywhere else. What a computer *can* do is act as an able and tireless assistant, running errands and sharpening the pencils, keeping accessible archives and performing tedious calculations – but never intruding where it is not wanted.

Concept design has always been the cinderella of cad. Back in the heady days of the 1960s, excited theorists – especially in architecture – mapped out schemes for automated or "systematic" design, comfortable perhaps in the knowledge that the means of implementing their visionary systems existed far out of reach in the distant future. In practice, more pragmatic and modest applications for computers, such as the 2D drafting systems that emulated the manual methods of the traditional drawing office, continued to rule ever since. The ubiquitous low-cost PC-based drafters, rather than liberating designers, merely perpetuated outdated conventions.

The problem with most mainstream cadcam systems was that designers usually had to know exactly what they wanted before sitting down in front of the screen. And this is exactly what the conceptual designer does *not* want; the initial sketch phase of design is the back-of-the-envelope stuff, in which the designers are struggling to formulate and externalize their ideas. The last thing they want is a computer pestering them for dimensions, angles and tolerances good enough to build a working prototype. Not yet, at least.

Then, in the 1980s, all of a sudden, the processor developers were calling the shots. The hardware with the horsepower to handle compute-intensive tasks and manage large amounts of memory was getting more affordable by the month. Cadcam developers were already using the excess processing power to make their systems more user-friendly and the software more "intelligent" by employing object-oriented programming techniques. Designers could then have more confidence that their designs had a good chance of being right first time, and they could try out "what if?" scenarios. Most importantly, they could take more responsibility for the ultimate success of the designed product.

Free from that "prior condition of completeness" forced upon the user by procedural-type languages like Fortran, designers could really begin to use their computers to design creatively. They could tell the system as much as they wanted it to know now, and more later; they could tell it what they wanted it to do instead of spending time explaining to the machine how to go about doing it and where to find the information.

In object-oriented systems, such as Intergraph's EMS, an "object" – which can be as primitive as a line or arc, or as complex as an assembly – is defined in terms of a set of data items plus all the procedures for manipulating and controlling it. The object not only knows what it is, but also what it is legally capable of doing and how it goes about doing it, and is aware of its relationship to other objects with which it may have to interact.

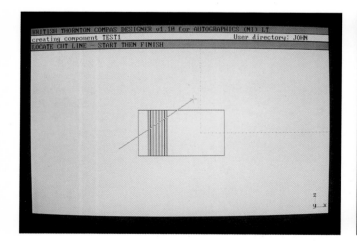

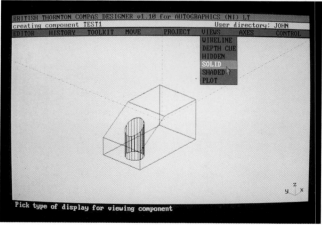

Similar objects are grouped into "classes" and these can be broken down into sub-classes which can "inherit" the data structures and functionality of the parent. The class "line" can have a sub-class "pipe" that will inherit the methods for moving, displaying and deleting, but whose data structure will also include such attributes as material and diameter. Thus new graphic elements can be defined with the minimum of duplication and least amount of disturbance, making it easier to reduce the maintenance of the software.

Common code can be shared by many classes in the system and where differences do exist it is necessary to indicate only the changes. Object-oriented programming allows software engineers – and designers – to develop new applications by taking advantage of previously developed objects, and all the intelligence inherent in them.

Objects take cad beyond the confines of physical geometry. The designer can try out variations of a design using different materials, sending off a stack say, for stress analysis, each of which can then be explored more readily.

Design Modeller was developed by Autographics, a Northern Ireland company set up by John and Julia Frazer, which runs on a Research Machines Nimbus or IBM PC/AT. In this package, the whole history of the design process is automatically recorded so it can be rerun, altered or evaluated at any time – a feature indispensible to concept designers who like to play around with ideas before committing themselves.

This "history" function also enables designers to gain an insight into the manufacturing implications of their styling decisions on a component's physical properties (weight, volume, moment of inertia) and the likely production cost penalties. "A need was identified for programs that allow designers to change their minds," says Frazer, "allowing precise definitions of components for the purposes of evaluation, but at the same time permitting the easy change of fundamental shapes or proportions. With CSG (constructive solid geometry) modellers like Geomod and Boxer, this is not always possible. Unless you can get at the tree of Boolean operators the design process is irreversible."

Design Modeller is also sympathetic to a designer's needs. Its menus use familiar words, taken mostly from manufacturing vocabulary, rather than computer-oriented ones like Boolean and Euler. They can create components from blocks, billets, sheets, turned parts or extrusions using commands such as drill, punch and chamfer.

The biggest handicap to working in 3D on a flattish 2D screen is being able to picture exactly where you are in space. Design Modeller uses a mouse-controlled 3D cursor, in the form of a conventional corner-of-a-cube x,y,z axes symbol. As the mouse is moved around, the cursor moves in the horizontal (x,y) plane. Press the left-hand mouse button and the cursor is restrained and moves only vertically (in z). Release the button, the vertical position locks and the cursor is free to move in the horizontal again. As the cursor moves around the screen, the nearest face or line on the current model is highlighted, usually in red.

The model being worked on is displayed in isometric or perspective wireframe. When a face is identified for drilling or cutting, the component is automatically rotated so that the view is perpendicular to the viewer – as if it were placed on a workshop bench with the designer looking down at it. When satisfied with an object, the designer can then get the system to generate hidden-line or shaded pictures of the components or assemblies (components can be "glued" together in limited ways). To satisfy the production office, first- or third-angle engineering drawings can be produced, as many as needed, in a consistent style. The program can also be linked directly to machine tools so that the part can be manufactured. Design Modeller cannot yet do everything a supermini-based solids modeller can do, or produce every conceivable kind of shape. It is more of a demonstrator of what could be done in the next generation of modeller.

Frazer sees it as a potential designer-friendly front-end to bigger systems. But it is well aware of its own limitations (it will not let you embark on a course of action that it cannot handle); it is difficult to crash and because of this has ensured a place for itself in education.

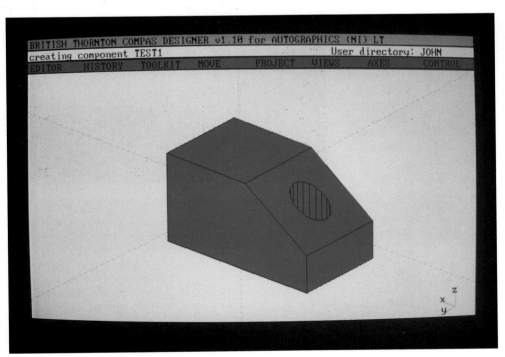

◄ Three stages in solid modelling using Design Modeller, showing the perpendicular view being prepared to have the corner cut; the whole object, with the cut made, in perspective; and, finally, the object with all hidden lines removed and rendered.

BRITISH THORNTON COMPAS DESIGNER v1.10 for AUTOGRAPHICS (NI) LT
creating component TEST1   User directory: JOHN
EDITOR   HISTORY   TOOLKIT   MOVE   PROJECT   VIEWS   AXES   CONTROL

Pro-engineer (distributed in Europe by Ferranti Infographics) is another system that promises to offer maximum flexibility of definition and modification during product conceptualization. It is described as an interactive feature-based parametric solids modeller, and runs on engineering workstations from DEC, Apollo and Sun.

Like Design Modeller it allows models to be constructed and modified dynamically: the designer can add to or delete from the base model without suffering the penalties incurred with conventional "static" solids modellers. The need for exact dimensional information has been eliminated – the general shape is captured parametrically, and dimensions can be modified either by inputting a value, by establishing a relationship to other parametric dimensions or by defining a relationship to a table of parts. A designer can establish datums, axes and space envelopes, sketch a part, then generate a component model that can be further refined by adding features, such as holes, bosses and flanges.

Pro-engineer is capable of modelling objects with any number of planar, cylindrical, conical, spherical, toroidal or sculptured surfaces. Models of assemblies or parts can be viewed and shaded from pre-set angles, interrogated for mass-property data, used to produce associative and automatically dimensioned 2D drawings, and exploded diagrams. The term "associative" means that amendments to the drawing are automatically updated in the model and vice versa.

The ability to generate unconstrained forms has also been a major concern to potential cadcam users. Sculptor William Latham has managed to tease "organic" forms from a solids modeller (IBM's Winsom) that is more used to handling chunky engineering components.

Latham is currently working at IBM's UK Scientific Centre in Winchester towards a PhD thesis entitled "An interactive computer graphics system for designing complex forms." The research base is the Royal College of Art (where Latham developed his rule-based "evolutionary tree" shape inspirer) and – showing the seriousness of the work – funding comes from the UK Science and Engineering Research Council. Latham's program Form Synth is intended to help designers with the sort of 3D products that have to fulfil certain functional requirements, but are still allowed scope in their overall shape: products such as sofas, light fittings and bottles.

Wireframes, which can be created and oriented interactively are sent off to be textured, lit, blended (softened by rounding off edges and filleting joins) and finally ray-traced for authentic appearance according to the laws of optics. Texture is generated in 3D using fractal techniques so the object looks as if it has been carved from a solid textured block. Latham has found that the smallest amount of texture added to a polished metal or glossy plastic object makes it appear even more realistic.

Hardcopy output – the bane of the computer-aided designer – is currently to a slide camera, but could be to holograms or physical objects using numerically controlled milling or the Fotoform stereolithography machine that builds up layers of ultraviolet curable polymer, pioneered by the US firm, 3D Systems.

At the concept stage of the design process, the designer is mostly concerned with evolving new and novel product forms while resolving the constraints of the design brief to his or her satisfaction. Rough sketches and freehand layouts, plus associated notes and calculations have been sufficient for this task in the past.

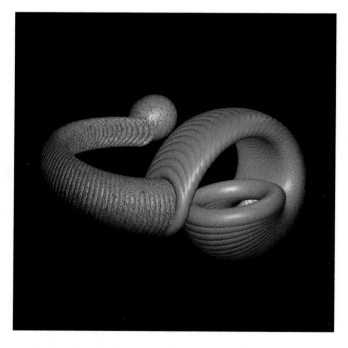

▼ William Latham has paved the way for designers to use conventional solids modellers to explore unconstrained free-form shapes, confident that the data exists in the computer to attempt manufacture.

Conventional cad at an early stage can stifle creativity by its insistence that the designer provides the system with exact dimensional and geometric information right from the start. But there are systems in development that can provide the designer with valuable analyses – weights, volumes, moments of inertia – and information on clearance and clash detection, while not committing anyone to a final shape or form. Until they are an inexpensive – and portable – reality, designers will still rely on the clutch pencil and the nearest used envelope to record their spontaneous conceptual thoughts.

◀ ▶ These cellphones were designed at Brand New for the West German manufacturer Hagenuk, using Deltacam's Duct surface modelling software running on Apollo workstations. Different views and colour schemes can easily be generated from one wireframe model.

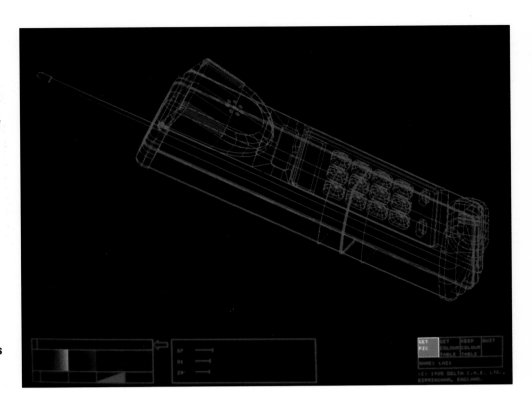

▼ William Latham's evolutionary tree, a detail of which is shown here, is described as an ideas generator for designers. Simple geometric forms, called primitives — such as a cube, a cylinder, a cone, and so on — are systematically distorted or added to according to a prescribed set of rules. Quite complex shapes can result in just a few generations. This is a process not unknown to the Bauhaus and to users of cad solids modellers.

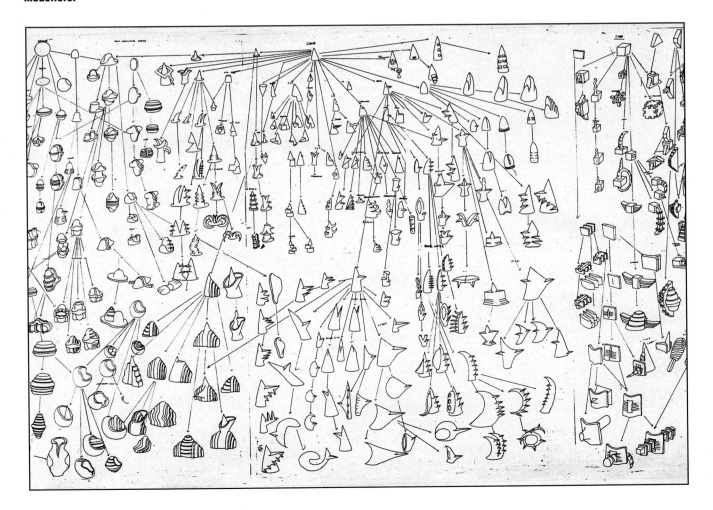

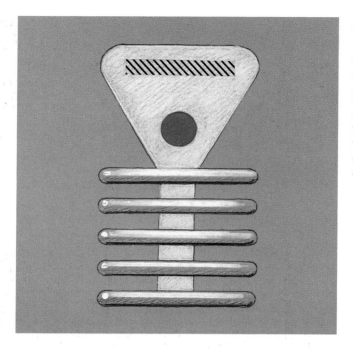

◀ Presentation sketch by King-Miranda for the key/information complex in a console for Olivetti's man-machine interface project of 1983. Representing the chosen configuration, it is rendered in coloured pencil on tinted card. A simple elevation with the merest hint of a third dimension, it has all the authority of a hieroglyph.

Case study: # King-Miranda Associates, Milan

Perry King and Santiago Miranda have been working together in Milan since 1976. Perry King was born in London and studied at Birmingham School of Art and in 1964 went on to work for Olivetti for five years, notably on the celebrated red Valentine typewriter with Ettore Sottsass. Santiago Miranda is Spanish-born, from Seville, and studied at the Escuela de Artes Aplicades there until he moved to Milan. The practice has an international reputation for graphics, furniture, lighting design for Arteluce/Flos and "interactive" industrial design, particularly for Olivetti, with both Sottsass and Mario Bellini.

Their Airmail chair was designed for Marcatré in 1984 and they have since worked for Disform in Barcelona, producing the Beato range of free-form upholstered easy chairs. The La Vuelta range of tables for the Basque manufacturer Akeba includes dining tables, conference tables, writing desks and receptionists' tables. A common element is a surreal leg made from cast aluminium in the form of the front fork of a bicycle, and tops like saddles – homage to Spain's obsession with cycle racing (see page 98). A research project for Olivetti in 1983 to improve the ergonomics of computer consoles for non-experienced operators and to remove aggression from the workplace resulted in the membrane keyboards shown here.

Drawing and illustration skills are key components of the creative design process for King–Miranda, who manage to combine high-tech research with whimsical artistry. For Marcatré, for example, they produced a series of five large drawings depicting the five senses. "There must be logic and discipline in the work," says King, "but there also is the need to stimulate the senses and give enjoyment."

◄ Preliminary sketches in coloured pencil on paper reveal an exploration of various concepts: the technique is as loose as the idea.

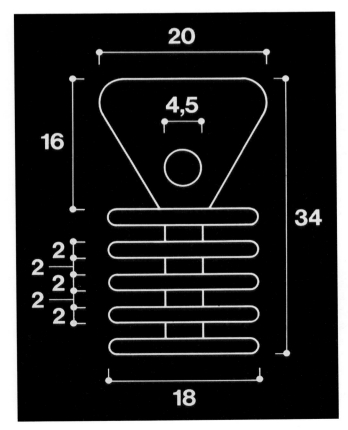

◄ A dimensioned drawing in ink on tracing paper consists of the outline of the presentation sketch (opposite page), with numbers added.

▲ Concept sketches in chalk and pencil on tracing paper, dating from 1988, show a design emerging for a new keyboard proposal which developed from the original one.

The designer has never resembled Rodin's "Thinker" who sits in solitary meditation, but has in contrast always externalised his thoughts, not only as an end product in the form of a design, but as an integral part of the process itself in the form of drawings and sketches

Bryan Lawson, "How Designers Think," 1980

6 Presentation Graphics and Visuals

Highly rendered pictorial presentation drawings became increasingly important as the engineers' orthographic drawings – in the quest to become complete and unambiguous representations of a designed object – became unreadable to the person being asked to foot the bills: the client, patron, manager or accountant. Early examples of presentation drawings were in fact working drawings executed in pen and ink with a watercolour wash, but with the need for legibility on multiple copies the colour washes were reluctantly replaced by cross-hatching.

With the growth of independent design consultancies from the 1940s onwards, there became a need to "sell" concepts to the client, and an engineering drawing was inadequate. Designers had to present a realistic rendering, showing the client exactly what he was going to get for his money. Rendering skills became important. Some designers employed watercolour artists to produce their presentation graphics. Raymond Loewy, a fashion illustrator by trade, was able to do his own. The Italian designers, all architecture-trained, had the edge: the act of drawing has always been a joy to architects. Gouache and airbrush ruled during the 1950s and 1960s, and Syd Mead in his work for Ford and US Steel was king; by the 1970s the marker drawing had become dominant.

The skills needed to produce presentation drawings or visuals are very different from those required in concept design. Designer Richard Seymour of the London practice Seymour Powell contends that a presentation drawing is "painting by numbers" and anyone following the exercises in his partner Dick Powell's excellent book *Presentation Techniques* will be able to produce acceptable results. Drawing for presentation is all about colouring and rendering, and is an aside from the process of designing a product. Nevertheless, without a successful presentation – and the approval of the client – the design is unlikely to proceed.

▼ This exhibition information counter for Nixdorf, designed for the 1987 Hanover-Messe by Schürer Design, was rendered in marker on A3 board.

Presentation Graphics and Visuals

Interestingly, after writing the book, Powell simplified his presentation style: he began using more physical models, with concept drawings conforming to the same colour scheme – rendered in white on graduated colour board with the shading in blue – so that a client would not be distracted or influenced in the choice of a design alternative so early in the process by the colours used in the presentation drawing. It is also true to say that the more famous the designer, the fewer presentation drawings he or she needs to submit. Star designers are known quantities and are engaged by a client to put their stamp on a product. They are given *carte blanche* and will often come up with one solution which in their consideration is the one that is right for this particular client. An "average" design consultancy will be expected to present perhaps four concepts, of which one may be the designer's own favourite, and it is down to the designer's persuasive powers and diplomacy to direct the client into choosing that particular approach.

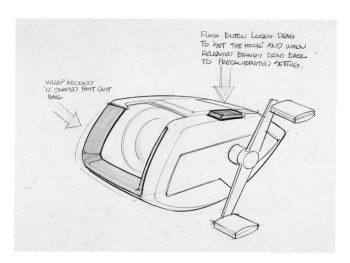

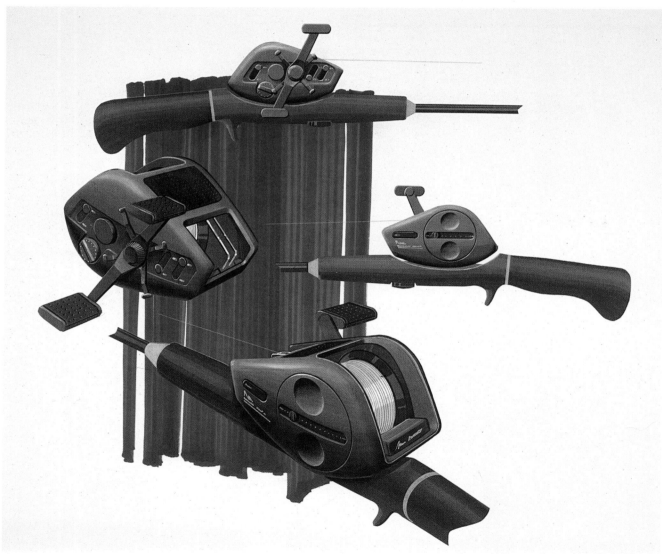

▲ John Betts of Henry Dreyfuss Associates in New York designed these baitcasting reels for Swedish manufacturer Abu Garcia Produktion. The multi-view marker rendering, with perspectives and elevations, was used with others to help the client determine two designs to be modelled. The sketch (top) by James Ryan was used to communicate to the client certain functional aspects of the design.

◀ The prototype of the baitcasting reel by Henry Dreyfuss Associates.

▼ Lyons-Ames in London produced Wine Saver proposal number 5 for Anglo Syphons. The main drawing is full size, using felt tip pen and marker. The cross-hatched sections, done in twice size, show the client that the designers were considering not only the aesthetics of the product's shape, but also how the size, centre of gravity and construction were to be tackled. The prototype of the final scheme chosen is shown below; note how it differs from the earlier concept sketch.

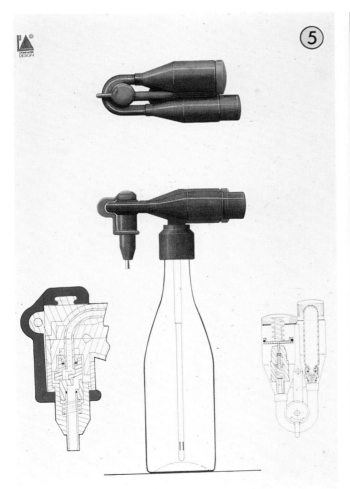

Presentation Graphics and Visuals

► Syd Mead was a designer for Ford in Detroit in the late 1950s, worked for US Steel in the 1960s and Giugiaro's ItalDesign studio in the 1970s. He was credited as "Futurist" on the science fiction film *Bladerunner.* The sequence shown here starts with a small-scale preliminary colour sketch in gouache to establish the composition and colour balance.

▲ The final artwork begins with a line drawing on 500×760mm illustration board.

Drawing for presentation is all about producing a stylish drawing – one that is likely to appeal to the client – as quickly as possible. Shortcuts and conventions will be used here, as elsewhere later in the process. Designers will also strive to make drawings recognizably theirs, whether they deny it or not. They are also not immune to changes in fashion. Thus Syd Mead's colourful fantasy cars for Ford can be placed squarely in the 1950s and 1960s; the striated marker lines behind the products of the 1980s will identify these drawings as belonging to their own decade.

As the profession of *design* evolved from "applied art," and commercial artists became designers, so they seemed almost ashamed of their artistic roots, preferring the businesslike tag of industrial problem-solver. Rendering skills inevitably suffered. But as design threatened to become just another branch of marketing, a backlash in the form of Post-modernism began to restore detail and decoration to product design (and why not?). Drawing skills have never been so greatly sought after.

▲ The drawing is blocked in with six or seven key colours in gouache, using a ½in wide flat brush. Secondary details are then filled in.

▲ Airbrush is used to refine the surface of the entrance soffit and the snow, and to soften the brush strokes generally. Finally, the figures, foliage and vehicle trim are highlighted with a fine brush.

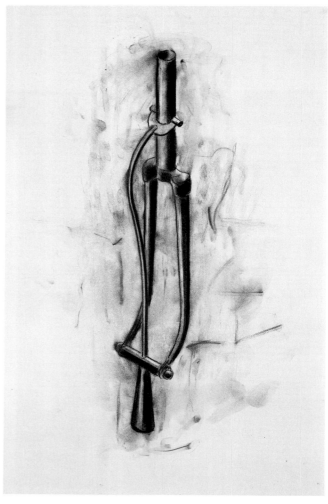

▲ King-Miranda Associates designed the "Vuelta" table for Akaba in 1987, inspired by Spain's obsession with cycle racing stars. The main picture is a perspective in acrylic paint and charcoal on paper; the detail of the table is in graphite on paper, and for the sketch of the leg they used charcoal on paper.

The influence of Memphis lives on in this selection of drawings. The designers represented here demonstrate that presentation drawings need not be restrained by the tenets of Modernism and the legacy of the "problem solving" 1960s, but can help in projecting joy and exuberance.

◄ Bořek Šípek's "Ota Otanek" chair for Vitra of 1988 is an askew orthographic that sets cool and rational design against the baroque and poetic, combining wood, steel and sheet copper into a gracious, wistful unity. The use of the half-elevation at the top left to represent a symmetrical object is reminiscent of boat design.

▼ Anthony Dunne produced this stark and moody hi-fi concept in chalk and pencil while at the Royal College of Art, London.

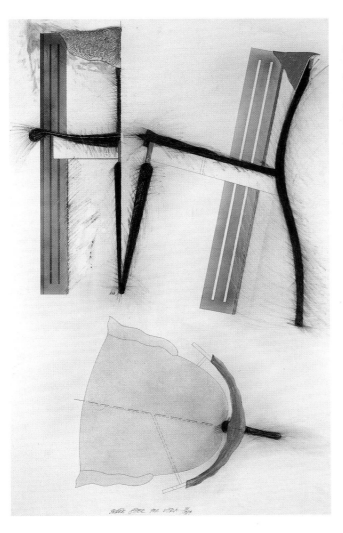

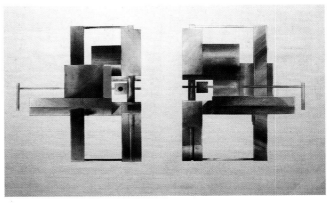

▼ A coloured pencil sketch on yellow trace of the final version of Mario Bellini's "ETP 55" portable typewriter for Olivetti of 1987 emphasizes

the dynamic of the diagonal: you can feel the copy shooting out. The hand explains the ergonomic curve on the keys, as well as giving scale.

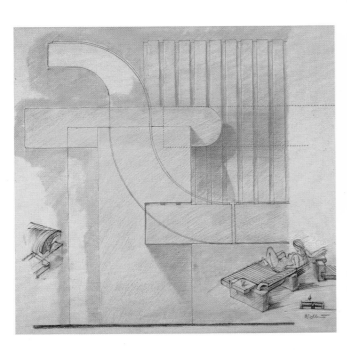

◄ Mario Bellini's 1985 partial elevation drawing and sketches for the "Forte Rosso" bench, to be made in red stone, is again executed in coloured pencil on yellow

trace, an affectation said to be peculiar to architects, and slightly at odds with the subject. Bellini also shows his skill as a life artist in the sketches at the bottom right.

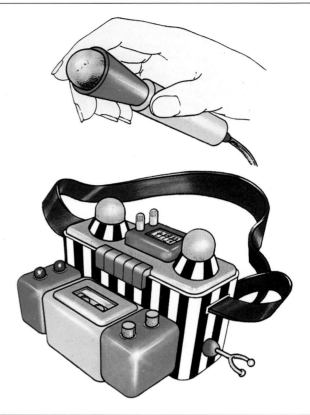

▲ Michele De Lucchi's garish cartoon-like renderings of a hi-fi for Memphis in 1980 were naturally meant to shock the more staid design community of the early 1980s. The technique, however, rapidly developed into a visual style and now itself looks dated. The main drawings are in exaggerated three-point perspective (Memphis designers more usually employed exotic metric projections). An oblique projection is used on the three boxes at the bottom right, where the front elevation is the only area of interest.

Composition

Good presentation drawing owes more to fine art than it does to reality, whatever that may be. Prospective designers will do well to study the masters – David Crisp of the London practice Crisp and Wilson sets Degas up as an example for students learning to draw; Tucker Viemeister of the New York practice Smart Design lists Leonardo da Vinci.

Photographic realism – for the photograph with its single viewpoint and fixed depth of field is the present-day paradigm for "reality" – is a limited aspiration. The lessons that painters have developed over the centuries for presenting visual clues that exploit the mind's ability to accept clues to previous experience should not be ignored.

Art – and presentation drawing – is more concerned with conveying a desired impression, and not necessarily with presenting geometric and physical accuracy. That comes later, in the general arrangement and detail production drawings. A presentation drawing should be like a cartoon, where features are exaggerated, albeit subtly and by choice of view, to get over a message with economy of effort. It should be remembered that artists such as Matisse and Picasso worked hard to make their drawings appear simple – Matisse would draw all day "to get his hand in," discarding pictures as he went, to produce in the evening just one perfect and fluid drawing that looked as if it had been dashed off in seconds.

There are many books available that give step-by-step examples for producing convincing visuals of a designer's concept, good enough for a client to make that important decision to commit finance to take the design further along the design cycle.

The designer should be bold, and approach the rendering in the knowledge that it will probably take two or three goes to build up the confidence to attack the final version. An outline "underlay" inserted beneath the translucent marker paper can be used as a guide, and it is well worth spending time to get it right in the first place – no amount of rendering skill can disguise a badly produced perspective.

Designers should develop a strong sense of graphic balance. That means composition, and there are rules and conventions (the golden section, the law of thirds, etc.) that

can be used – and abused. Drawing from life is advised. Drawing is all about looking – careful observation of the disposition of tone, reflections, highlights and shadow. Conversely, the act of drawing is an aid to understanding the structure of objects. The process is iterative, with the designer's skills improving and the visual vocabulary increasing all the time.

Economy leads to visual clichés, and these can be put to good use only if the designer is aware of them. "California chrome," for example – a trick of the airbrush artist – assumes that the glossy object being drawn stands surrounded by yellow sand surmounted by a deep blue sky which graduates to white at the horizon where it meets the dark desert. This is patently ludicrous in many situations, but it is used with great effect almost universally, on the aerials of radios for example, regardless of the product's location and background. Shiny automobile bodies often reflect a city roofline of skyscrapers. The details, not always apparent at first glance, give the viewer visual clues as to the lifestyle of the aspiring end user.

There are other conventions that add to the vocabulary of the presentation drawing. When a curved object is depicted, it is common to leave a thin band of "reflected" light instead of taking the shadow right to the edge bounding the surface. Square windows, preferably with old-fashioned quartered panes, make effective highlights (also called "farkles" or "chings") on a shiny product, even if such a window would not be found in the depicted environment. Comic books are a good source to be studied for tips on rendering, for how to use high-contrast reflections and theatrical lighting. Marker drawings in particular exaggerate the qualities of a surface to be informative and convey excitement.

Markers are used for presentation drawings for their immediacy and quick results, their colour range – which is increasing all the time – and their compatibility with other media. They require little preparation and no cleaning up afterwards. Marker drawings are at least as good and often more appropriate than drawings done by airbrush, in gouache or watercolour. They offer a limited opportunity to blend and manipulate tonal value, nevertheless they help the design process move at the pace expected of today's designer, and allow a greater number of concepts to be communicated to the client and the other members of the design team.

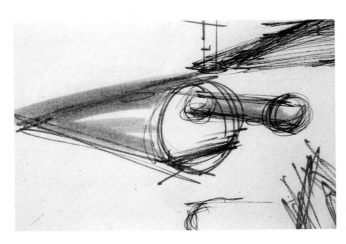

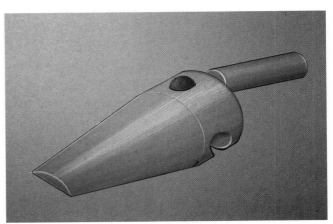

▲ Another no-nonsense, sufficient-realism sketch and subsequent marker visual by Michael Cousins of Cousins Design, New York, showing the

"Dynamic" car vacuum cleaner (see also his hairdryer on page 82 and compare his style with that of Raymond Loewy on page 11).

▲ In this sequence of drawings, Julian Quincey demonstrates how to render a drawing of an automobile in markers. He begins by lightly tracing the drawing from a first sketch on A2 sized layout paper, using a Bic fine ballpoint pen which will become invisible when covered by marker. The wheel ellipses are drawn in using guides. He always has a sheet of clean paper to lean his hand on, to keep the surface clean.

▼ The sides of the vehicle are blocked in using Edding cool grey 7 for the upper body and Magic Marker cool grey 3 for the lower area. While this is still wet, Magic Marker cool grey 4 is used to shade the lower portion, thus avoiding a distinct edge or "tide mark." The feature line is emphasized with Bic fine ballpoint to stop it from disappearing.

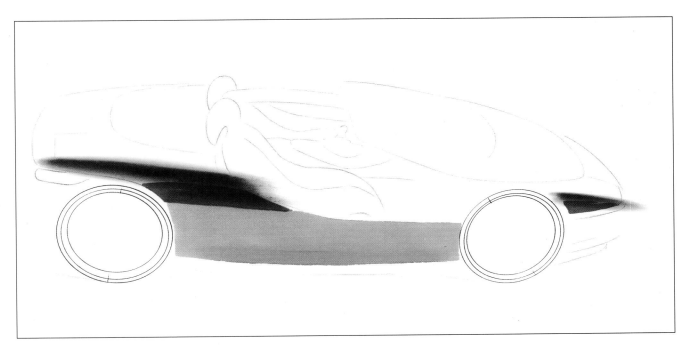

▲ The graduated colour on the top edge of the body is achieved by sweeping a cotton handypad loaded with a 5:1 mixture of Rembrandt black pastel and talcum powder. The pastel is scraped into powder using a scalpel blade. Another pad containing talcum powder alone is wiped over the lighter part to achieve an even smoother graduation of colour. For a constant tone, it is necessary to go over the edges of the car. The excess can be rubbed out using an eraser, or the picture can be cut out when completed and remounted.

▼ Magic Marker black on top of cool grey 7 is used to represent the reflected horizon on the upper portion of the body side. This is further accentuated by adding a white pencil line, faded upwards by changing the pressure of application. White pencil is also used to delineate the upper edge of the lower plastic cladding. A mixture of Rembrandt mid grey, black and talcum powder is used to tone down the area below the white pencil. The seats are blocked in using an Edding yellow ochre marker, with Parisian blue to denote shadowed areas. The centres of the wheels are picked up using Magic Marker cool grey 2. Black marker was used to express the horizon line, and the cast shadow from the bodywork above, on the chrome exhaust pipe below the rear indicator.

▲ The car's upper surface is next. Cool grey markers (2, 3, 4, 5 and 7) are used to suggest the instrument panel behind the glass and cool grey 7 is used to render side reflections on the bodywork. A good hint is to study photographs of cars and their "authentic" reflections to get this right. In general, the car's side should be thought of as a highly reflective barrel shape, picking up reflections from the sky, represented by graduated pastel, and from buildings and the horizon, with additional reflected earthy/sandy tones or reflected shadows below, rendered in marker. Texture has been added to the interior by rubbing a coloured pencil over aluminium mesh placed under the paper, a technique called frottage. All manner of textures can be created in this way, experimenting with anything from Perspex bathroom tiles to highly textured vinyl.

▼ Parisian blue marker is now added to the interior and some cast shadowing to the gearshift and gaiter. Pastel is again scraped and mixed with talcum powder and, after lightly dusting and wiping the drawing with talc to smooth off the surface, applied in long clean sweeps until the required level of even graduation is reached. It is best not to put too much paste! on at a time, so that it retains its clean quality, and each layer should be fixed with a little matt spray, left to dry before proceeding with the next.

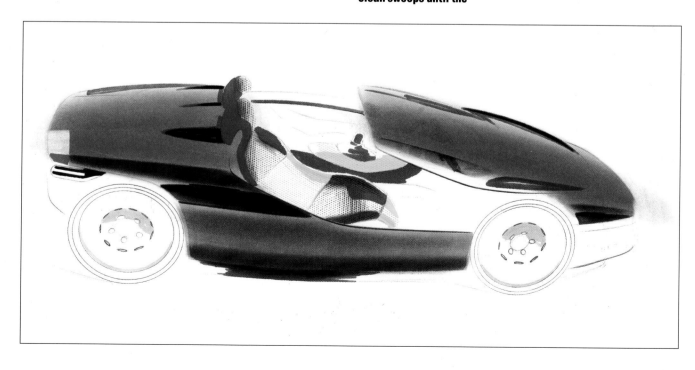

▲ Another layer of blue pastel has been added, followed by a little black to achieve the intensity required. It is important to keep both the hands and the paper clean, to avoid smudges: lean on a piece of paper while working, and clean up any excess pastel immediately with a soft eraser. At this level of finish, the lines of the car should be brought out by making them heavier and thicker. This has the effect of tightening up the whole picture. Lastly, a white pencil is used on the tops and edges of the wings and to highlight the top edges of the lower panels. This can be accentuated by adding white gouache with a fine brush, remembering to maintain a constant direction to represent this imaginary cast light.

▼ To finish off the drawing, crude graduations of cool greys are added to the wheels, and the car's cast shadow is blocked in. On this base, black and white pencils are used to create a smoother graduation of tones. A layer of yellow pastel is added to the far side of the car; grey and beige pastel is applied to the wheels. The front and rear bumpers are both treated the same way as the lower panel earlier, and more white pencil, gouache and black ballpoint pen are added to bring out the details. Normally the completed drawing would then be cut out and mounted on either a plain white sheet or a spattered background created by spraying aerosol very lightly so that the nozzle clogs and spatters the paint in a pattern.

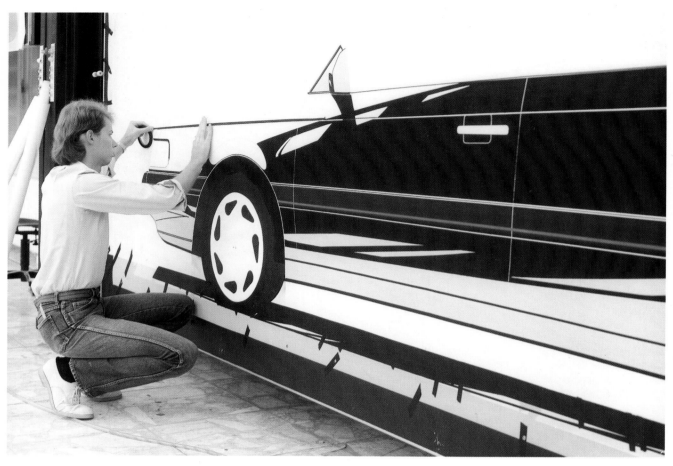

Automotive design has its own breed of designers and illustrators, with one thing in common: to sell speed and "lifestyle" to the client and consumer. Marker is the preferred medium for visualizations, although airbrush is invariably used for the technical illustrations which follow manufacture (see chapter 8).

◄ ▲ Full-size elevations of the latest model, like these of the Volkswagen Passat, are produced using tape for the linework and paper stencils for airbrushing. The completely stylized diagonal reflections make the car appear far more streamlined than it actually is.

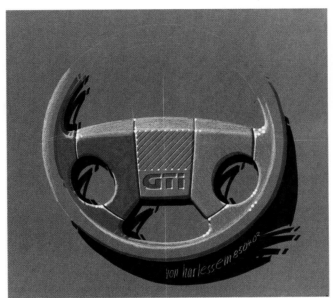

◄ This steering wheel, also from Volkswagen, uses chalk on coloured paper with frottage to express texture. The incomplete circle and dynamic marker strokes, especially in the lower shadow, all suggest aggressive speed.

► This study of a dashboard and seating from the Bertone Studio is remarkably restrained for most automotive designers. Extensive use of frottage has been made to convey the upholstery.

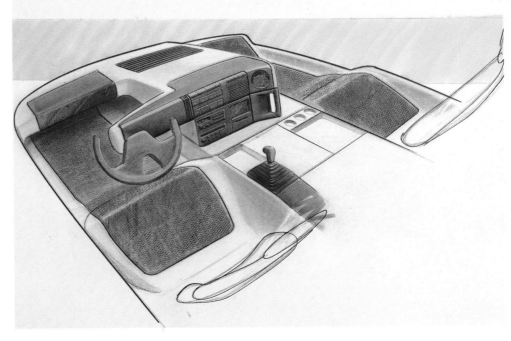

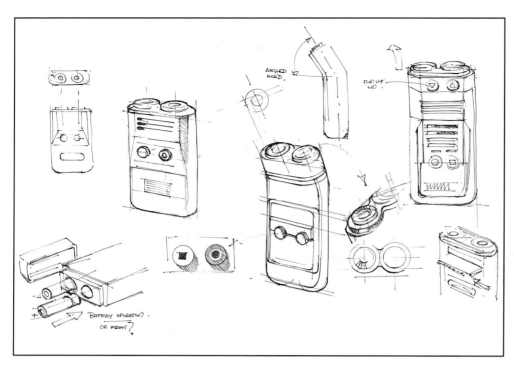

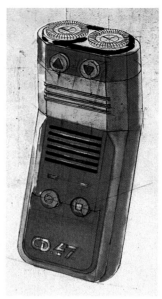

▼ Once the image has been lightly transferred to board, Frisk film is laid over the entire illustration, so that the areas to be successively sprayed can be cut out before airbrushing. First, the areas to be sprayed cerulean blue on the front face and down the right-hand side are removed and flat colour sprayed on the front, fading to white (for reflected light) on the right-hand side. When the paint is dry, the masks are replaced.

Next, the masks running around the front face are removed and the area is sprayed from mid-blue on the right and underside to light blue/white on the left-hand side. A light blue vignette is then sprayed on to the top left face. Finally, the top face on which the cutters are mounted is sprayed a light blue with dark blue reflections, to suggest a glossy surface. All masks are then replaced.

▼ The next stage is to add a darker blue to areas of the cerulean, fading off to the right. To check colours in relation to each other during spraying, a cotton bud can be used to rub paint gently from the masks.

▼ The masks on the front face are removed and sprayed with cadmium yellow to full strength. The left-hand side is then treated with a light vignette on the upper left-hand face and lower left face. The masks for the top right-hand side are removed and the exposed area sprayed with yellow ochre, making the top, downward-facing, side slightly darker in tone by an application of sepia. Sepia is also used on the bottom yellow edge. All masks are replaced.

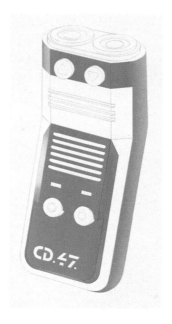

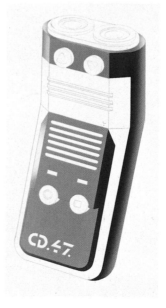

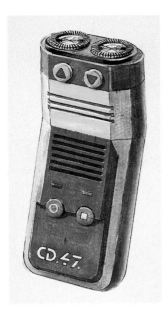

◄◄ In this sequence, John Scorey uses a step-by-step approach to produce an airbrush rendering of a mains-rechargeable shaver. First a design is selected from an A3 sheet of concept sketches – the chosen solution is in the top right-hand corner – and a working drawing made on tracing paper. This is then photocopied on to tracing paper of at least 90 gsm weight. The back of the photocopy is sprinkled with graphite dust which is rubbed in with a tissue or cotton wool swab. Using a sharp instrument, the lines of the image are then pushed through on to CS10 board.

▼ The top of the shaver is modelled by spraying indigo/black to the front edge using loose paper masks for soft edges, leaving the turning edge white as if it were picking up reflected light. The top face is sprayed to mid-grey, and the reflection of the cutters sprayed using an ellipse guide held 2mm from the board's surface to act as a loose mask. The outer edge of the cutters is sprayed a blue/grey tone on the right-hand side, a loose mask leaving the outer edge white. The cutters should be treated as short vertical cylinders and rendered with highlight, lowlight and reflected light.

◄ Separate photocopies are worked on with coloured pencils to produce a colour rough. If no other colour reference exists, this can help resolve any colour problems before airbrushing commences. The reason for using a photocopy at this stage is that the original remains intact should anything go wrong.

▼ The soft shadows under the buttons also require the use of loose masks. The shadows for the top set of buttons are sprayed with separate colours: yellow ochre and sepia for the yellow face; blue for the cerulean blue face. Highlights are added using permanent white gouache. Those running along straight edges can be put in using a fine sable brush along a ruler's edge. A darker line next to the highlighted edge emphasizes the corners and makes the highlights appear brighter. Highlights can also be created by removing pigment with a scalpel blade. The slots on the cutters are drawn in using a Rotring pen.

▼ The recessed grooves are sprayed next. The masks are removed from the upward faces and a pale yellow sprayed on. The vertical recessed faces which are in shadow are sprayed with yellow ochre and sepia. The ventilation slots on the blue face are unmasked and an indigo/black mixture sprayed on. The buttons, which are curved, are sprayed with cadmium yellow, darkening into a crescent towards the bottom right with yellow ochre.

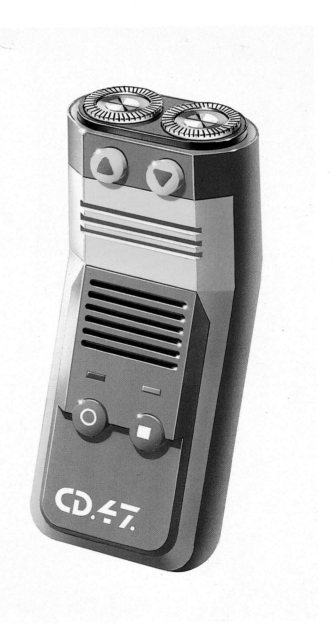

Computer-aided styling

The main and most fundamental difference between a marker or airbrush drawing rendered manually and a computer-generated visual is that the conventional paper drawing is a 2D illlusion; the computer drawing, if it has been modelled in 3D, exists in three dimensions.

A computer visualization can be looked at from any angle or viewpoint (though not simultaneously in real time, since a new view may take some minutes to compute) and the aim of a so-called "computer-aided styling" system is to shade, texture and light the wireframe model, sending the same stimuli to the brain as a viewer might experience seeing a physical object in a naturalistic setting.

First a 3D model must be built within the computer that defines the entire geometry of the object and its environment. The simplest way of constructing the model is to use the software tool called a solids modeller (discussed in Chapter 4), which will produce a complete and unambiguous description of the model in 3D space by performing either Boolean operations (union, intersection, difference) on "primitive" shapes such as cones, cubes, cylinders and spheres, or by extruding a 2D profile, or by sweeping a profile around an axis, or some combination of all of these methods. The resulting shapes are welded together or bits are subtracted until you arrive at the desired form. Built-in checks make sure the topology is always correct and that you are not creating Escher-like impossible objects.

Alternatively, a designer can use a "skin-deep" object generated on a surface modeller as input. This class of modeller is particularly adept at handling the doubly curved "fair" shapes loved by the designers of automobile bodies and telephone handsets. When rendered they look just as substantial as a "solid" model, but do not exhibit the same attributes – mass properties will be more difficult to extract, for example.

Each vertex of the model is then mathematically transformed to generate a perspective picture of the object in wireframe on the image plane, and the correct depth information is stored in the computer's database. On most systems the model can be moved around at this stage, to find the most aesthetically pleasing position. At present, the wireframe view has to be fixed and "sent away" to the computer for a while (maybe overnight) to be rendered and lit. The computer then works out which surfaces should be visible and which are hidden to the viewer, and uses a light reflection routine to predict the colours and spatial distribution of the light rays reflected from, refracted through or absorbed by each surface in the scene. Finally, the image is rendered by the computer selecting the appropriate red, green and blue intensities for each pixel on the screen.

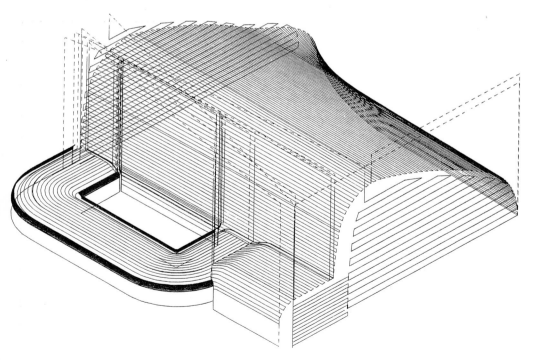

◄ ► Deltacam's surface modelling software, Duct, running on an Apollo workstation, is used here to model and visualize a plastic jug kettle. The 3D data can also be used to create the 2D orthographic drawings (right); the mesh required for finite element and plastic flow analyses (above right), and to generate and verify the path of the machine tool that will make a full-size model and eventually cut the moulds (left).

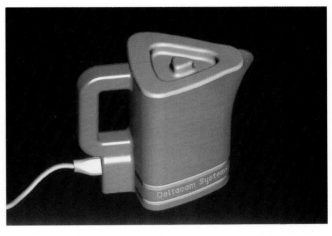

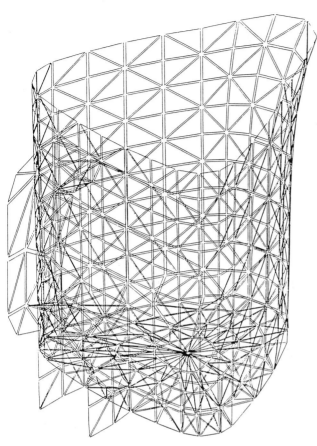

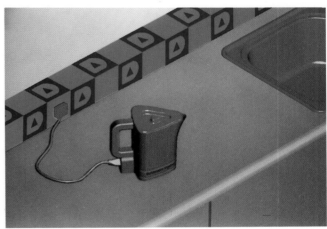

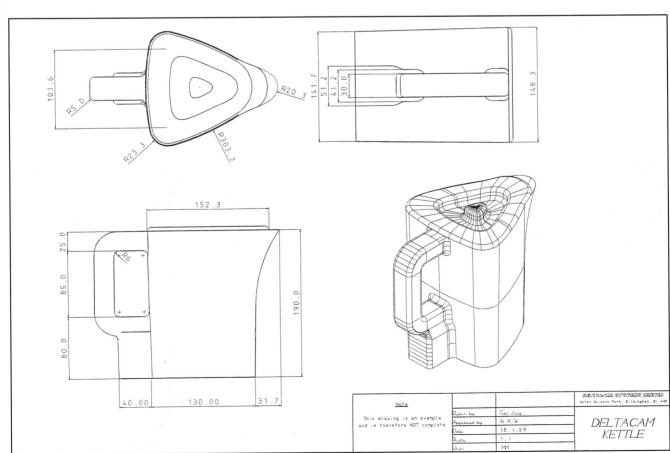

Note	DELTACAM SYSTEMS LIMITED
This drawing is an example and is therefore NOT complete	Aston Science Park, Birmingham, B7 4AP

Drawn by	Carl Jung
Approved by	N.K.W
Date	18.1.89
Scale	1:1
Units	MM

DELTACAM KETTLE

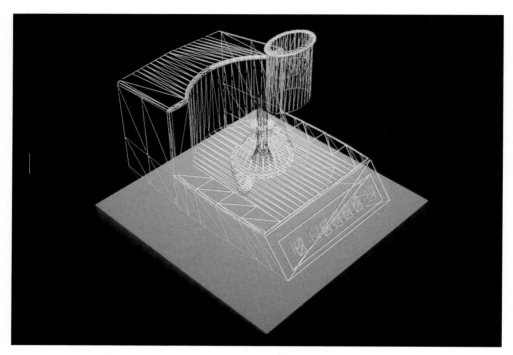

◀ ▼ This visualization of a food processor was made using Ardent's Doré software. It shows how an image is built up from a wireframe model, which can be rotated and manipulated in real time, then solid shaded, and finally ray traced to generate a realistic image with transparency, reflections and marble-like solid-texture mapping.

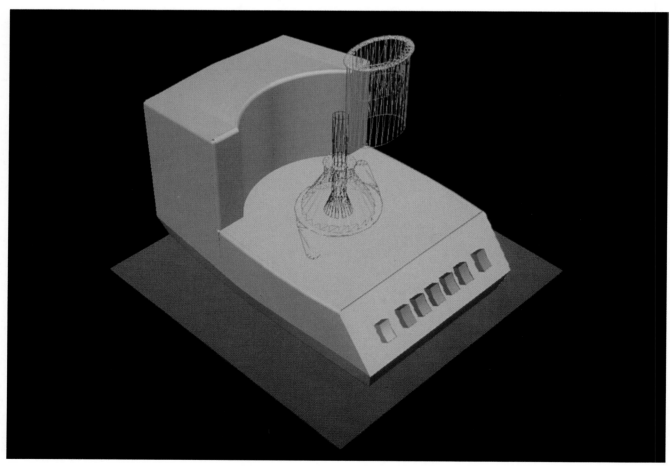

Realism

The search for photorealism (and a simulated *photograph* with its restricted depth of field, motion blur and out-of-focus backgrounds seems somehow more "real" than pin-sharp accuracy) has added weird and wonderful words to the computer graphics vocabulary: Phong and Gourand shading, fractals, ray tracing, and radiosity. How near are researchers to producing the perfect simulation, indistinguishable from actuality? The answer as you can see from the illustrations is that it can be done – but at a price, albeit a price that falls by the month.

Computer graphics journals were once filled with elaborate and ingenious algorithms for producing hidden-line and hidden-surface line drawings. Neatly, however, the newer colour raster displays, with polygon fill, have by-passed the problem of hidden-line removal. If the designer paints a scene from the back, surfaces nearer the viewer will automatically obscure objects or parts of objects that could not possibly be seen. It is also possible to fake (non-refracted) transparency by overlaying paler shades with "perforated" pixels, so that you can simulate being able to see inside the workings of a car engine, for example.

Because of constraints imposed by available processing power and the limitations of computer memory, many shortcuts have been taken to produce acceptable results. Models are often displayed as a collection of planar facets – so that a cylinder will look like the kind of pencil designed not to roll off your desk. The more facets there are, the smoother the object. But adding more facets means increasing the time needed for computation.

Lighting effects

First attempts at realism used constant value shading – the computer calculates a single intensity for the whole polygonal facet, coloured lighter or darker depending on whether it pointed towards or away from the light source. Now the faceted pencil appears to be a fluted column from a Greek temple, as something called the Mach band effect accentuates the boundaries of the faceted surfaces. Gourand shading was invented in 1971: it interpolates the shading linearly across the polygon to provide a smooth transition between edges.

Specular reflection introduces highlights, and a shading scheme developed by Phong Bui-Tuong in 1975 was based on an empirical observation that shiny surfaces reflect light unequally in different directions. Only in a perfect mirror are the angles of incidence and reflection equal. Both Gourand and Phong shading are now accessible as "firmware" on displays such as Lexidata's Solidview – i.e. software in the form of a chip that becomes part of the processor itself. They are also available as conventional software elsewhere.

An illuminated object does not look real unless shadows are present and to the computer the problem is similar to that of hidden surfaces – a shadowing algorithm determines which surfaces can be "seen" by the light source. These techniques can take account of multiple light sources, both ambient and local – and the lights can be any colour. The designer is thus able to light the object dramatically and theatrically, with no restrictions on where the lights are placed. Diffuse shadows are tedious to calculate, but a trick that is sometimes effective is to place a "negative" light source, which has the effect of sucking away the light, somewhere behind the object.

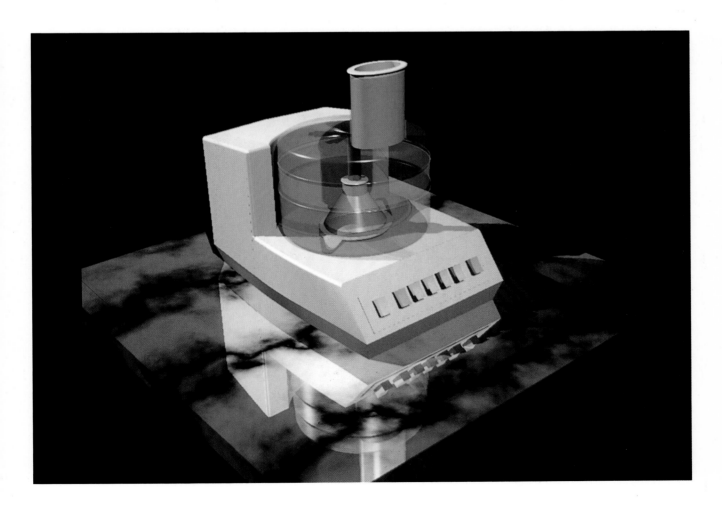

Presentation Graphics and Visuals

None of the techniques discussed so far takes account of the light-transmitting properties of surfaces, and if they are ignored the results can look limp and lacking in sparkle. Any painter knows that it is the subtle colours found in shadows and reflections that bring a picture to life.

Ray tracing was worked out in 1980, when Turner Whitted went back to basics and applied the laws of physics to the light ray's journey round a scene. He established that every time a ray encounters a surface, it divides into three parts: into diffusely reflected light; into specularly reflected light; and into transmitted or refracted light. Each ray leaving a surface is the sum of varying contributions from these three sources.

If you think of each ray growing a "tree" each time it hits a facet, it does not take a great deal of mathematical ability to

deduce that the amount of computation required to arrive at the correct optics for a scene is enormous, if not infinite.

Luckily, most of these rays shoot off to oblivion and so to pare down the number of sums needed, the calculation is done in reverse – rays are traced back from the viewpoint (shot, in effect, through the pixels of the display's screen), bounced around the scene, and arrive eventually back at the light source. Hence the term ray tracing.

Even with these economies, the task for the processor is still colossal. A display with a resolution of 1024×1024 pixels has over a million rays to deal with, and with even a modest scene containing, say, 10,000 polygons, it is obvious how the technique can strain the most powerful supercomputer. Early ray-traced images were created on a Cray; and even with progressive software improvements the process can take 40

▲ Ray tracing renders the lighting, refraction and reflectivity of this assembly of packaging concepts for Colgate. The software is Intergraph's ModelView and the processing took many hours.

▶ Radiosity is an advanced technique that can render true ambient light and the subtle colour reflections that it creates on objects next to each other. An orange placed against a white wall, for example, will transmit colour

that simple ray tracing could not calculate. These demonstration globes were modelled on an Iris 3130 workstation and rendered on an Elxsi 6400 processor at Amazing Array Productions, London.

hours of numbercrunching on a Vax minicomputer. Special graphics engines dedicated to the task are coming to the rescue, however, and ray tracing is now a possibility on an engineering workstation – and, if you have the patience, on a PC turbocharged with a go-faster graphics card.

Despite the global approach, ray tracing does fall down in certain circumstances – it will not show the glow from obscured local lights, colour bleeding or "blushes" from one object to another, for example. And each image is dependent on the current position of the observer – shift the viewpoint and the whole lot has to be recalculated.

Radiosity is an approach that determines the light energy equilibrium of all the surfaces in a static environment, independently of the observer's position. This requires the computer to solve large numbers of simultaneous equations, but once the scene has been computed in terms of its form factors and intensities, it is then only necessary to render any further views. If the first picture takes five hours of computer time, lights can be altered or turned off without having to recalculate the geometry, and the next view is produced in, say, only half an hour. Change the position of the viewer and only the rendering process has to be repeated, which can take just 15 minutes.

For sophisticated lighting models, such as radiosity, the computational requirement increases exponentially with the number of surfaces depicting the environment. The technique awaits advances in hardware, but on current form (the MIPS ratings of machines is doubling each year), designers should not have to wait too long for desktop radiosity.

Presentation Graphics and Visuals

Surfaces and texture

Most real surfaces are not smooth; they have texture, and various techniques have been developed to give a surface microscopic detail. The earliest method was to "map" or wrap around a scanned-in photograph or 2D texture that was artificially produced (on a "paint" system, such as Quantel's Paintbox, for example) on to the curved surface of the object.

James Blinn of the Jet Propulsion Labs in Pasadena was the pioneer of this effect, using it successfully on his simulations of the planets Saturn and Neptune for the Voyager 2 mission publicity. When the real image-processed pictures arrived from the space vehicle, they were remarkably similar to the simulations. Other methods "perturb" the surface to render the effect of roughness. It is now possible to reproduce synthetically almost any surface texture, and it is not difficult these days to produce 3D textures such as wood or marbling that go right through the object and appear correctly when the object is sliced.

To create natural-looking objects such as mountain ranges and clouds using facets would be a herculean task, and even then, being fabricated by humans, the results would probably not look random enough. So computer graphics enthusiasts turned to the work done in the 1930s by a man called Benoit Mandlebrot to make sense of the seemingly haphazard bits of nature. He had originally set out to measure the length of a coastline, but found the job frustratingly difficult. The details are just as complicated at each level as you home in from a bay to a cove to individual pebbles. What he did discover, however, was that there is a degree of self-similarity between the macro shape and the micro shape, and looking around he found this principle repeated throughout nature – a twig, for instance, looks just like a tree – a fact not unnoticed by model railway enthusiasts. The result of his research was a book entitled *The Fractal Geometry of Nature*.

Fractals in computer graphics start with a generator – a series of coordinate points or, for a mountain range, a mesh of polygons. This shape is scaled and rotated to fit between an initial pair of points, called the initiator, and each new pair of points on the resulting shape further subdivided recursively. All this can be implemented with just a few lines of code and produces a surface of infinite complexity. A fractal is defined as "a curve of infinite length with an infinite level of detail." No matter how closely you look, fresh detail is forever revealed.

The most spectacular examples of fractals are the mountainscapes by Loren Carpenter of Boeing Aerospace, but they have also been put to practical use by Adrian Bower when at Bath University to generate texture – such as simulated rust on an automobile's air filter.

Particles are similar to fractals, but are free floating and are used to create naturalistic "assemblies" like fire, smoke, clouds and leaves.

▲ Texture-mapping can help a designer to visualize the final appearance of a product. These pots and bowls were produced for ceramics firm Queensbury Hunt by designers Peter Hardie and Peter Comninos, using an Apollo-based CGAL system.

Programs

Commercially available computer-aided styling systems that incorporate all or most of the tools described above include Doré (dynamic object-rendering environment), a set of high-level modelling and rendering software developed for the Ardent Titan supercomputers. Scenes are built up using primitives (from single points to nurbs – non-uniform rational B-splines), attributes and other so called "studio objects," such as local light sources. An integral renderer produces wireframes, Gourand and Phong shading, solid texturing and ray tracing from a single abstract database. Doré can be tightly coupled to applications programs, sharing data and code, for kinematics and animation.

Eidostation, from the Italian computer graphics house Eidos, is aimed at computer-aided styling and runs in a Unix environment on Apollo, Sun or Silicon Graphics workstations. It is intended to integrate the modelling power of existing cadcam systems with the kind of rendering and animation techniques found in the broadcast TV and film industries.

The price of a system in 1989 was around £50,000, and for this the software allows a designer to create the geometry, then define the colour, reflectivity, translucency, iridescence and surface texture of a computer model. A sub-program gives the model animated movement: it can be rotated in space, observed from unusual angles and the shadows can be altered. Backgrounds can be montaged into the scene.

Styling software from the Canadian company Alias Research has been taken up mainly by the automotive industry. The first system was installed in 1985, at General Motors, and is currently in use at Volvo, Boeing, Subaru, NASA and Honda. It runs on Iris workstations from Silicon Graphics. As well as incorporating a powerful surface modeller, the system can create and animate environments, such as haze, fog and fire. The system boasts strong links, via standard data interchange formats IGES, DES and VDAFS, to IBM's Catia, Computervision and Intergraph cadcam systems.

Computervision (owned by Prime) was also, by the late 1980s, supplying "entertainment quality" graphics as a result of a deal with Wavefront Technologies to license, distribute and support that company's image software. This software also uses ray tracing and texture mapping to produce amazingly photorealistic shaded images of computer model prototypes. They are complete with physically correct shadows and authentic reflections.

For centuries, designers have been forced to struggle with the handicap of externalizing and communicating their 3D thoughts for 3D artefacts in two dimensions – with pencil and paper. In recent years, computer-aided design has perpetuated this convention by concentrating on speeding up and making more accurate the production drawing end of the design cycle.

▲ The woodgrain texture gives an idea of computer-generated possibilities: it was created on Wavefront software from Computervision data. The unfortunate scale makes this visual from Peugeot look like a design for a model car!

Presentation Graphics and Visuals

While the so-called 3D solids modellers on the market have been used mainly to produce visualizations or check out potential clashes in complex assemblies only *after* the design has been fixed and signed-off as a set of 2D orthographic projections, the impetus for using the computer as a tool for designing at the concept stage is more likely to come from work in TV computer graphics or computer-aided fine art.

In many applications for consumer-oriented products, such as cars, there is a demand for a much closer relationship between stylists and engineers. Expensive automobiles are bought for their looks, and the specular reflection of the horizon on a car's surface is a design element now as important as its profile or proportions. Cost-effective and credible realism early in the design process, when financiers are deciding to underwrite a project, and integration with manufacture to maintain the designer's intentions throughout the process, are key parameters in any future system.

It must not be forgotten that the principal role of a presentation drawing is to make the clients feel happy that the project is proceeding satisfactorily and that they were right in their choice of designer. Anything goes, and the presentation style is often carefully tailored to the client. With a longstanding relationship, a designer may be able to get away with the most cursory and sketchy presentation visuals – and these may be entirely appropriate for a more designerly and fashion-conscious client.

A more conventional captain of industry using a particular consultancy for the first time may require more subtle wooing and a theatrical advertisement agency performance (which could include video and computer-generated concepts). The purpose is to get the ideas across successfully and to inspire confidence in a client – who may be committing substantial development costs to an as-yet-intangible project – as expediently, but as effectively, as is humanly possible.

◄ Animation adds a fourth dimension to a drawing – time. This sequence of an interior with chair and uplighter was modelled and rendered by Giuliano Zampi at Amazing Array Productions, London, using a ray tracing trick: to save computation time, each element was ray traced and the surface then turned into a "texture map" for the computation.

▶ In most animations of product drawings, it is the viewpoint only that changes while the rendering remains static in space. "Twisting Jake" is an Amazing Array demonstration of flexible patch modelling that enables the form of the product itself to be manipulated dynamically.

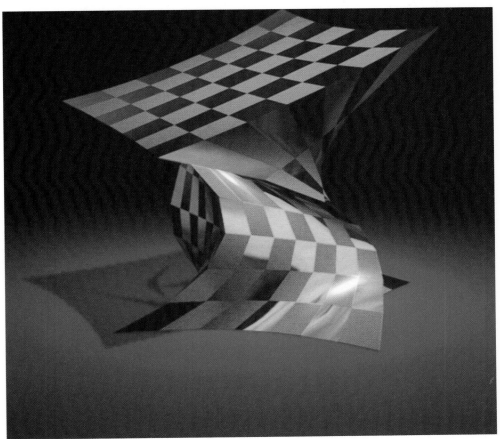

Case study: **D-Team, Schondorf**

For the past 18 years, D-Team has been conceiving and realizing ideas for new products, with skills in design conception, analysis, styling, ergonomics, engineering, modelmaking and prototyping. D-Team was founded in 1970 by Rainer Bohl, who had studied interior design and industrial design in Berlin. Dorothee Hiller trained as a carpenter, and studied interior design and furniture-making in Stuttgart before joining Bohl in 1971. Their clients include Drabert (with the first patented self-adapting office chair in 1969), Ford, Röder, Bosch, Herman Miller, Ideal Standard (they designed one of the best-selling wash-basins in the world), Philips, Bundespost and Fissler.

D-Team's first office was in Stuttgart. In 1978 a Bavarian office was opened in Schondorf, southwest of Munich, 584 metres above sea level, and said to be a good place for creative work. The "D" in the name D-Team comes from the observation that there are different categories of project, designated A to D. A is for little information; little time. D is perfection: there is enough information for what is required, and an optimum amount of time in which to get things done. The "Team" part of the name derives from the group's philosophy: *Design ist Teamsache*, Design is teamwork.

◄ ▼ **Models (left) and**
presentation sketches (below)
of various tools that form part
of the kitchen range for
Fissler, marketed in 1986.

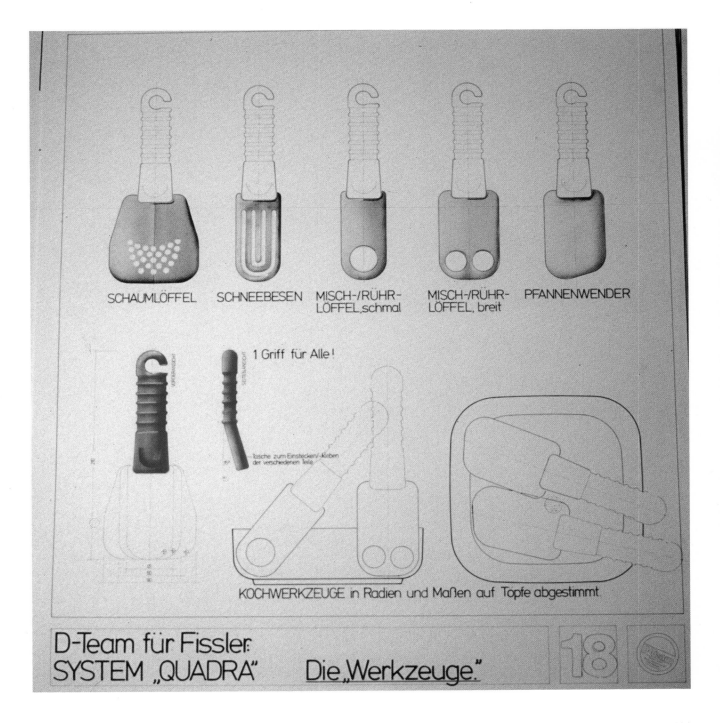

SCHAUMLÖFFEL   SCHNEEBESEN   MISCH-/RÜHR-   MISCH-/RÜHR-   PFANNENWENDER
                               LÖFFEL, schmal   LÖFFEL, breit

1 Griff für Alle!

Tasche zum Einstecken/-kleben
der verschiedenen Teile

KOCHWERKZEUGE in Radien und Maßen auf Topfe abgestimmt.

D-Team für Fissler:
SYSTEM „QUADRA"   Die „Werkzeuge."

18

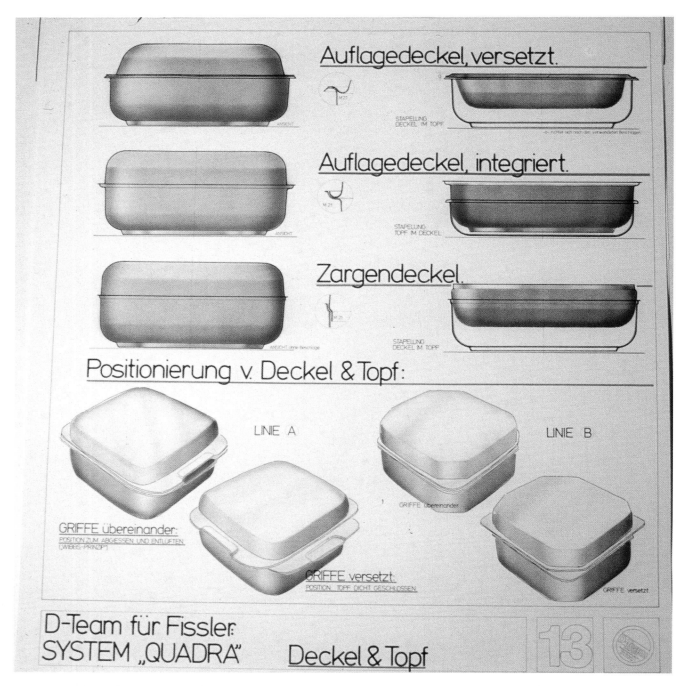

In the project for Fissler, the task was to develop a series of pots, pans and ancillary kitchen equipment that could be used both on the cooker hob and in the oven. The designs also had to make use of a production facility that enables the fully automatic polishing of non-rotationally symmetrical objects. "We can't stand any more round pots . . . Innovation is necessary," said Fissler. The result after one and a half years of work was design program FD 90, in moulded 18/10 stainless steel – "quadrature of the circle" with easy-pour edges and heat-insulated handles. They were put on the market in 1986, and have won many design prizes.

The designs have a functional point to make, too: square forms make better use of space in ovens and cupboards. Angular vessels hold the same amount as circular ones, while looking smaller and neater due to their lower profile.

At D-Team, early concepts are made with a 6B pencil or felt-tip pen. The client presentations shown here are plans and elevations with a precision look. Dorothee Hiller generally uses mixed techniques and media, and when she is designing furniture sometimes uses airbrush. D-Team also makes use of foam models which are photographed and enlarged to stimulate further discussion. Production drawings are usually the responsibility of the client, although D-Team does get involved in the production of detailed drawings for patent applications.

D-Team is not concerned with just the surface styling of a product, but considers its function, and will tackle the whole design using a thorough and rigorous approach. That is not to say that the appearance of a product is not important. "Design," according to Hiller, "does not only live out of its functionality, but also out of the narrative quality of the form."

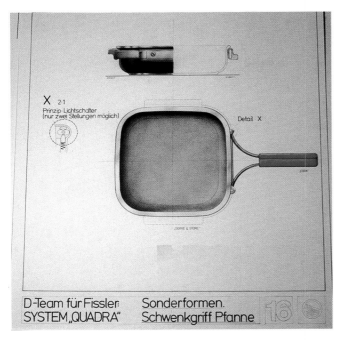

D-Team für Fissler: Sonderformen.
SYSTEM „QUADRA" Schwenkgriff Pfanne 16

D-Team für Fissler: Sonderformen.
SYSTEM „QUADRA" Schnellkochtopf 14

◄ ▲ Highly finished presentation sketches for the Fissler range of pots, pans and other cooking equipment. Though they are plans and elevations, they are arranged unconventionally. The rendering is confident, precise and realistic, at a scale of 1:1. They were made with markers on semi-transparent paper, with Letraset Pantone film overlays.

▼ Prototype of one of the saucepans in the range.

A working drawing is merely a letter to a builder telling him precisely what is required of him – and not a picture wherewith to charm an idiotic client

Sir Edwin Lutyens

7 From General Arrangement to Production

A product designer's background can always be detected from his or her detail drawings: a product "engineer" will do them by the book; more artistic types might take liberties, and are in real danger of infuriating the sticklers down on the shopfloor in production, or even in the designer's own model workshop.

The familiar engineering drawing, in ink or polymer pencil on Mylar film, has one purpose: to communicate a designer's concepts to those responsible for manufacturing the components of the product and assembling them with pre-sourced proprietory items to create the finished object. As such the drawings must be complete and unambiguous. To prevent any misinterpretation, production drawings are highly codified, and to the untrained eye can appear confusing and difficult to read; it is often hard to see the form of the object for the dimensioning and tolerancing information.

Engineering drawings are always executed in orthographic projection, in the USA and the UK using third-angle projection, elsewhere in first-angle projection (see pages 105-6). The type of projection must be indicated on the drawing, usually by means of a conventional symbol. The orthographic projection is often accompanied by auxiliary views (i.e. ones not orthogonal to the x,y, or z axes), scrap views of details requiring close scrutiny, and perhaps a pictorial view in isometric or perspective.

▶ **This model drawing of a stopper to keep wine fresh was rendered in marker to help clients decide on a final colour scheme for the product (see page 95 for an earlier proposal and the final product).**

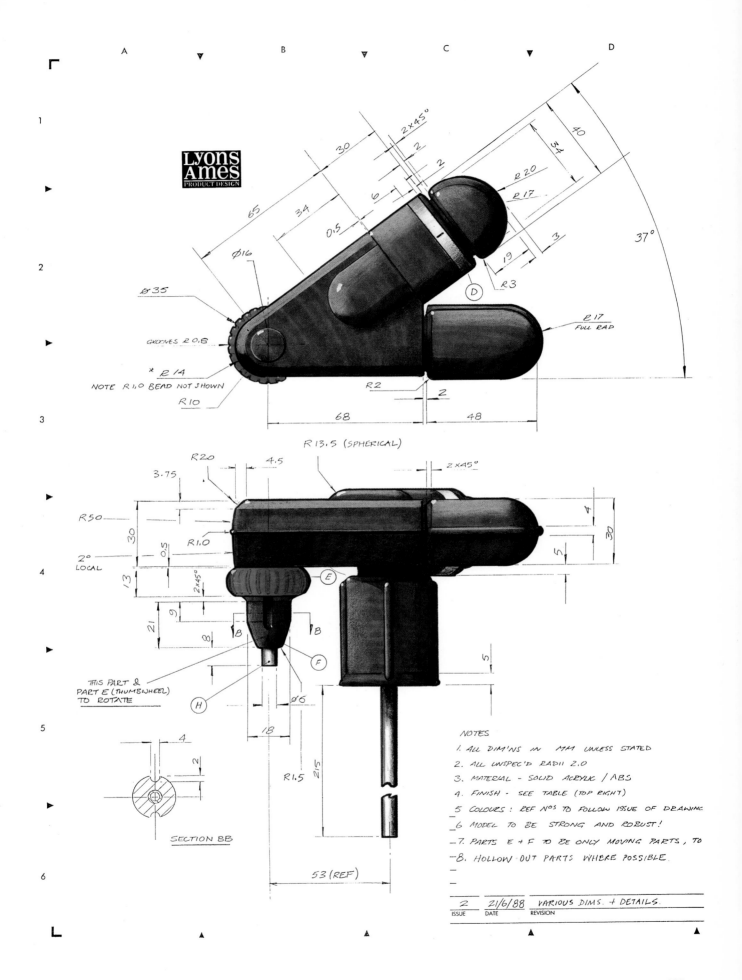

Lyons Ames PRODUCT DESIGN

2×45°

30   2   2

65   34   6   R 20

Ø 16   0.5   R 17

Ø 35   54   40

GROOVES R 0.8   37°

* R 14   19   3

NOTE R 1.0 BEAD NOT SHOWN   R 3

R 10   R 17 FULL RAD

R 2   2

68   48

R 13.5 (SPHERICAL)

R 20   4.5   2×45°

3.75

R 50   R 1.0   4

30   2°   0.5   30

2° LOCAL   13   2×45°   5

21   9   E

8   B   B

THIS PART & PART E (THUMBWHEEL) TO ROTATE   F

H   Ø 6

4   18

2   R 1.5   215

SECTION BB

53 (REF)

NOTES

1. ALL DIM'NS IN MM UNLESS STATED

2. ALL UNSPEC'D RADII 2.0

3. MATERIAL - SOLID ACRYLIC / ABS

4. FINISH - SEE TABLE (TOP RIGHT)

5. COLOURS : REF Nᵒˢ TO FOLLOW ISSUE OF DRAWING

6. MODEL TO BE STRONG AND ROBUST!

7. PARTS E + F TO BE ONLY MOVING PARTS, TO

8. HOLLOW OUT PARTS WHERE POSSIBLE.

2	21/6/88	VARIOUS DIMS. + DETAILS.
ISSUE	DATE	REVISION

The GA drawing

The GA (or general arrangement) drawing is the key to all the other drawings. It is here that the final layout is decided, dimensions are fixed, ergonomic considerations resolved and the methods of production finalized. The client is satisfied and the designer is, in theory, ready to embark on the task of producing the fully dimensioned drawings required by production: the detail drawings, and the drawings of the press tools, progressive dies or moulds, plus all the assorted jigs and fixtures that will be needed to manufacture the product. There may also be a need for assembly drawings showing how the component parts are to be put together. All these drawings, which could run to hundreds, might be at different scales and are coordinated with reference to the GA.

In the early days of the industrial revolution, one drawing – a rendered GA – often sufficed. A drawing of a pump or steam engine by Boulton and Watt, for example, would incorporate the basic dimensions for erection, but none concerned with manufacture. As they were almost invariably unique productions, the making of the parts was left to skilled craftsmen. As machinery became more standardized, more and more drawings were needed and their production was delegated to draftsmen and (mainly female) tracers.

The GA gives the overall disposition of the product, the arrangement of its component parts and the way they are to be put together. It gives the overall dimensions and usually includes a parts list that refers the reader to the whole hierarchy of the other more detailed drawings: sub-assembly and discrete assemblies, and the individual detail and sub-detail drawings. These show more manageable sections of the product, with every essential dimension and allowable tolerance documented. These drawings also include information detailing the material the part is to be made from, its surface finish and treatment (ground, anodized, painted, and so on). The tolerance and finish of a part have a significant effect on the type and precision of tools that can be used and hence the cost of manufacture, so they must be chosen and documented with great care. If a part is to be cast and subsequently machined, the designer may be expected to provide as-cast drawings. Any way a designer can help optimize the production cycle is bound to be appreciated.

The drawings from GA onwards are produced using technical pen and ink, or polymer pencil, on to sheets (generally A0 size) of Mylar film preprinted with a border and a title block into which will be placed information about the drawing: its unique number and its relationship with any other drawings, the name of the designer, the date, a symbol indicating the projection being used (first-angle or third-angle), the original scale, and the title of the drawing.

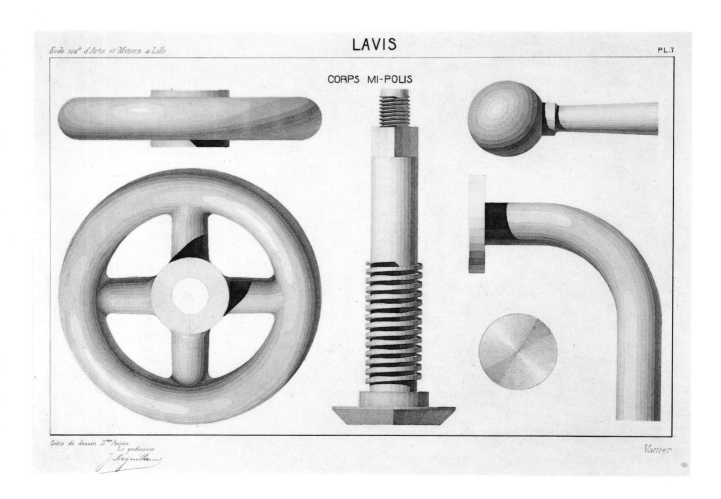

LAVIS

CORPS MI-POLIS

Ecole nat^{le} d'Arts et Métiers de Lille

PL.7

Cours de dessin 2me Année
Le professeur

Vanier

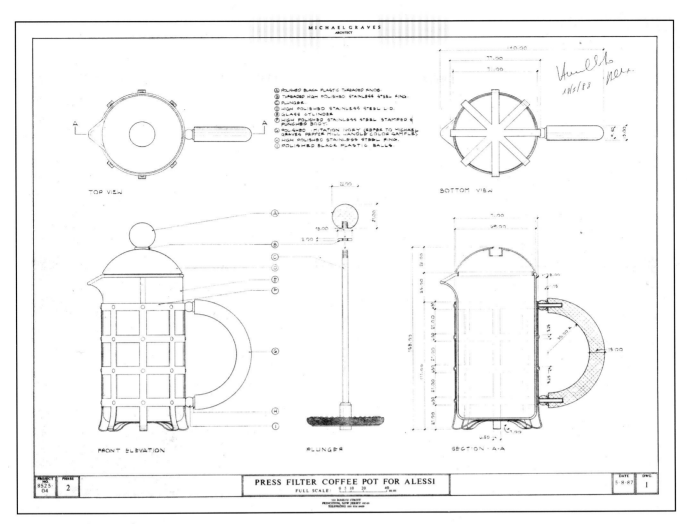

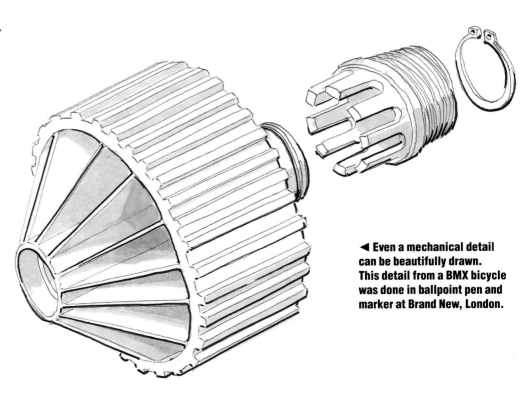

▲ Most technical drawings are notoriously difficult to read, but this orthographic of Michael Graves's coffee maker for Alessi of 1989 tells the viewer just as much about the product as a drawing by Aldo Rossi ever could (see page 163).

◄ Studies for mechanical designs by Vanier in pen and ink with watercolour over pencil, dating from the late 19th century. The mannered watercolour shading and the shadows heighten the sense of realism.

◄ Even a mechanical detail can be beautifully drawn. This detail from a BMX bicycle was done in ballpoint pen and marker at Brand New, London.

From General Arrangement to Production

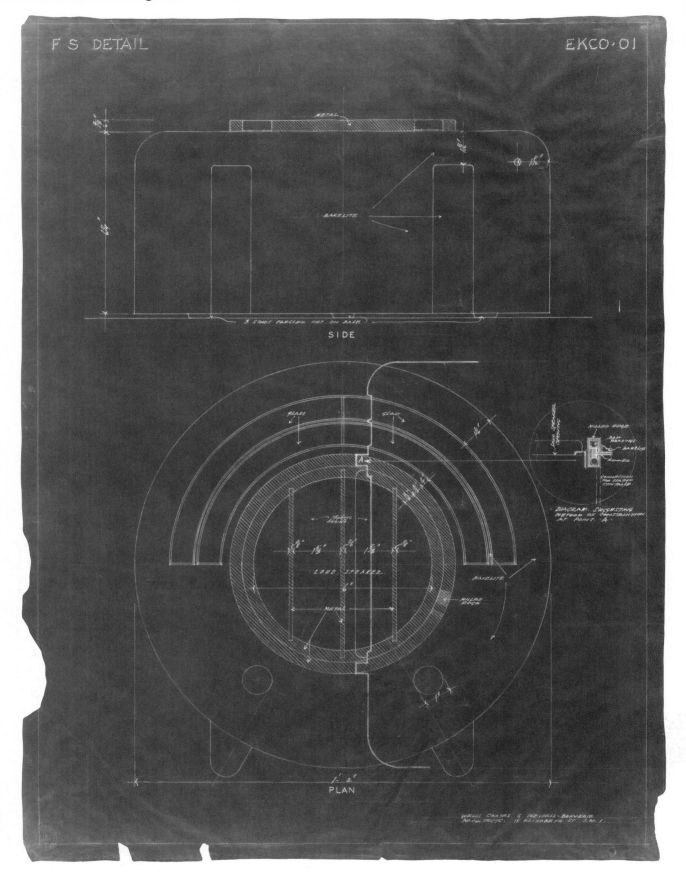

Drawing standards

BS308, the first standard in the world for orthographic engineering drawings, celebrated its 50th anniversary in 1987 and has grown to three large volumes (two of which are devoted solely to tolerancing) in which are detailed the way dimensions, tolerances, cross-hatching and so on ought to be presented for consistency and clarity. It is probably unique in that it is universally accepted in the UK by both industry and the armed forces. The American standard ASA Y14-1, published by the American Society of Mechanical Engineers, is only one of a number of standards issued by bodies such as NASA, the utilities and the armed services. There are equivalent DIN standards in Germany and international standards issued by the International Standards Organization in Geneva. These date back to the 1950s when the UK, the USA, Canada and Australia cooperated on a proposed world standard. Inevitably, however, these are less up-to-date than national standards.

The purpose of a drawing standard is twofold: first and foremost it is a universally agreed codification of practice to aid in the communication of ideas between different professionals and disciplines; second, as stated in the 1943 foreword to BS308, it is "a useful guide which will enable young engineers and draughtsmen to proceed with much of their work without too frequent reference to their seniors."

Drawing standards such as BS308 will advise the designer on such matters as recommended scales (1:1, 1:2, 1:5, 1:10, 1:20 and so on), the type of linework to be used (continuous thick lines for visible outlines and edges; chained thin lines for centrelines, trajectories and pitch lines; continuous thin with zigzags for indicating the limits of partial or interrupted views and so on); and how to draw the arrowheads used on dimension and leader lines. There are recommendations on lettering, the simplified representation of symmetrical parts, how to draw "interrupted" views of long simple objects, and repetitive features such as holes on a circular pitch. The drawing of sections and sectional views is treated in great detail, as are the methods and conventions of hatching.

But not everything is so straightforward: by convention, when a sectional view passes longitudinally through fasteners such as bolts, nuts, shafts, ribs, webs and the spokes of wheels, it is the practice to show them in external view. Intersection lines, too, are often approximated by arcs and straight lines where the projection of true lines of intersection is unnecessary. Flat surfaces on a shaft, for example, can be indicated by crossed diagonals; and knurling is hinted at by showing only part of the surface so treated. There are also conventional representations for bearings and screw threads. Surface finish is indicated by a tick symbol with the maximum permissible roughness shown numerically. Commonly used items, such as bolts, springs and gears, are not drawn realistically but are represented by symbols.

According to the standard, each dimension necessary for the complete definition of a finished product should be given on the drawing and should appear once only. There are all kinds of regulations governing the placement of dimension lines and the method of dimensioning (parallel, superimposed running, or chained dimensioning). American and European methods of dimensioning differ in that all dimensions on drawings produced in the USA can be read from the horizontal; drawings produced in Europe keep the dimensions parallel to the dimensioning lines – verticals are thus turned on their sides and must be read from the right.

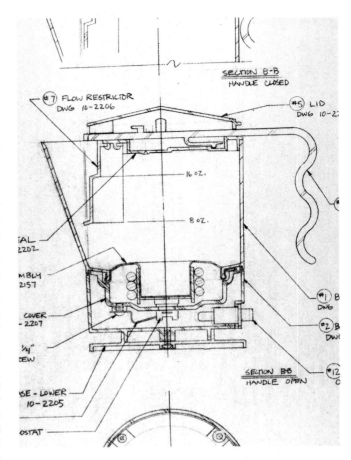

▲ The assembly drawing of the "Bellhop" kettle by Tucker Viemeister of New York's Smart Design is to scale, but undimensioned. It refers the user to other, numbered, parts drawings. Below is the finished prototype.

From General Arrangement to Production

Tolerances

All dimensions are subject to tolerances, and tolerances are a subject in themselves. More than two thirds of BS308 is devoted to tolerancing and most of the major revisions to the standard since it was introduced in 1927 have a direct relationship to the way tolerance information is represented. A tolerance specifies the limits of size of the dimension and is crucially important if an assembly of parts is to fit together and function properly. A tolerance should not be too stringent, however, or the cost of machining the part will begin to escalate dramatically. It has to be just right, and selecting the right tolerance is part of the skill of the designer. What the standard does is ensure that the designer's instructions are conveyed to production with the minimum possibility of misinterpretation.

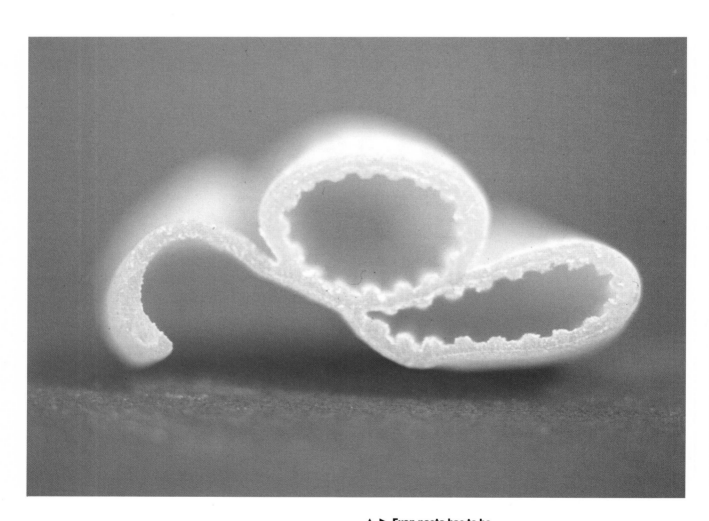

▲ ▶ Even pasta has to be designed by someone! Pasta is basically a 2½D shape: a 2D x, y profile extruded into the z-direction. Giorgio Giugiaro's "Marille" pasta for Voiello was designed for perfect straining and to capture the optimum amount of sauce.

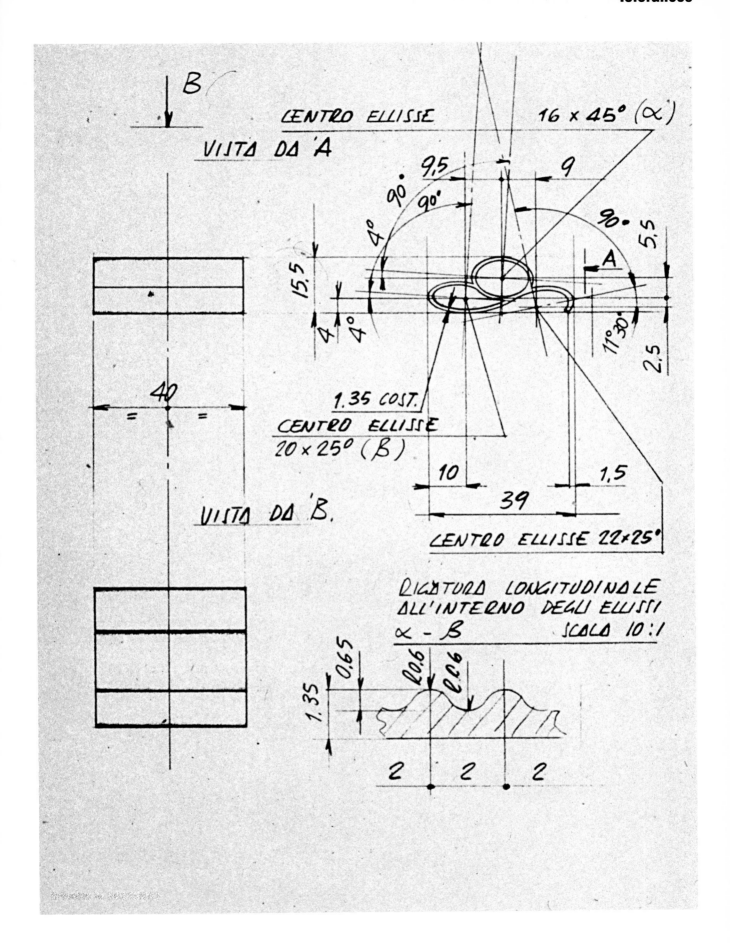

B

VISTA DA 'A

CENTRO ELLISSE   16 × 45° (α)

9,5   9

90°
90°
90°

4°
4°   90°   5,5

15,5   A

4°   11°30'
4°   2,5

1.35 COST.
CENTRO ELLISSE
20 × 25° (β)

40
=   =

VISTA DA 'B.

10   1,5
39

CENTRO ELLISSE 22×25°

RIGATURA LONGITUDINALE
ALL'INTERNO DEGLI ELLISSI
α - β   SCALA 10:1

0.65   R0.6   0.06
1.35

2   2   2

Computer-aided GA drawings

Most designers will claim that of course they can produce drawings to BS308 or other equivalent national standards if they are really pushed. The good news is that these rules and conventions can be programmed into cad systems to ensure that designers always keep on the straight and narrow. Some systems will even convert a drawing done to BS308 to its American ANSI or European DIN or ISO equivalent at the push of a button, or allow dimensions to be input in a mixture of imperial and metric units.

The rudiments of engineering drawing have been well documented elsewhere. This chapter aims to show what a cad system can do to help designers produce the necessary evil of fully dimensioned and toleranced orthographic drawings.

With cad, it is possible for the designer to work at full-size (1:1) on a "master" drawing of the product, regardless of its size and complexity, using the system's capacity to pan and zoom in order to window in to the portion of the overall product currently being worked on. Most commercial cad systems arrange the drawing in layers or levels which are equivalent to overlays, so that, for example, a relatively uncomplicated GA can be put on one layer, with detail kept separate on further layers. However, because the computer has so many layers available, and the means for managing them, it is usual to install even the simplest drawing on several layers to aid later modification: the construction lines on one, the outline on another, the text on a third, and so on.

These layers can be viewed and worked on in isolation or combination and coordinated variations can be output in various forms and scales. All the different craftspeople involved in the production process can then have their own individual customized drawing, rather than – as is traditional – a barely legible scribbled-on dieline blueprint, up-to-date and signed off with recent amendments.

With systems connected together in a network, it is also possible for different members of a multi-disciplinary team to work on the same master drawing, some of them having no more than read-only access, while others have the authority to make changes.

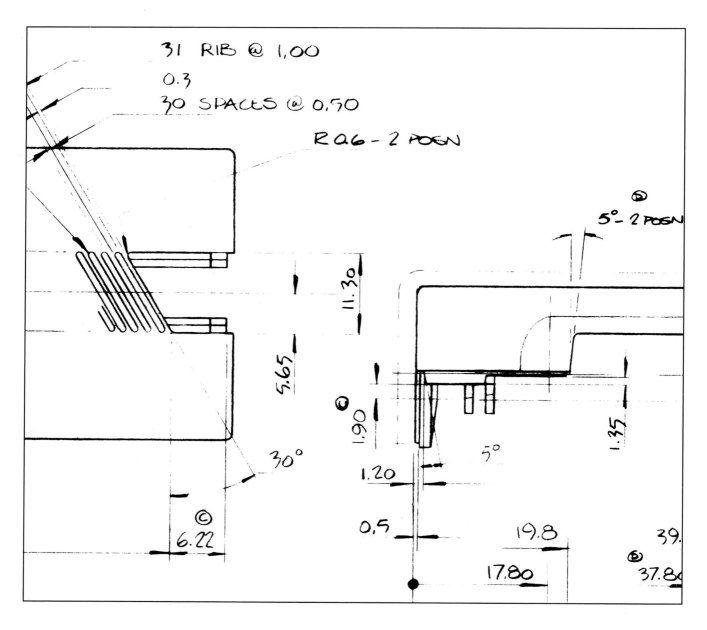

Geometric constructions

Cad systems are at their most productive at the detail design stage. These productivity increases are usually attributed to the use of "library" symbols or components – those that can be drawn once, and used over and over again – or to parametric programming (more of this later) for generating families of parts. But even on one-off products it is possible to score over manual methods by making use of all the geometric constructions that a cad system has to offer.

The simplest PC-based systems have commands that can draw circles tangent to lines, arcs or other circles. A circle can be drawn through any three points, inscribed inside a triangle or polygon, or, say, tangent to two converging lines and another given circle lying between those lines. Fillets, blends and chamfers can be generated automatically. Commands like these plus on-screen rulers and calculators can sometimes make the tedious preliminaries of setting up construction lines unnecessary. Lines will always be straight, circles always true, and right angles always square.

Manual dimensioning is a matter of annotating a drawing with the number you know it ought to be. A designer would never "scale" a drawing to ascertain the true length, because he knows that manually produced drawings are too inaccurate for fabrication. With cad, it is the other way round: entering points accurately in the first place ensures that the drawing (or more correctly, the computer model) is precise. You can also "take off" other dimensions from the drawing with confidence, and most systems will have some form of automatic and associative dimensioning in metric or imperial units, conforming to a national or international standard such as BS308 or its equivalent.

The snapping of points to a pre-defined grid ensures that a profile, for example, will be closed with no gaps or "grey areas," so fudging is not allowed. Manual drawing is always restricted by the limits of a designer's visual accuracy, not so cad. Editing – with commands like delete, alter, move, rotate, translate, mirror, trim, copy – is much simpler with cad and therefore more likely to be done.

◄ ► **These engineering drawings from Brand New, defining a remote transmitter and cordless headphones for Ross Electronics, show the difference between the output from a cad system (Pafec's Dogs) and drawings produced manually (left). Cad drawings (right) are consistent in line quality and lettering and are far clearer to read.**

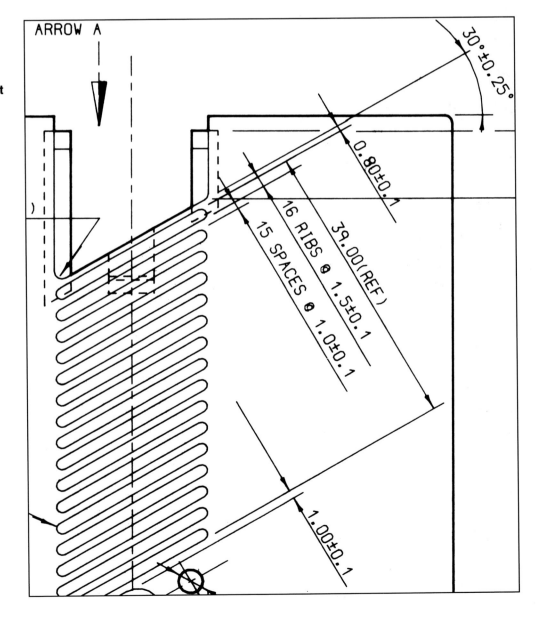

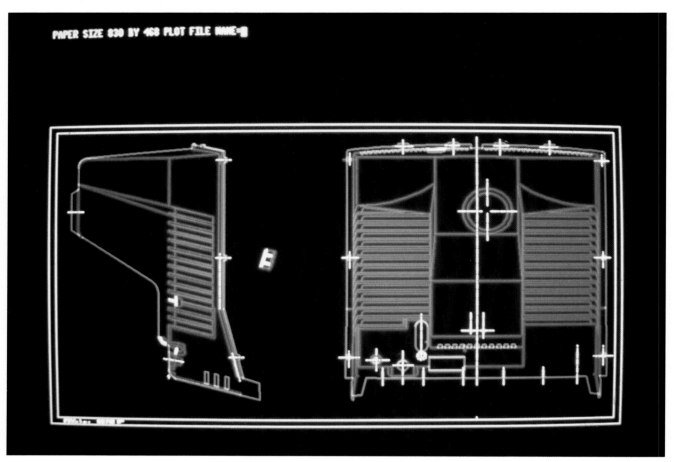

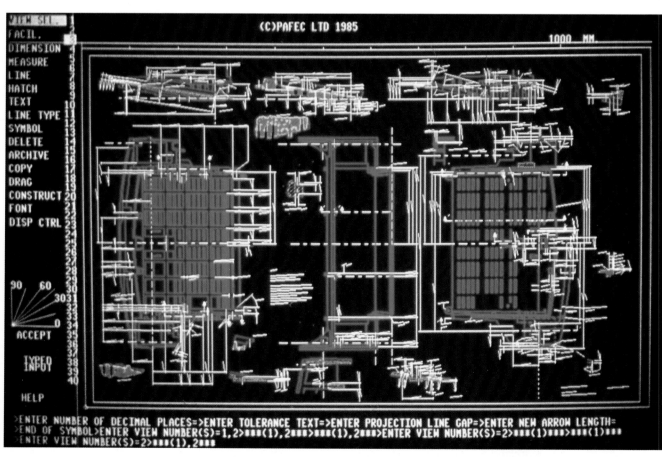

◄ ▼ Screen shots (left) from
an Apollo workstation running
the Dogs 2D drafting program
at Brand New show how colour
can be used to distinguish
between "layers" of a
drawing. The product is the
MX3000 television set for
Bang & Olufsen (below), and
the use of cad cut the time to
the tooling stage from 26 to 12
weeks.

From General Arrangement to Production

Curves

Before the advent of computers, designers did not seem to care very much about the accuracy of their curves. If it could not be done with compasses or an ellipse template, they would reach for the nearest French curve or one of those bendy rulers and leave the rest to the patternmaker on the shopfloor to sort out. Motorway designers and the skilled loftsmen (patternmakers who worked on full-size templates) of the shipbuilding and aerospace industries had their own tricks of the trade – using piano wire and weights, or plywood "splines" held in positions of tension with lead "ducks" – to generate the long "fair" lines required by their particular applications.

When numerically controlled point-to-point contouring machine tools became available in the 1960s, they demanded software that could deal with parametric spaces and define totally and accurately complex doubly curved surfaces. Strangely enough, the problems associated with *surfaces* were tackled before simple 2D curves, in the work of Steven Coons in the USA and Pierre Bézier at Renault in France.

Complex surfaces are important to the designer for two different reasons. First there are the shapes that have been optimized by rigorous experimentation – turbine blades, boat hulls and so on – and second there are the aesthetic curves created by stylists, like car body panels, that must assemble with or keep clear of neighbouring parts. In both cases an accurate, predictable and controllable means of defining the curves and surfaces is paramount. The representation should also be economical in terms of the computer memory needed and the speed of response.

Early systems joined up the dots defined by the x,y,z cartesian coordinates measured at various points on the surface to create a net of curves, with each mesh of the net (the "patch") defined by an algorithm which ensured continuity of slope or curvature between adjacent patches. The operator could often adjust the derivatives to improve the general shape, without altering the general continuity.

The parametric cubic segment is the most commonly used curve in cadcam. This requires the cartesian coordinates x,y,z to be expressed in terms of a parameter t, with the x,y,z coordinates varying as polynomials of t, in this case containing a term of t to the power of 3. The Bézier form is defined in terms of four points: a start point, an end point, and two points lying on the respective end tangents. The positioning of the tangent points is critical – the further they are moved along the tangent line, the more highly curved the segment.

The designer starts with an initial first guess – say placing the tangent point a distance along the tangent line a third the chord length – and successively improves the positioning interactively until the overall curve shape is right.

Most cad systems have a spline routine that automates the definition of curves built up of several parametric cubic segments. The designer specifies the end points of the segments and the system supplies the end tangent vectors. The result is called a spline curve and models the loftsman's physical lath which always rests in the position of least tension. The underlying theory is a tangle of assumptions and for the maths, consult a book such as John Woodwark's *Computing*

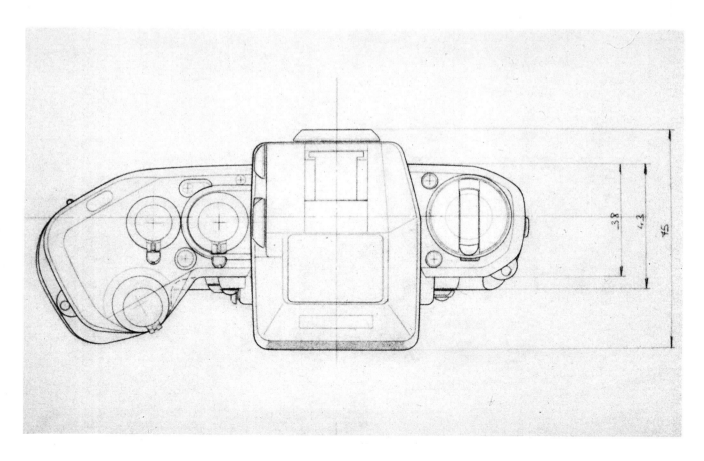

Shape (see Further Reading). Spline routines are simply programs for assigning tangent vectors in a reasonably sensible way to achieve overall smoothness.

Modifying the curve thus created is another problem altogether. A spline is an entity in its own right and can only be altered into another spline. Direct and total control is a chimera, especially if you only want to change bits of the curve. Local data changes can cause global shape changes. The B-spline is an optimal definition that confines the extent of shape changes and gives designers direct – but not total – control over their creations. A B-spline with two segments is defined by five points; one with three segments by six points and so on. The designer inputs the segment end points V1, V2 . . . Vn+1 and the system creates a polygon framework of points P1, P2 . . . Pn+3 around the curve. From then on the designer works with the "polygon" points and the disturbing effects of localized changes are restricted to around four segments at most.

Higher order Bézier curves are often offered as an alternative form in some cad systems. The designer specifies the points and the program generates a curve passing through them. Subsequently, the designer works directly with the vertices of the Bézier polygon with direct and total control of the definition, but cannot make localized shape changes.

Autocad has cubic B-spline curves, to which all the standard editing commands can be applied. The spline subcommand uses the vertices of the selected polyline as the control points or frame of the curve, which can be open or closed. The curve passes through the end-points and towards but not necessarily through the others. Robocad 4 has cubic Bézier curves interpolated about four points, B-splines about any number of points and something called a Q-spline (Q stands for cubic!) that automatically constructs a smooth curve through any number of user-defined points.

The rational cubic is a versatile form and can define a wide range of shapes including spline curves and cubic sections (circles, ellipses, parabolas and hyperbolas). It is the basis of in-house systems in the aerospace and automotive industries.

The non-uniform rational B-spline (nurbs) has been adopted by leading turnkey vendors Intergraph and Computervision (though not in Personal Designer which uses Bézier curves in the microCADDS surfacing option) as a mathematical means of unifying their wireframe, surfacing and solids modellers. The first PC implementation of nurbs was in MCS's Anvil-5000 pc.

Nurbs can be trimmed to arbitrary boundaries, and have more modest database requirements. Large curves, such as an entire automobile body panel, can be modelled with single, low-degree entities. Operations such as smoothing, intersecting and offsetting are faster and more stable, and nurbs are very good for fitting fair curves through large numbers of points (up to 3000 on the CV system) even when the points are unevenly spaced. In addition, nurbs geometry can exactly represent points, arcs, conics, Bézier curves and uniform B-spline curves without approximation – for better geometry transfer between different makes of system.

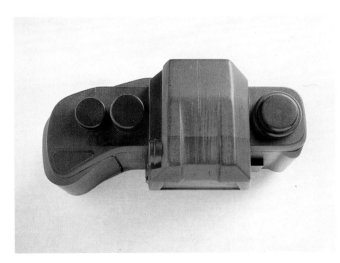

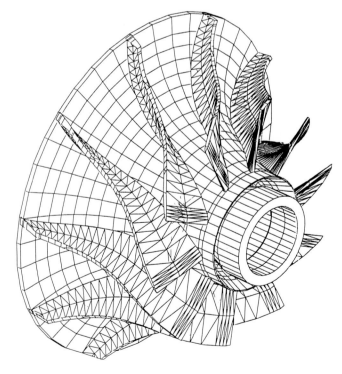

◀ ▲ **Giugiaro Design's "friendly, intelligent and comfortable" designs for the Nikon F4 camera, dating from 1985-88, are represented in orthographic form. Cad was used to analyse and smooth the surface at model stage. Note that a "schematic" model (above) cannot contain the detail of a drawing.**

▶ **Surface modellers are used to design products containing complex curves, such as this compressor wheel, which was developed using a combination of Diad solid modeller and Diad surface modeller.**

From General Arrangement to Production

Parametrics

Early cad systems merely modelled the drafting task, simulating pencil on paper. Most present-day cad systems contain some degree of "intelligence." A system may remember how items connect with one another, when items are tangent to others, and may associate fillets and chamfers with their master lines. These features save time when making alterations to the drawing, and reassure the designer that the drawing has not lost its integrity. For example, in Deltacam's Ductdraft the radii of all the fillets around a profile can be changed with a single command. All connecting lines will automatically adjust to the new tangent positions. Dimensions and cross-hatching are linked to the geometry they reference and change automatically when it is appropriate to do so.

Parametrics are useful for creating a set of parts having a family resemblance from an initial "generalized" drawing. A bolt, for example, can be short and fat or long and thin. The topology is the same; the dimensions (angles and lengths) may be different. By replacing the exact dimensions with parameters l for length, b for breadth and w for width, and so on, the real dimensions can be keyed in at a later stage to generate automatically the production drawings for the specific part. Parametrization is also a useful tool at the concept stage of design when final dimensions – to fit around a sourced component, for example – may not be known.

Conventionally, parametrization is achieved by entering into a computer file all the commands necessary to draw a part, perhaps by recording the key strokes made during the construction of a drawing. Ductdraft lets the designer define the parameters as the shape is drawn. Once drawn, the shape can be altered interactively by a command to change the parameter to a new value. Any items dependent on that parameter will be automatically redefined. Any parametrized geometry can be converted into a "symbol" by pointing to the appropriate area. The symbol can then be stored in a library and recalled on to another drawing. On recall, the system will prompt the designer for each parameter value in turn. This kind of relational geometry can also be used to draw linked views and mechanisms.

Cad benefits

Computer-aided drafting is less like copying and much more akin to *designing*. Designers have the time to try out "what if?" ideas with the confidence that they can always return to the original design if the variant being tested does not look likely to succeed. Whether the 2D orthographic drawings are derived from a 3D solid or surface model, or worked up from scratch from the original concept sketch, the designer can rest assured that the cad drawing will be accurate, legible, coordinated and easily amended should the client have a change of mind or a pre-sourced component turn out to have different dimensions from its specification.

Many design consultancies, especially those practising in mainland Europe and those from a more architectural background, do not usually concern themselves with the nuts and bolts of engineering drawing. Their involvement with a design project ends with the layout drawing or the GA. In the USA and UK, on the other hand, there is a longstanding tradition in engineering, and designers will wish to see the design right through to production. Some designers insist that this is the only way that their original concepts can be realized with integrity and without compromise. The production of all the many hundreds of detail drawings needed to manufacture a product is a very labour-intensive and time-consuming activity, and the designer often has to rely on the cooperation of the client and the client's drawing office, or possibly use contract draftsmen to do the work. A cad system in-house, while not a panacea, can give the design consultancy control over the entire design-to-production cycle. With time scales reduced, a great competitive edge is gained.

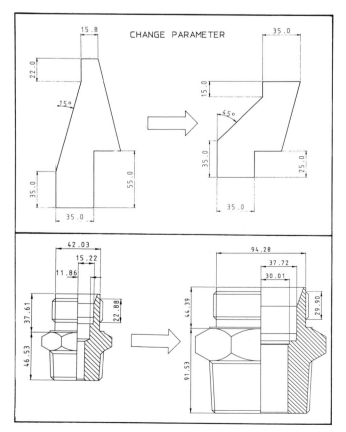

◀ **Parametric programming can help a designer generate a set of drawings for parts with a family resemblance almost automatically.**

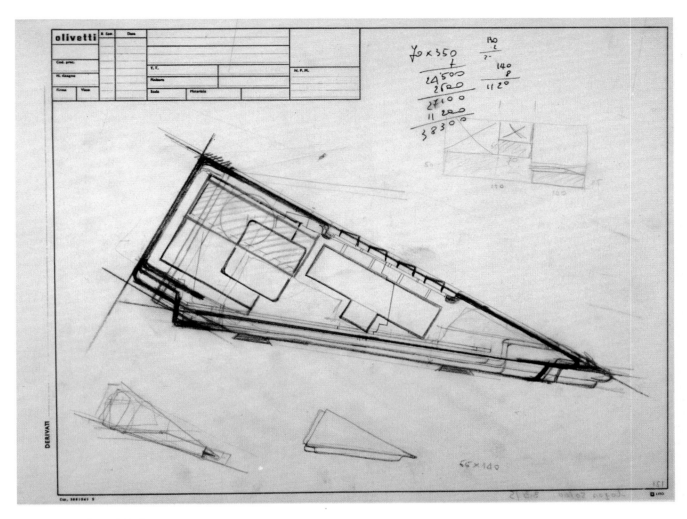

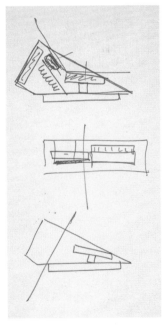

▲ These drawings of Mario Bellini's 1973 "50/60" desktop calculator for Olivetti show the development of a project. Preliminary concept sketches in coloured pencil on tracing paper (above) are developed into a more detailed scale drawing, showing the position of internal components, also in coloured pencil on preprinted vellum (top). The final stage is a fully dimensioned general arrangement drawing in ink.

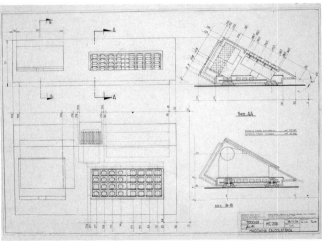

▶ Early concept sketches were done in marker and pastel on photocopies of line drawings (right). Later investigations of particular options are shown in isometric and axonometric projection (far right). They are neater versions of the concepts, used as support for arguments during meetings.

▶ Prototype of the Trane air-conditioning project, which involved about 14 designers at BIB for almost two years.

Case study: # BIB Design Consultants, London

Nick Butler is chairman and joint managing director of industrial design group BIB Design Consultants and a visiting professor of industrial design at the Royal College of Art, London. Originally called Butler Isherwood Bartlett, the consultancy was named after the three founding partners, Royal College of Art graduates who set it up in 1967. Because Nick Butler was first in the list he always seemed to have to take the phone calls, so he soon contrived to abbreviate the unwieldy title to BIB. From humble beginnings, the firm now runs a 25-strong design office and a nearby modelmaking/prototyping shop in West London. Nick Butler and Stephen Bartlett are still with the firm; Peter Isherwood left BIB in the mid-1970s and the third partner is now Lin Williams.

From the start the practice has concentrated purely on product design, handling graphics only when necessary to a product-based project. The traditional workload has been split equally between capital goods and consumer durables, with the emphasis shifting recently towards consumer goods – their best known designs are the fliptop Durabeam torch and the Minolta 7000 camera. For the past 10 or 11 years, half of BIB's work has come from abroad, mainly Japan, USA, the European Community countries and, lately, Australia. Unlike some other practices, however, BIB does not maintain nor does it plan to open an overseas office.

The practice has for the past three years been running a five-screen HP9000-based cad system using Dogs 2D drafting software to drive the NC machine tools in the model shop. "It is no exaggeration to say that we have found cad to be incredibly useful," says Butler, a designer with a declared affection for

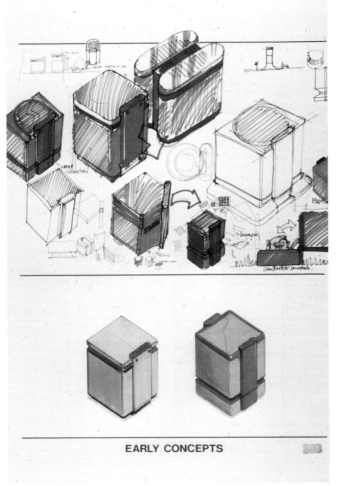

EARLY CONCEPTS

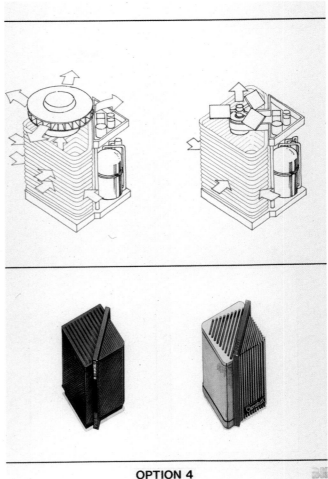

OPTION 4

engineering. "Cost aside, cad take-up among design groups has been slow, but that has been because the wrong people have been trained to use it. At BIB we don't have cad operators – all the designers have been trained or are undergoing training on the system. It's not cheap to do that, and clients tend to forget that design groups are tiny compared with themselves, but the benefits are worth it. The efficiency of cad allows our designers to spend more time at the concept stage of a project (where the drawings are mainly manually produced) without lengthening the lead time. Cad is going to have a profound effect on design groups: talent has traditionally been the most expensive resource, now consultancies can buy a strap-on facility to offer a guaranteed service."

BIB's first customer was Decca – Butler designed their radar, navigational equipment and echo sounders. Now the client list includes British Telecom, Thorn EMI, Ferguson, JVC, Antler, Duracell, Black and Decker and Prestige in the UK; Kone Lift Group in Finland; The Trane Company and Apple Computer in the USA, and Minolta Cameras in Japan.

BIB's projects are multi-disciplinary, in terms of both scale and marketplace, taking products from concept to pre-production. If a client company has a big enough in-house design engineering resource, BIB may undertake only concept work and design development, but will always insist on taking the project to the model or prototype stage. Multinationals with a limited in-house design resource may still sometimes call in a BIB designer to act as an overseer, as someone who can sort out the wood from the trees and help with initial concepts or with resolving problems later in the cycle.

BIB has a good track record of getting projects through to production – "sticking with the project further into the process to pre-production gives a designer more control over the concept and more confidence in its ultimate success," says Butler. Many proven products are out in the marketplace; for example, Duracell's Durabeam range has sold over 14 million units and has captured 30 per cent of the torch market.

Clients are offered a ten-stage programme, with the concept and design development phases given equal importance. The briefing is followed by a feasibility study (stage 1) to check out the data contained in the original brief. "If you don't get this right," says Butler, "you're designing the wrong product." When he is confident he has all the data – on how the product is to be made, what the manufacturing resources of the client are, and so on – he will put together a team of two to eight people tailored to the complexity of the product. This "fusing of intellect," says Butler, "sparks off ideas and is the most exciting part of the process." Although design is a team effort and no one can claim individual credit for designing something these days, one designer usually takes the conceptual lead.

Early concepts (stage 2) are done on layout pads, using as many as three or four 100-page pads on one idea. Clients are presented with a minimum of three and a maximum of ten "routes." Presentation drawings are always produced on A2-sized paper – "It's a good size to pin on walls," says Butler. "It's also a comfortable size to take on planes and will store behind the seat on trains." Designers at BIB use markers, ballpoint pens, montage on cartridge, coloured paper or film – it is a matter of personal choice, but there is some consistency in

141

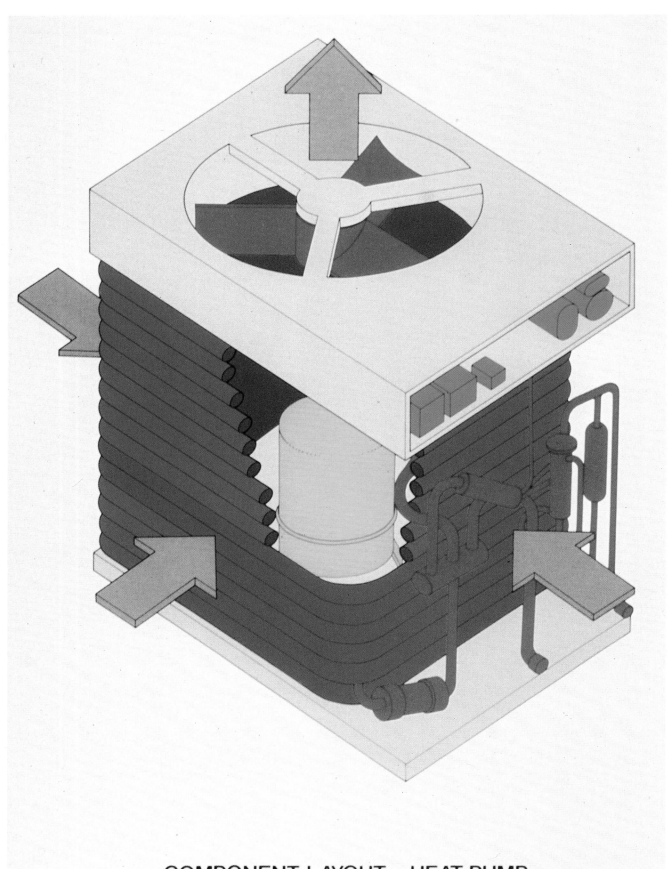

COMPONENT LAYOUT – HEAT PUMP

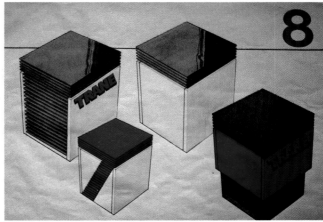

◄ **More finished presentation sketches, exploring two different styling possibilities for the units.**

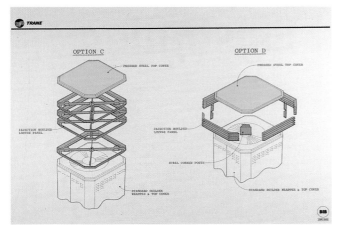

◄ **Exploded detailed diagrams show the proposed construction of two different options. At BIB the drawings are never considered in isolation, but are adjuncts to full-size schematic models. The details, however, are always better expressed in drawings.**

◄ **Explanatory line diagrams, such as this heat pump layout, accompany presentation sketches during meetings. At BIB these are often blocked in with flat colour.**

presentation. The drawings are described as "loose but clear" cartoons (in the Raphael sense), plans for action that steer the client towards two possible conceptual approaches (stage 3), and ultimately gain approval to proceed.

Once the two favoured routes have been selected by the clients, BIB moves to the design development phase – making schematic block models and general arrangement drawings (stage 4). The design is still conceptual – the fine details can make or break a product – but now the designer works on how the components of the product will go together. At this stage, the designer must be able to justify both of the two designs as final products, right down to how much they will cost to make. All through the process there are interim meetings with the clients, to involve them in the authorship of the design.

The process then continues to finished shell models and prototypes (stage 5), and a final selection is then made against all the parameters. The chosen design is tested by market research. There may be revisions and a second prototype. Only then will the designer produce the final production drawings (stage 6). In the case of the Ferguson TV range of five models, a four-person team working for nine months produced over 2,000 drawings, 900 of which were detailed engineering drawings. In mid-project the sourcing of the tubes was changed and the tolerancing found to be different, but it was possible – with cad – to update all the drawings in only six working days. Implementing the design through pre-production tooling and manufacture take up stages 7 to 10.

Butler is convinced that anyone can be taught to draw: "Look at children two or three years old. They design the most wonderful structures. The innate ability is there. So draw for pleasure, draw from life. Drawing should be as easy as tying your shoelaces, as natural as handwriting. If you have to think of the technique you're using, you're restricting the flow of ideas from your head to your hand."

*One picture is worth more than
ten thousand words*

Chinese proverb

8   Technical Illustration

Technical illustration is a skill akin to still-life painting, in that the artist (for it is not always cost-effective for the designer to be involved at this stage) has a tangible object – or at least a set of plans – to look at and base the illustration on. A technical illustrator is an accessory after the fact. And the job of the technical illustration is to explain the mysteries of the designed object to those whose responsibility it is to assemble, market, service and ultimately use the product.

Technical illustration can be traced back to the earliest times, when perhaps some primitive man, wanting to explain the theory of the wheel to a colleague, scratched out a diagram in the sand. The drawings of Georgius Agricola from the *De re metallica* of 1556, showing the workings of such machines as the chain-and-dipper pump, are the best known precursors of today's cutaway and exploded diagrams. Leonardo da Vinci, too, has left many examples of exploded diagrams, although whether these were of objects that really existed or mere fancies is open to conjecture.

Diderot's Encyclopedia in the 19th century created a requirement for "instructive" drawings, as did the many patent applications around the time of the industrial revolution. Technical illustrations can also trace their lineage from the "as-fitted" drawings of ships, usually undertaken by apprentices, and the "contract drawings" of steam locomotives, which were handed over to the client as part of the design contract, on completion of the work. But it was the forces that revived the need for technical illustrations after the First World War, when manuals were produced to help keep all the military equipment serviceable.

▲ Two airbrush renderings by Stuart Spencer, Principal Designer in the Styling Department of Jaguar UK. Top is the Daimler Double Six, and below a Jaguar XJ13 engine.

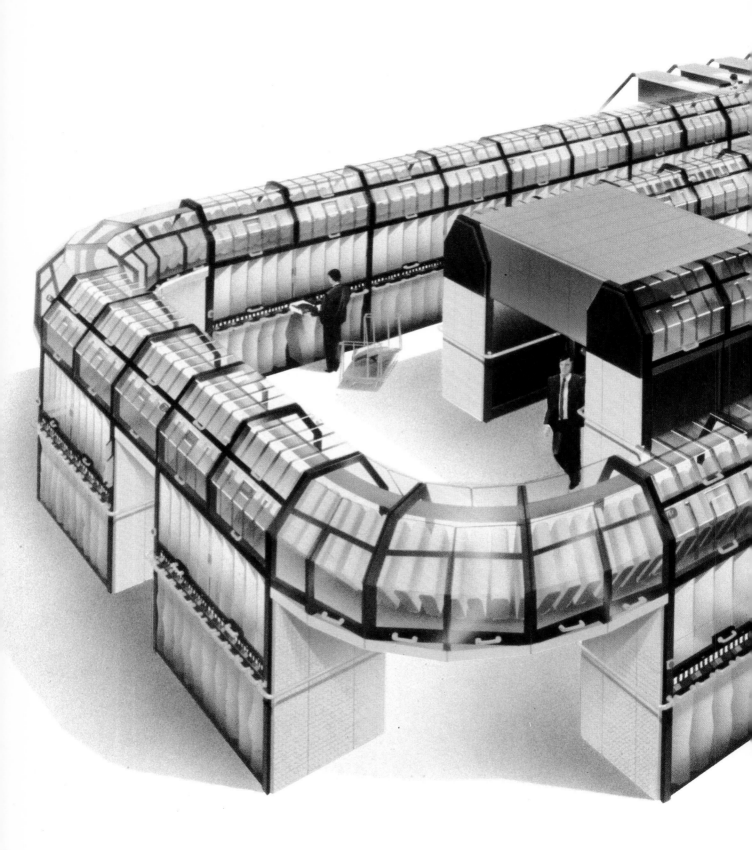

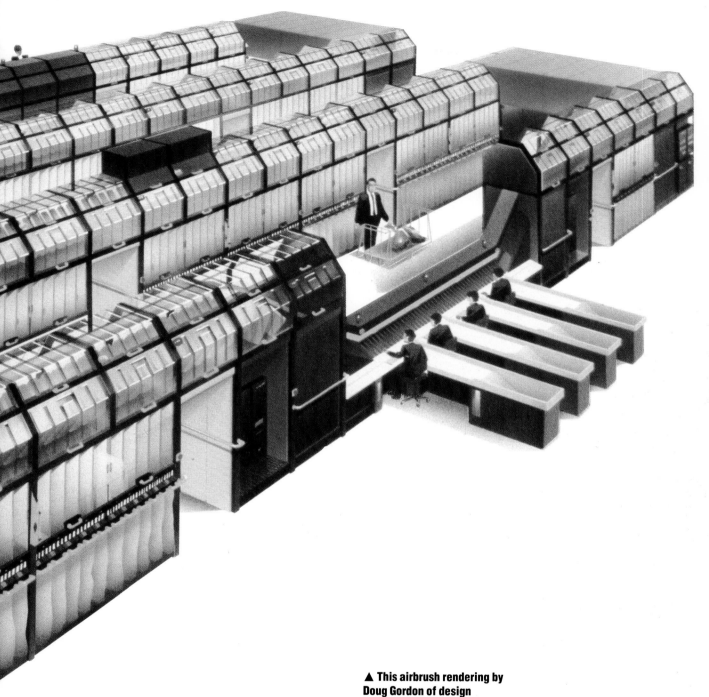

▲ This airbrush rendering by
Doug Gordon of design
consultants Warwick Evans
shows an automatic parcel
sorting machine for the UK
Post Office. It is claimed to be
the longest piece of industrial
design in the world.

Technical Illustration

The skills of the technical illustrator have always been in demand in the aircraft and automotive industries, and the intricate cutaway diagrams that revealed the mysteries of the inner workings of the then "modern wonders" were a popular feature of the trade magazines and the "how it works" books until the 1950s.

"The job of a technical illustrator falls squarely between the artist and the engineering draftsman," it states in the introduction to a "how to draw" book of the 1940s. "On one hand the artist generally draws an object as it appears to him personally, whilst on the other, the draftsman proceeds with great pains to ensure an accurate reproduction complete with dimensions, to enable the craftsman to make the part with no possibility of error. The only way to do this is by orthographic projection, which is difficult for the layman to understand. The technical illustrator is the link. The technical illustrator's life-like portrayal, not only of the component's exterior, but also of a comprehensive section of the internal structure, make possible quick and easy reading of a machine drawing."

A good technical illustrator must be more than a good artist. By his or her knowledge of how the product functions and a mastery of technique, the illustrator will be able to simplify an engineering drawing, bringing out the important details without sacrificing the overall shape and form of the product. The most appropriate viewpoint must be chosen for clarity, decisions made as to what and how much material can be cut away while leaving the whole coherent and credible looking, and all the time aiming for an elegant and pleasing composition. The illustrator must have the insight and X-ray vision to generate drawings that would be impossible to produce by any other means.

The constraints of printing technology have dictated the methods and media used by technical illustrators. Water-colour, gouache – even marker – can be used for colour work, but airbrush has always been the favoured medium. For line work, intended for cheaply produced manuals often printed on poor quality paper, the illustrator has turned to black ink on board or to scraperboard – a medium which is unusual in any other application.

A sharp tool – a scalpel or proprietory cutter – is used to scratch away the smooth black surface of a specially coated board, revealing a layer of clay or chalk, resulting in whites of great clarity and sparkle. Some illustrators prefer white board, which can be coated with black Indian ink where there are areas to be scraped out. Mistakes or areas for further detailed work can be scratched out or inked over, left to dry thoroughly and redrawn. Boards with a grained or stippled surface mechanically embossed into the material are also available.

In order to aid execution and reading alike, line drawings for technical illustration are almost as stylized in their way as comic-book illustrations. A single light source usually comes from the top left corner; shadows and shading are included only to enhance the three-dimensionality of the product being illustrated and are left out if they obstruct the view of some essential detail. The method of shading and cross-hatching must be consistent, too. As in engineering drawing, there are conventional ways of rendering such common objects as springs, screw threads and gear wheels.

▶ **This drawing started life as an enlarged sketch of Julian Quincey's original stereo perspective (see pages 68-71). The sketch helped him to construct perspective lines across the page, which become the basis for an exploded detail drawing. The first stage is to trace off one component from the sketch underneath – in this case, the top half of the casing. Then the sketch is moved slightly to separate this part from what is above or below it. The next component is chosen, usually one that is visible on the original view, and again traced off. It may be necessary to readjust the perspective of each part and its relative size.**

► A large number of components are visible in the original sketch, so it is not difficult to trace off most of the parts, enlarging the objects nearer to the viewer. The remainder are drawn directly from the finished prototype, disassembled to assist in the drawing.

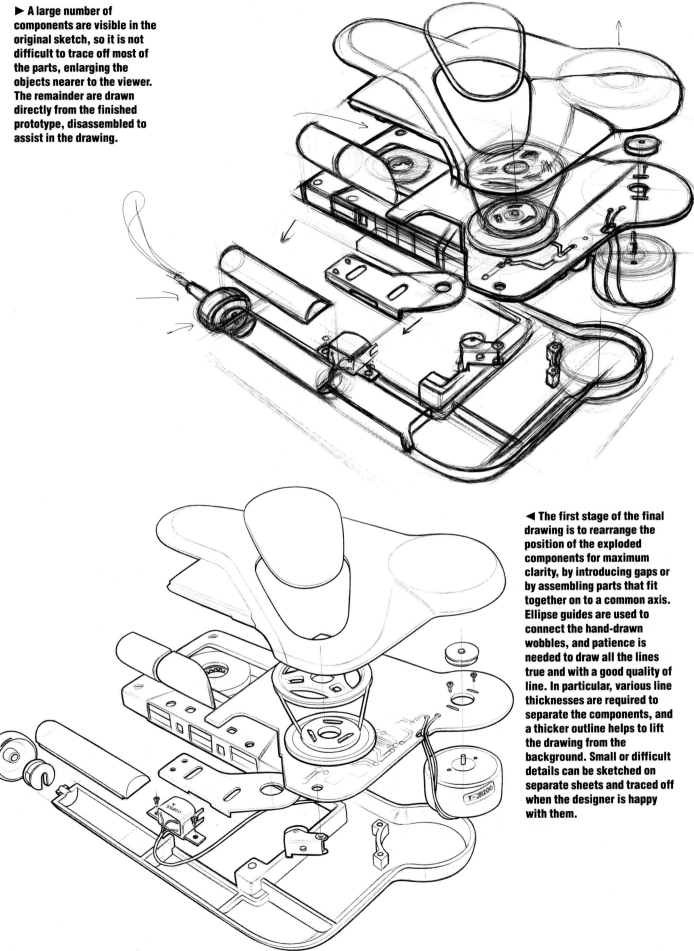

◄ The first stage of the final drawing is to rearrange the position of the exploded components for maximum clarity, by introducing gaps or by assembling parts that fit together on to a common axis. Ellipse guides are used to connect the hand-drawn wobbles, and patience is needed to draw all the lines true and with a good quality of line. In particular, various line thicknesses are required to separate the components, and a thicker outline helps to lift the drawing from the background. Small or difficult details can be sketched on separate sheets and traced off when the designer is happy with them.

Airbrush

Airbrush is used in technical illustration because of its capacity to make soft gradations of tone, which subtly models 3D form and gives a smoother finish than ordinary brushwork. Its mechanical "untouched by human hand" finish is ideal for the technological nature of the objects being depicted. Airbrushing, too, is a technique with conventions. Paradoxically, the aim of the airbrush illustration is not to attempt photographic realism, but to combine assumption and observation in a logical fashion to produce a convincing image that is well defined and technically accurate, but easily assimilated by the buyer of the product.

Machines are shown in gleaming condition against pristine backgrounds, clean and unused. Shiny and matt surfaces are kept separate and distinct, and the differences exaggerated. Reflections which might confuse a reading of the product's structure or which interrupt plain surfaces are avoided. There is a constant balance of light and shade throughout the illustration, with edges defined by the sharp contrast between light and shade rather than by using delineation devices. In cutaways, light backlit edges are used to bring forms such as cylinders, shafts and bolts forward from the heavier tones behind.

An airbrush illustration can take months to complete and it is not uncommon for one person to be responsible for the initial linework, while another is responsible for the colouring by airbrush. As well as being skilled in the techniques of airbrushing and competent at being able to read engineering drawings, the illustrator must develop a keen eye to judge tonal values and an efficient visual memory to retain a mental plan of the overall scheme as the work in progress is ever disguised by the many stencils and masks.

Technical illustration is one of the older branches of illustration, but it is by no means a static technique. Present-day illustrators working in airbrush tend to favour a "ghosted" look, using subtle airbrushing to make the outer casing of the product look as if it were made of glass, resulting in a more coherent and solid drawing, rather than the more severe and hitherto conventional cutaway drawing that can have the effect of mutilating a form.

Technical illustration today is a lot freer than it once was, and is used in many more applications, mostly in marketing: in advertisements, sales brochures, posters and so on. Some technical illustrations are indistinguishable from presentation drawings in their sketchiness, and there has been a vogue for reproducing "designer concepts" to spell out to a more design-conscious public that this or that go-ahead company is actually employing design consultants on their products – of course, the truth is that they always did!

▼ Highly finished onthographics of the Jaguar XJ220 by Stuart Spencer. They are rendered on cad output plots from Jaguar's Computervision system; the airbrushing took 40 to 50 hours.

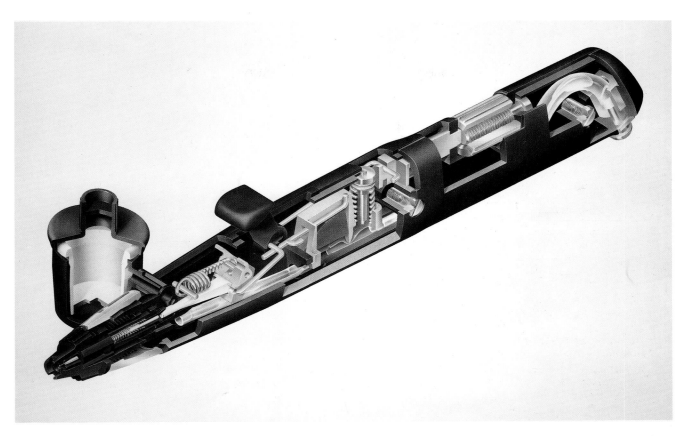

▼ Cutaway airbrush rendering, with some ghosting, of the Jaguar XJ220 by Stuart Spencer. Because this model was a one-off, "artisan-designed," few working drawings exist. The airbrush perspective was therefore drawn direct from a bodyshell, engine and assorted components, using watercolour and gouache. It represents 120 hours of work.

▲ This airbrushed cutaway drawing of the Aztek airbrush by Ray Mumford explains the inner workings of the device.

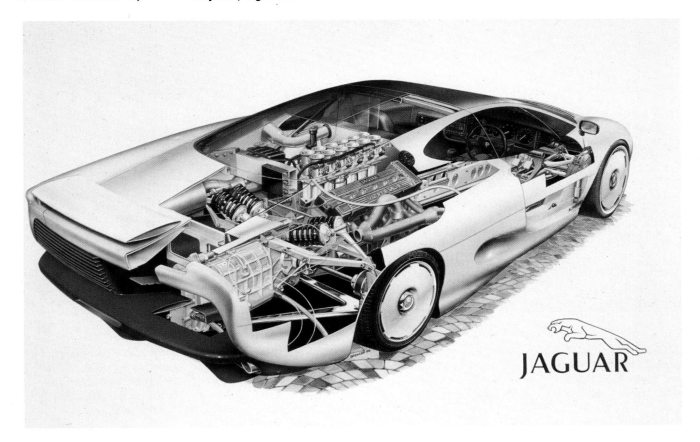

JAGUAR

▲ This fantasy of the Fiat Uno, in the style of Syd Mead (see pages 96-97), has a space-shuttle backdrop. It was produced in 1983 by Alessandro Porta of Form Design for the ItalDesign studio of Giorgio Giugiaro.

► In contrast to Stuart Spencer's finely finished, labour-intensive work (pages 150-151), Nick Hull's sketchier interiors of the Jaguar XJ220, rendered in Derwent pencils and marker, took less than an hour. The cut out of a D-Type Jaguar was pasted on as a reference to a similar sports model of 30 years ago.

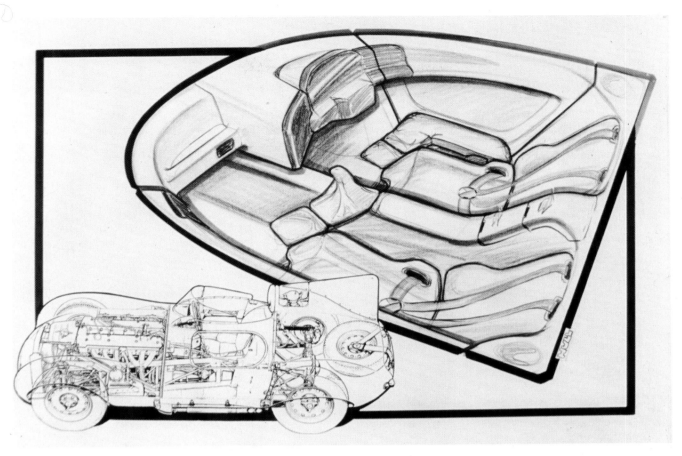

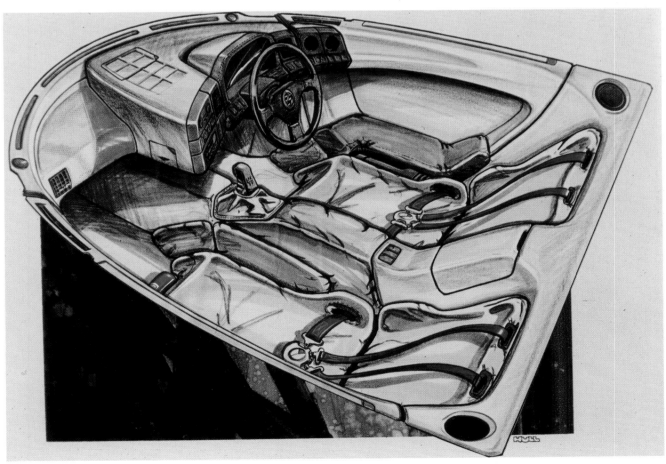

Desktop publishing

Computers usually mean that nothing has to be done twice. Technical illustration, however, is perhaps the exception. In theory it should be possible to re-use drawings created earlier in the design process for technical publications. In practice, however, engineering drawings contain too much information and are generally too complex to reproduce well; concept/presentation drawings will be inevitably obsolete or too inexact. It will fall to someone – the technical illustrator – to create new drawings based on the latest update of the production drawings, or the product itself. These will be drawn from scratch specifically for the purpose, commissioned to illustrate an operating manual, for example.

Several computer programs are available for technical illustration which are completely unrelated to programs for computer-aided design, although they do share some cad features. The end product of a computer-aided design system is the product itself; the end product of a computer-aided technical illustration package is the drawing, which can subsequently be incorporated into a printed publication.

Programs such as Adobe Illustrator, Cricket Draw and Aldus Freehand are more closely linked to word-processing and page-layout packages than cad systems. On a computer such as the Macintosh, there are two different ways of producing illustrations, referred to as "draw" and "paint". While it may be amusing to argue about the differences between drawing and painting in 20th-century art, in computing these terms can be defined exactly. A "paint" document is stored in the computer's memory as a bit map, a one-to-one

▲ **This dramatic isometric cutaway of the workings of a Rolex watch was created by Duncan Hearnden, using Adobe Illustrator. It was made to demonstrate the software's potential for technical illustration.**

array corresponding to the pixels on the screen. This is also known as wysiwyg (what you see is what you get). A "draw" document is stored in the computer's memory as a "display list" of the point and line coordinates and formulae for circles, etc., that make up the drawing. This is also known as object-oriented graphics, because every "object" – a circle, line or curve – can be accounted for separately. In a paint program, a circle intersected by a line, say, is just a pattern of dots and can only be moved en bloc. It is not possible to edit *globally,* i.e. modify all the components of a particular shape in a drawing. In a draw program, it is possible to move the line without affecting the integrity of the circle. And the output resolution to, say, a pen plotter is quite independent of the screen resolution.

▼ Concept drawings for a hairdryer by Roger Davies, when he was a student at the Royal College of Art, London. He used SDRC's Geomod to demonstrate that disassembling components in wireframe (top left) and rendering the casing transparent (bottom left) can produce highly convincing technical illustrations.

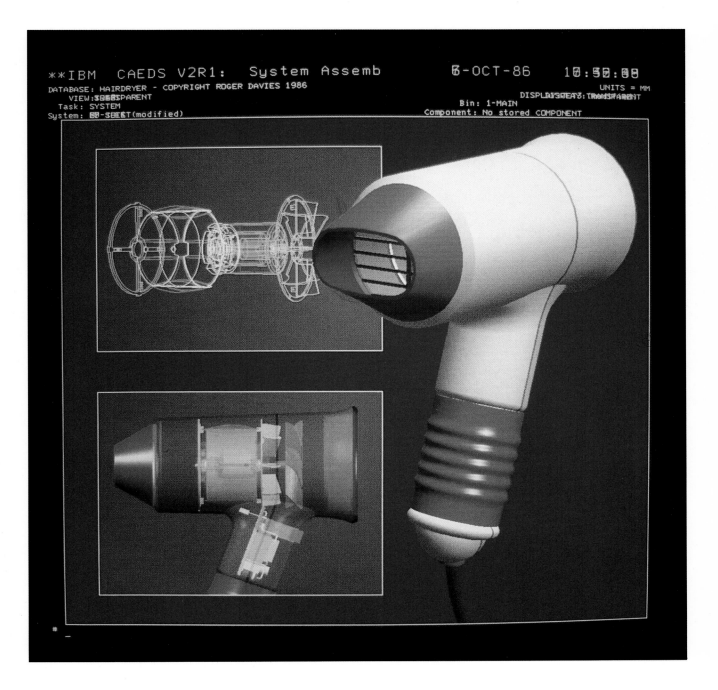

MacPaint was the first program for the Macintosh to use bit-mapped graphics, and is good for producing freehand irregular-shaded objects and airbrush effects. MacDraw, now completely rewritten to make it more like a 2D drafting program with multiple layering, was the first object-oriented program. Some programs, such as Silicon Beach's Superpaint, use both techniques on separate layers, and images can be transferred from one layer to another. The early draw packages were restricted to drawings made up of simple geometric primitives, such as lines, boxes, circles, polygons and arcs, which can be combined and grouped together.

Adobe Illustrator's objects are mostly Bézier curves which can be manipulated to produce complex drawings. Bit-mapped and scanned images can be "imported" and traced over. Cricket Draw is aimed at business users of presentation graphics and includes many functions for manipulating and modifying text. Both are intended to produce output on a laser plotter.

Aldus Freehand, despite its name, is an object-oriented program and not intended for spontaneously loose drawing. It uses a "join the dots" approach to create Bézier shapes – but it is not always clear what is going on until you move to "preview" mode. Other tools create boxes, lines, ellipses and corners at any angle. The program has 200 layers available, so that the drawing can be split up into separate elements that can be displayed and edited individually. Line attributes, fills and colours can be saved on a "style sheet" and applied to other elements later to maintain a consistency throughout a series of illustrations. There are commands for rotating, scaling, mirroring, skewing and stretching elements, and text can be wrapped around a line or shape. And it can produce graduated tones in "spot" or the four process colours needed for print separations, complete with registration and centre marks. Drawings thus created can be exported to page-layout packages such as Interleaf Publisher, Aldus PageMaker or Xerox's Ventura and combined with text originated on a word-processing system.

Designers do not spend all their time drawing, and a desktop publishing system can prove beneficial in many other ways: producing typeset-quality reports and proposals, for example, with a greater degree of in-house control, while helping to project a better image of the consultancy to the world outside.

▼ Power drill section illustrations by Robert Harrington, using Adobe Illustrator 88 running on a Macintosh II and output on a laser printer. They show the level of detail that can be obtained from a package developed for desktop publishing.

► A cad solid model can be used as the basis for a set of exploded assembly drawings. This spray mechanism assembly for a plastic container was designed using McDonnell-Douglas's Unigraphics system.

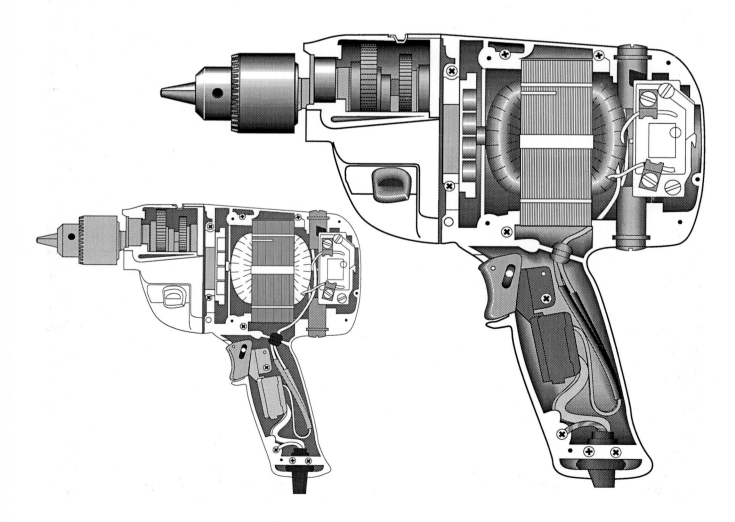

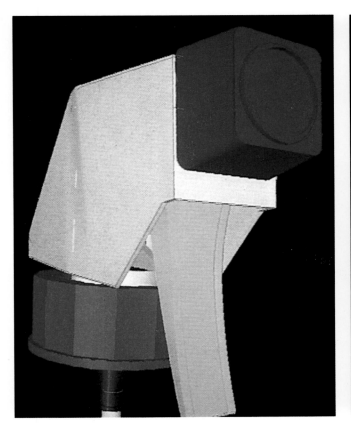

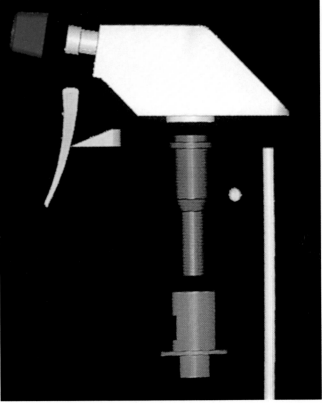

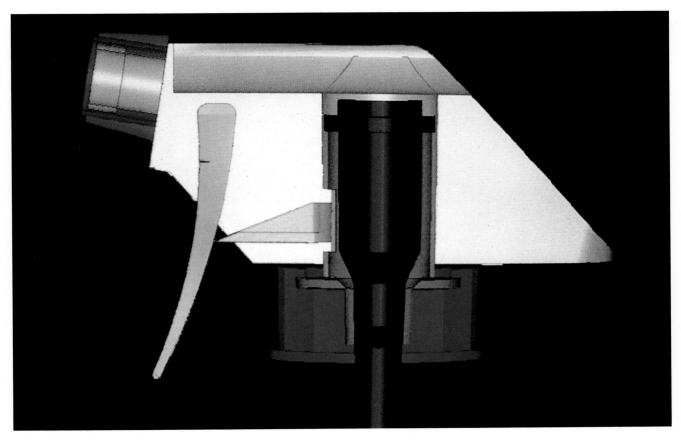

◄ Prototype of the "Post Card" travel iron, designed by a team of five designers at Smart Design.

Case study: **Smart Design, New York**

Smart Design was founded in New York City by Davin Stowell and Tucker Viemeister in 1985, and grew out of Davin Stowell Associates. It is a multi-faceted group of 15 product designers, graphic designers and ergonomics experts, with clients including Corning Glass Works, Eastman Kodak, Sanyei, Singer and Swatch. Tucker Viemeister is the son of Read Viemeister who was responsible, when at Lippincott & Margolies in 1947, for the industrial design on the revolutionary but ill-fated Tucker Torpedo automobile. Tucker Viemeister, born a year later, was named after the car. He graduated from the Pratt Institute in 1974, taught in Portugal and worked on the graphics and street furniture for Washington zoo. He was the co-designer, with Lisa Krohn, of Phonebook, a telephone answering machine whose form is a metaphor for its intended use.

Phonebook has linked Viemeister with the Cranbrook school of designers, but he likes to position his work in a wider context. "I do not think there is an American 'school,' but American designers do have a unique way of looking at design: practical, economic, functional. We don't have the balls of the Italians nor the design public of the Germans. But we are in the middle of the biggest commercial market. In the past we have been controlled by the marketing guys ('More chrome! More woodgrain!'), but today we are learning that our holistic approach to design is giving us a special perspective in the product development process. We are realizing that, to make a truly popular product, we have to instill it with the ability to connect emotionally (as well as functionally) with the user."

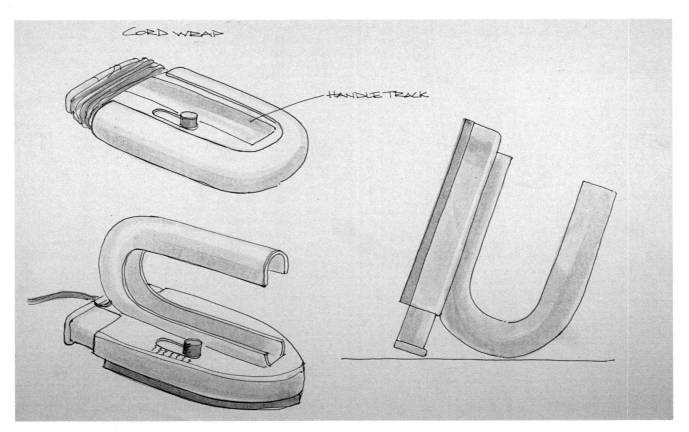

▲ One of many concept sketches on A3 paper, in pen and rendered with marker, showing the way the travel iron folds flat for packing. The perspective presentations, mainly in linework, are always simple and straightforward. Sketching does not just help refine an idea, according to Viemeister, but often triggers a new one. He uses rough underlays to help with colour sketches.

The name Smart Design was picked because "it was easy to say, easy to remember, could be the name of a person (although we are a group and did not want one of our names to be the name of the office), and it expressed our combination of practical and imaginative design." He is proud to say that his products are good-looking: "Today things like ergonomics and efficiency are taken for granted. You don't make a product that doesn't work. So we are moving on to the next level – or rather we are rediscovering what designers like Raymond Loewy used to do – making products that are seductively beautiful, meaningful, and interesting." But Viemeister tempers beauty with concern. "Industrial designers will play an increasingly critical role in the solution of the world's problems – from Aids to hunger, from the elderly to the ozone. Designers give form to our dreams. We make our ideas real."

On drawing, Viemeister believes that the designer's media have a great and direct influence on the shapes and forms of the products created, "analogous to the role that words play in the development of ideas. Eskimos have something like 137 different words for snow. Pantone dictates the number of colours we can use. Magic Marker technique suggests sharp shapes; pastels, smooth forms; Fome-Cor, crisp boxes; cad, tricky intersections and repetitious vents and textures. You can see an obvious parallel between modern styles and design media. Automotive and point-of-purchase designers love markers. Designers of medical equipment and office furniture, on the other hand, like breadboard mock-ups.

"Industrial designers make things in space. Sketching is a two-way shortcut between ideas in my head and 3D reality. On paper, ideas can be checked quickly, but drawing is only one of the weapons in my arsenal – and each is used for its special qualities. I use these tools to evolve an idea: sketching either triggers new ideas or helps refine the one I'm working on.

"The act of drawing for a designer is simply a tool used to create or develop an idea or to present the idea to someone else. The product of this activity is a design not a drawing although, as a by-product, the drawing may have intrinsic value – as an historic document, souvenir, or art-like artefact that can be framed and hung on the wall."

"Study Leonardo and Mies van der Rohe," advises Viemeister. He also recommends drawing from life. "Drawing is hand/eye exercise and figure drawing is to the designer as jogging is to the boxer. It is fun, it is traditionally part of all art. A big part of design is art. It is important."

Viemeister tries to save drawings and models that have a direct relationship with successful product development – or ones that look good – from the post-project clean-up: "I believe that Leonardo became famous mostly because his drawings were not thrown out by his tidy mother."

On presentation he says: "Designs are ideas which need to be 'sold' to the client, and we use the most appropriate media to communicate the idea. They can be models, photos, renderings, and we usually sketch during the actual presentation. We show anything that helps explain our idea clearly.

Case study: Smart Design

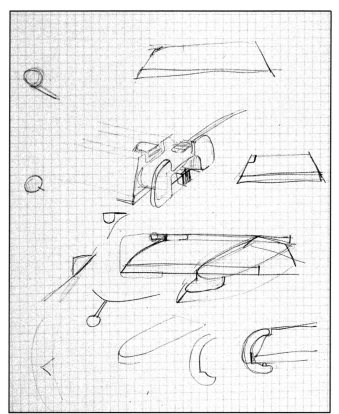

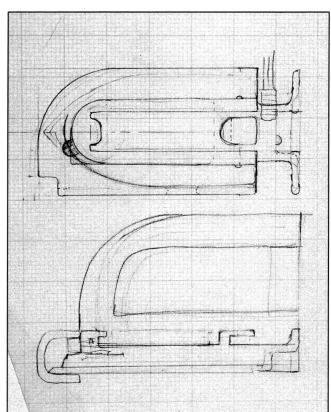

▲ Line sketches work out the details (above left) and the structure (above). Squared paper helps in taking off measurements.

"It is important that the design should drive the drawing technique selection. We use photo-montage, airbrush, markers, pastels, crayons, photocopies, collage, Color-aid and Pantone paper. Sometimes we present just one drawing; other times 300 – it depends." He uses perspective for rendering because "personally I think isometric and axonometric projections don't look like anything in the real world. They are simply a trick that architects use to fool the client as well as themselves into buying their design.

"The final products of our industrial design are the mechanical drawings that are used by the manufacturer to create prototypes, the tools, and therefore the product itself. Depending on the client's requirements, the control drawings may contain only overall dimensions or be fully dimensioned. Engineering drawings, if necessary, are based on these drawings."

The Post Card travel iron for Sanyei America Corporation was designed by John Lonczak, Davin Stowell, Tucker Viemeister, Tom Dair and Daniel Formosa. "It is easy to design something that pleases the designer," says Viemeister. "It is harder to design something that appeals to diverse consumer taste. Smart Design's challenge is to create things that please both the designer and 'middle America' through innovative, sensitive and fresh approaches. Sanyei appliances are sold everywhere from Macy's to True Value hardware stores!" The shape of the iron is derived from its archetype: the antique flat-iron. The concept of the handle as a case was "humanized and humorized," in an attempt to make an acitivity usually associated with drudgery more fun.

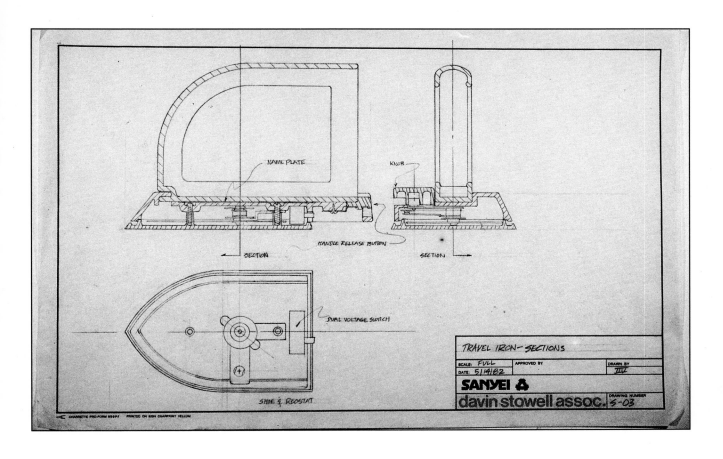

NAME PLATE

KNOB

HANDLE RELEASE BUTTON

SECTION

SECTION

DUAL VOLTAGE SWITCH

SHOE & REOSTAT

TRAVEL IRON — SECTIONS

SCALE: FULL	APPROVED BY	DRAWN BY
DATE: 5/14/82		ꗱ

SANYEI △
davin stowell assoc. DRAWING NUMBER S-03

◄ A simple sketch to help communicate to the modelmaker exactly what the designer intends at the manufacturing stage.

▲ General arrangement drawing showing the iron's sections.

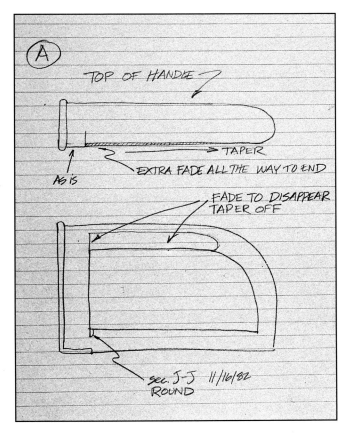

(A)

TOP OF HANDLE

TAPER

EXTRA FADE ALL THE WAY TO END

AS IS

FADE TO DISAPPEAR
TAPER OFF

sec. J-J 11/16/82
ROUND

Drawings are witness to the creative process . . . and more immediately than published works give an insight into the spiritual life of an artist. They are thus weighty documents for the study and understanding of his activity

Waldemar von Seidlitz, treatise on Leonardo da Vinci, 1909

9 The Future of the Design Drawing

The drawing, as a means of externalizing ideas and communicating them to others, has been used by artists and designers since the beginnings of civilization. The industrial revolution, with its need to separate the designer from the maker, endowed the drawing with a new importance: that of a symbolic representation of the designed object that could be worked on, tested and approved before the final form was committed in an expensive model or prototype.

Up until the 1930s, design theorists and the teachers of drawing were concerned with drawing as a formal and codified language. The European tradition of modernism, refined at the Bauhaus, placed emphasis on harmony through geometry, with its building blocks of circle, square and triangle. It was not so much "form follows function" as form follows drawing style.

From the end of the 1940s, product design has been carried out in group practices and consultancies, usually outside the organizational structure of the client company. And despite the media's demand for "design stars," it is often difficult to attribute authorship of a particular design to a particular individual. Present-day design is a complex activity requiring teamwork and a range of skills. The Sony Walkman, for example, is a virtuoso piece of 3D geometry in which the motors and electronic circuitry inside are clearly integrated with the functional and aesthetically pleasing (and hence marketable) exterior. This was not a case of a stylist being brought in at a later stage to add the "cosmetics" to already "designed" machinery.

▶ **Aldo Rossi has led the way in making the designer's drawing more visible, as with this press filter coffee maker of 1985 for Alessi, complete with Doric column. A sumptuous book of his drawings has been published to appeal directly to the targetted consumers of the product.**

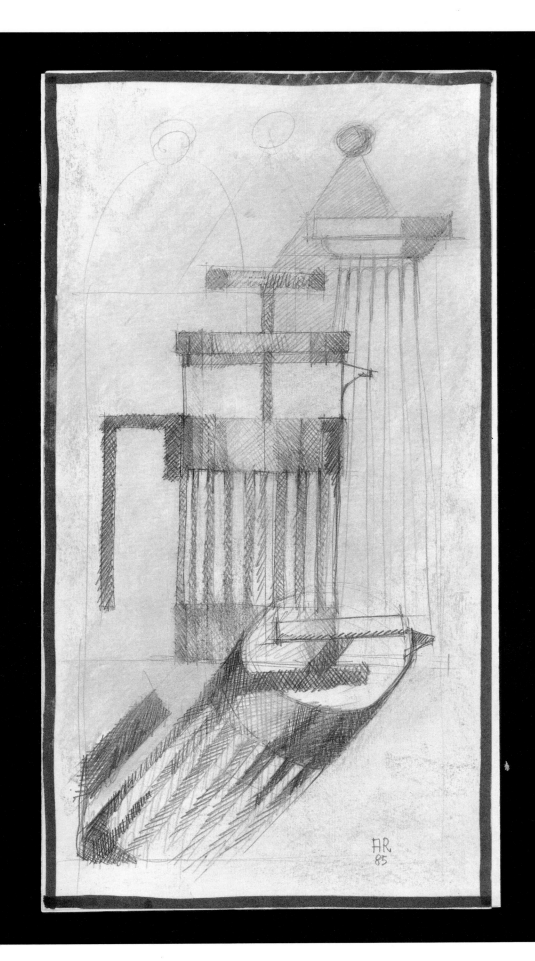

The Future of the Design Drawing

Ergonomics and psychological considerations are being added to the functional specifications of a product, and designers are studying the "semantics" of design, using simile, metaphor and hyperbole to help explain the function and operation of products spawned by the information technology age to "naive" users. These products, typified by the US-led "Cranbrook School" designers – Design Logic in Chicago, Seattle-based Technology Design, and New York's Smart Design – have a Cubist/organic look that has much in common with the "bio-form" designs of Luigi Colani. They are all breaking free from the Euclidean straightjacket of rectilinear boxes with rounded edges imposed by outdated drawing methods and manufacturing techniques.

Drawing has always been about attempting to express the three-dimensionality of the real world on the two dimensions of paper. Inevitably, something will be lost, and the almost insurmountable difficulties inherent in describing complex "sculptural" shapes on a two-dimensional plane must have deterred many designers from even attempting to draw them. If a drawing for manufacture has to be complete and unambiguous, then it may as well be rectilinear, and the design theory can be post-rationalized by using the geometric tenets of the Modern Movement.

With more versatile tools, however, and the time made available to use them, designers will be able to explore less conventional solutions. With the proviso that the system is easy to learn and to use, and that it *will* be used, cad promises to liberate the mainstream designer to try out more free-form shapes, thereby enriching the designed environment and ultimately offering more choice to the consumer.

▼ ▶ **Most products will have some degree of interaction with the human hand, so obviously a computerized hand about the place to test the ergonomic interface of products will pay for itself time and time again. This study, modelled on Duct at Brand New, London, was created from statistical anthropometric data, and can be bent and splayed to any logical position.**

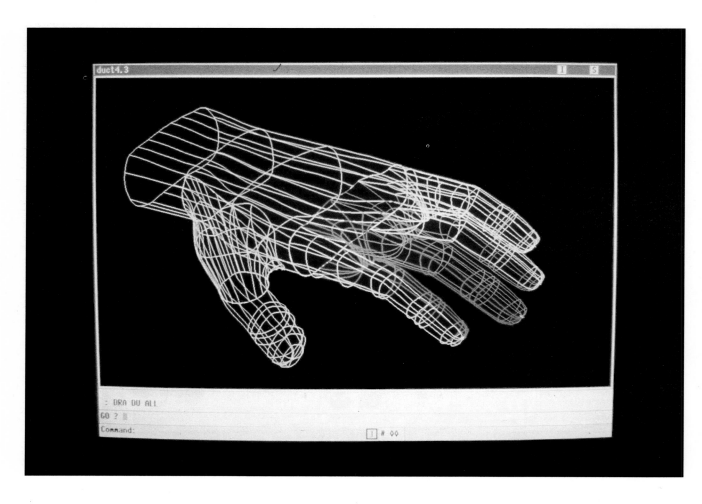

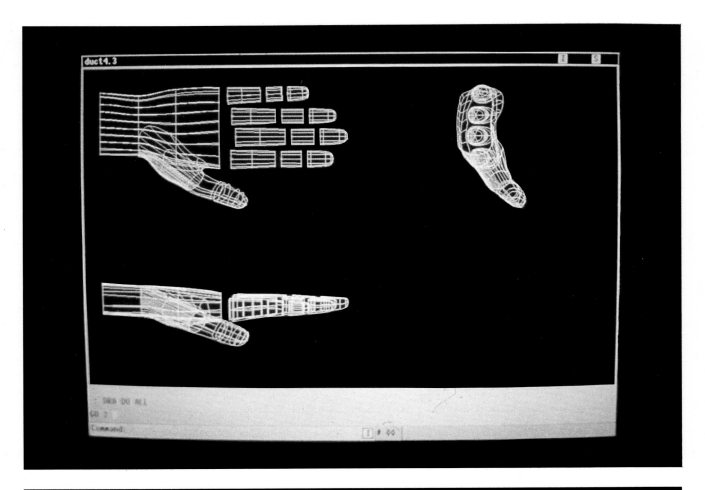

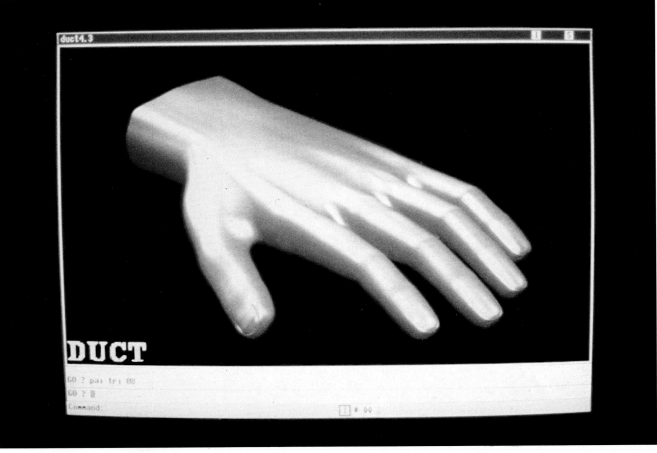

The Future of the Design Drawing

Cad is more than just the slick visuals of ray tracing and the productivity increases of 2D drafting. It enables the designer to explore new shapes and forms. With solid modelling a designer can "draw" in three dimensions, working on an electronic model that can be viewed from any angle. A designer can also be confident that, during experiments with form, any essential functional specifications, such as weight, strength, wall thicknesses, clearances and tolerances with pre-sourced components are always adhered to.

As computer hardware prices continue to fall, the cad system will become just another tool available to the designer. Cad systems are already found in design offices, mostly brought in first to handle the huge amount of drafting required at the pre-production stages of the design process. Once they are installed, designers begin to realize their potential for helping in the earlier stages of concept design and for producing presentation drawings. Graduates of design schools, who are increasingly educated in the techniques of cad, will come to expect those resources to be available to them in the workplace.

Computer screens may eventually replace drawing boards, but the drawing will always be a necessary part of the design process. The concept of a paperless office has become something of a joke; computerization has in fact created an enormous demand for paper. More data, in more and different forms, is the consequence of the information revolution. "If the computer can do it, then we want it," is the exhortation of management. Drawings, in the form of diagrams and charts, are helping make sense of all this "decision support" information and computers will aid the designer in all kinds of other ways: in producing illustrated reports, in project management, in marketing and in archiving previous designs. Just as Achille Castiglioni's studio contained a museum of inspirational objects, so can a present-day product designer have a CD-rom full of instantly accessible source images at his or her fingertips.

Some commentators, notably Mike Cooley in *Design After Modernism,* have expressed reservations about the blind take-up of cadcam, with consultancies buying it to impress clients rather than to increase the quality (and quantity) of service. Cooley has always argued that cadcam would spread division of labour, known as Taylorism, to more intellectual activities, namely designing. Taylorism was named after Frederick W. Taylor (1856–1915), who evolved the theory of "scientific management," promoting the rationalization, standardization and automation of production to save labour.

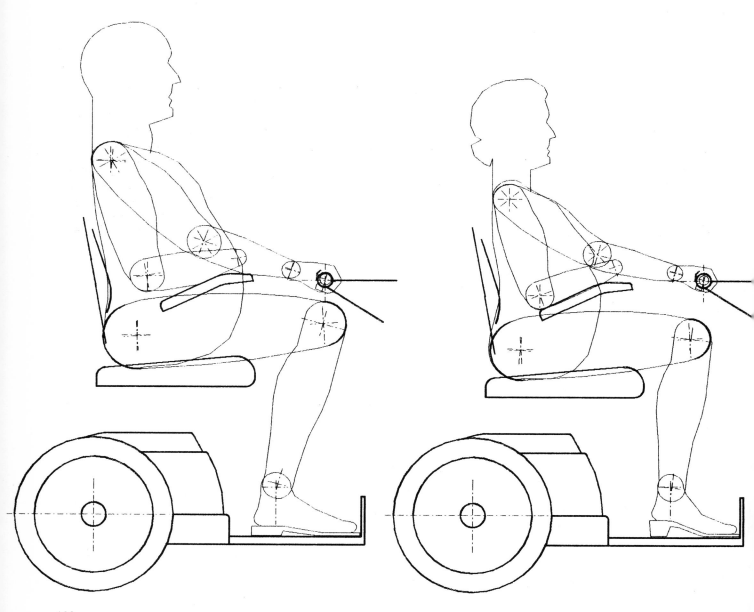

Cooley's theory has symmetry and elegance, but has been overtaken by events. Whether the teamwork seen in today's multi-disciplinary design projects can be treated as white-collar Taylorism is debatable, and would happen whether cadcam were involved or not. Shiftwork, introduced by large firms when the cost of cadcam was outrageously expensive, was recognized to be counter-productive. The use of cad-trained operators, acting as technicians to reluctant designers, is likewise out of favour. The best work comes when the designer has access to his or her own system to be used as and when necessary. Cooley's warnings that working with cad can be alienating, fragmented and stressful because of the ever-increasing tempo have been received and understood.

Instead of sub-dividing the designer's traditional job, cad can expand a designer's conceptual span and give him or her a holistic view of the project and more overall control over more stages of the design-to-production process. It is conceivable that a computer-aided designer could single-handedly tackle an entire large-scale project from conception to the gener-ation of tapes to drive machine tools. Cad equipment has enabled many designers to set up one- or two-person practices with the minimum of office space with the capacity to undertake quite complex projects.

Cooley is wary that "tacit knowledge" will be lost in rule-based and so-called expert systems, that designers will lose the ability to visualize, say, 3D objects from a plan and elevation. But just as calculators have removed the need to learn long division, so designers with cad are, in theory, released to concentrate on the more creative aspects of the job. Thinking time, however, preferably away from the screen, must be allowed for, and it is a fool indeed who accepts uncritically that the computer is infallible. "Alternatives exist," says Cooley, after Dürer, "which reject neither human judgement, tacit knowledge, intuition and imagination, nor the scientific or rule-based method, and we should unite them in a symbiotic totality." The key word in computer-aided design is *aided*. A system should build on human skill rather than marginalize it.

John Frazer, director of cad at the University of Ulster, sees the future cad system as an electronic muse and critic. It would be able to elicit from designers the purpose of the present design activity and then discuss with them the approach being taken. When they become stuck, the cad system could helpfully suggest alternative strategies, find previous analogous approaches or make random suggestions to help them clarify their ideas.

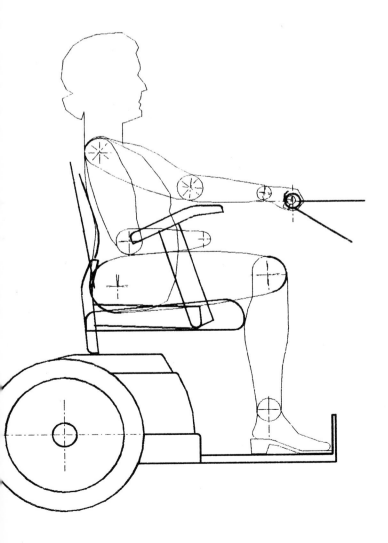

◄ Cad for the future is not all ray tracing and powerful numbercrunchers, it will also enable smaller practices to take on more socially sound projects with fewer cost penalties. Designer Chris Rust produced this ergonomic study for a Booster electric wheelchair, using a cad system based on an Atari micro running GFA Draft software. The print-out is reproduced at its original size.

The Future of the Design Drawing

Current cad acts as an amplifier or turbo-charger – it amplifies ability but also amplifies ignorance indiscriminately. Rather than being stressful to their users, in Cooley's sense, computers can cure designers of the boredom and under-challenge that, according to Frazer, produced "the peripheral intellectual flippancy of Post-modern styling." Rather than mimicking the "scruffy sketch, [cad] mimics the process of juggling with ideas." In product design, programs should model not two- and three-dimensional form, but the *process* of manufacture and the process of assembly that produces that form. This, says Frazer, re-establishes for the designer the power the craftsperson has when designing a craft object, and helps to overcome the alienation and separation of designer and machine that has existed since the industrial revolution.

The designer's drawing: collector's piece?

As the artist's drawing achieved increased stature early this century, and as galleries have sought out new media to fill the wallspace, so will the designer's drawing increasingly find the appreciation it deserves. As well as giving an insight into the creative processes at work, designers' drawings are now appraised as works of art, following the revival of interest in architects' drawings as decorative objects.

Yu-Chee Chong's gallery in London is claimed to be the first specializing in drawings by designers. She concentrates on drawings from 1780 to the 1930s, chosen for their aesthetic appearance rather than their design historic value. Exhibitions so far have included one entitled "Magnificent Machines," on engineering drawings rendered between 1820 and 1850, and one on furniture designs 1830–1930.

There was a sale of Raymond Loewy memorabilia at auction at the Château Rambouillet, Paris in June 1987, and the London office of Sotheby's holds an annual spring auction of architectural drawings and watercolours, which usually includes some examples of furniture and 19th-century engineering drawings. According to Charles Hind, the expert responsible for these sales, there are some problems for collectors, including the difficulty of telling hand-coloured copies from the genuine "original," and the fact that working drawings can often be marred with later annotations and alterations. If a drawing has been stored in reasonable conditions, however, it can be unaffected by light damage and glow with colour in a way rare among watercolours which have been hanging (and fading) for years.

More recently, manufacturers have been making a selling point with their designers' drawings. Suppliers such as Alessi have produced limited edition reprints of drawings, done either during the design process or after the object has been put into production. The trend started with a drawing by Afra and Tobia Scarpa of their Miss chair for Molteni, on sale at the Milan furniture fair in 1987, which cost more than the piece of furniture illustrated. Undoubtedly, the designer's drawing, now identified as a marketing tool, will become more and more visible in companies' advertisements.

Finally, here are some sobering words from the days when designing meant nothing more than adding ornamentation, which the practising product designer would do well to heed. R.Ll.B. Rathbone wrote in the metalwork section (the closest to today's product design) of *Practical Designing: A Hand-book on the Preparation of Working Drawings* (1893): "It is generally worthwhile giving the workman a rough perspective sketch of the whole design, so that he may picture it in his mind more easily than he can do from plans and elevations alone. To avoid the dangers of subdivided labour, the designer should endeavour to obtain free intercourse with the workman who is going to actually carry out the design; but not until he has either had some practical manual training, or else has made himself as conversant with the construction and processes of metal-work as theoretical study will permit. Our British workmen are apt to hold the ideas and attainments of designers in high disdain, and perhaps even to take a certain degree of pleasure in overwhelming them with all the practical difficulties in the way of working out what looks so nice on paper . . . The designer who has had the patience to follow these dry, technical details, should now be able to avoid falling into those errors of construction which make the British (or other) workman scratch his head, and wonder why designers were created for the apparent purpose of setting him problems which he can never solve – errors which cause the enemy of the division of labour to blaspheme, not without reason."

Today's product designers may never even meet the workers responsible for manufacturing their designs and so must be confident that the drawings, whether they are orthographic projections, more pictorial perspectives or metrics, or a computer-aided solid model, set out their aims and intentions, concerns and aspirations as explicitly and emphatically as the technology of drawing will allow.

▼ This drawing of the "Miss" chair for Molteni, by Afra and Tobia Scarpa, was on sale at the 1987 Milan Furniture Fair. Many manufacturers are now producing limited editions of screenprints that reproduce designers' drawings; paradoxically, they cost as much or sometimes more than the designed objects they were meant to help create.

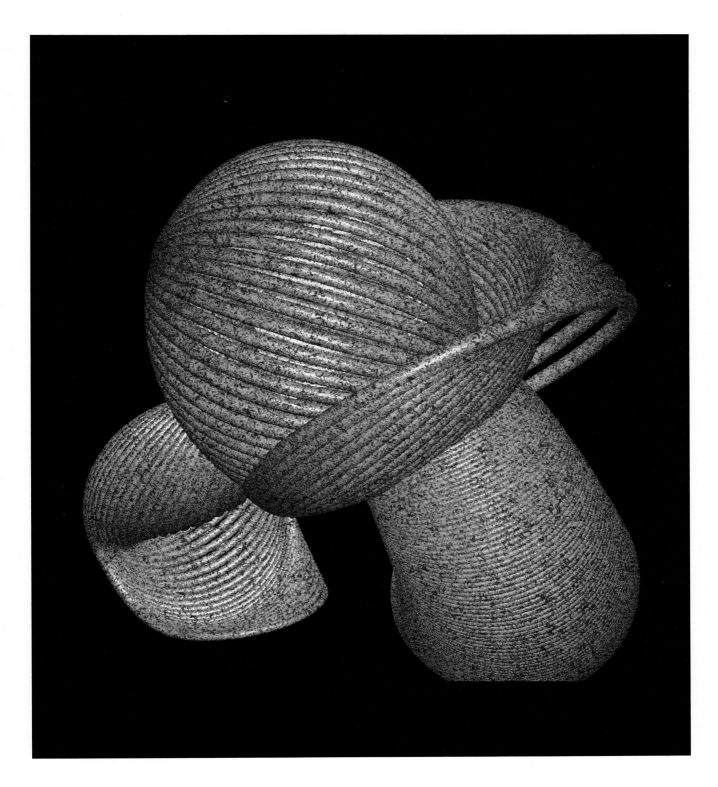

▲ William Latham's computer
sculptures show designers the
shape of things to come – the
most complex and organic of
forms can be modelled,
rendered and even
manufactured using cad.

Acknowledgements

The author and the publishers would like to thank the following for their help:

Julia Engelhardt for researching the illustrations for this book;
John and Julia Frazer of Autographics Software (NI) Ltd, Toye, Downpatrick, Northern Ireland, for the artworks on pages 63–4, 66–7, 73 top and 74 left;
Ed Matthews of Brand New Ltd, London;
Julian Quincey for the illustrations on pages 68–71, 102–5 and 148–9;
John Scorey for the illustrations on pages 108–9;
Wade Greenwood Design for the diagram on page 37 and the charts on pages 47, 49 and 55.

The examples of first- and third-angle projection on page 62 are an extract from BS308: Part 1: 1984, reproduced by courtesy of the British Standards Institution (BSI). Complete copies of the Standard can be obtained through National Standards bodies.

Permission to reproduce other illustrations was kindly provided by:
Alessi SpA, Crusinallo (page 127 top, 163);
Alias Research, Toronto (page 72);
Amazing Array Productions, London (page 115, 118–9);
Apollo Computer, Milton Keynes (page 45 centre);
Ardent Computer, Milton Keynes (page 9 bottom right, 112–3);
Artemide SpA, Milan (page 83 top);
Dott. Arch. Sergio Asti, Milan (page 27 bottom);
Autographics Software, Toye, Downpatrick (pages 86–7);
Aztek Ltd, London (page 34, 151 top);
Dott. Arch. Mario Bellini, Milan (page 30, 99 bottom left and bottom right, 139);
Berol, King's Lynn, Norfolk (page 29);
Carrozzeria Bertone SpA, Turin (page 35, 107 bottom);
BIB Design Consultants Ltd, London (page 36, 65 bottom, 140–3);
Bibliothèque Nationale, Paris (page 8);
Borough of Ipswich Museum (page 21);
Brand New Ltd, London (page 33, 52, 54, 88 top, 89 top, 127 bottom, 132–3, 134–5, 164–5);
British Architectural Library, RIBA, London (page 22, 128);
Cadcentre, Cambridge (page 137 right);
Capella Medicée, Florence (page 18);
Dott. Arch. Achille Castiglioni, Milan (page 81 bottom right);
Centraal Museum, Utrecht, © Stichting Beldrecht (page 24);
Cousins Design, New York (page 82, 101);
D-Team, Schondorf (pages 120–3);
Daimler-Benz AG, Stuttgart (page 32);
Deltacam Systems, Birmingham (page 73 bottom, 110–1, 138);
Dott. Arch. Michele De Lucchi, Milan (page 78);
Dorset Institute, Bournemouth, Dept of Communications and Media (pages 14–5, 116);
Henry Dreyfuss Associates, New York (page 94, 95 top);
Anthony Dunne, Fareham (page 83 bottom, 99 top right);
Electrolux Archive/Conran Foundation, London (page 11 bottom);
Peter Engelhardt, Idealdesign, Nieder-Olm (page 31);
Giugiaro Design SrL, Turin (pages 130–1, 136, 137 left);
Robert Harrington, London (page 156);
Hunterian Art Gallery, University of Glasgow, Mackintosh Collection (page 12);
IBM UK Scientific Centre, Winchester (page 74 right, 75 top left and top right, 88 bottom, 169);
Iittala Glass Museum/Museum of Finnish Architecture, Helsinki (page 77);
Intergraph, Swindon (page 43, 45 bottom, 114);
Italdesign SIRP SpA, Turin (page 153);
Jaguar Cars Ltd, Coventry (page 145, 150, 151 bottom, 153);
King-Miranda Associates, Milan (pages 90–1, 98);
William Latham, London (page 89 bottom);
Library of the French Institute, Paris (page 19);
Lovegrove & Brown, London (page 61 bottom, 79);
Lyons-Ames Design, London (page 95 bottom, 125);
McDonnell-Douglas, Woking (page 157);
McQueen Ltd, Galashiels (page 154);
Syd Mead Inc., Los Angeles (pages 96–7);
Moggridge Associates, London (page 27 top, 56–9, 80, 81 bottom left);
Molteni & C., Milan (page 168);
National Maritime Museum, Greenwich, London (page 9 top);
National Motor Museum, Beaulieu (page 81 top);
Pentel, New Malden, Surrey (page 28);
Pepysian Library, Magdalene College, Cambridge (page 10, 61 top);
Pfalzgalerie, Kaiserslauten (page 23);
The Post Office, London (pages 146–7);
Royal College of Art, London, Dept of Industrial Design (page 75 centre and bottom);
Chris Rust, Dean Clough, Halifax (pages 166–7);
Scala, Florence (page 9 bottom left; 18, 19, 20);
Schlumberger Graphics, Bristol (page 53);
Schürer Design, Bielefeld (page 93);
SDRC, Hitchin, Hertfordshire (page 155);
Studio Šípek, Amsterdam (page 7, 99 top left);
Smart Design, New York (pages 129, 158–61);
Oscar Tusquets Blanca, Barcelona (pages 38–41);
Venturi Rauch & Scott Brown, Philadelphia (pages 84–5);
Volkswagen AG, Wolfsburg (page 50, 51, 106, 107 top and centre);
Wavefront Technologies/Computervision, Basingstoke (page 117);
Daniel Weil & Gerard Taylor, London (title page, 17);
Westward Technology, Tewkesbury (page 45 top);
Yu-Chee Chong Fine Art, London (page 13, 126).

Glossary

Auxiliary projection A view of a component taken from an angle which is not at right angles, and hence not orthogonal, to any of the three views in an *orthographic projection*. It is usually included to help clarify the reading of a drawing.

Axonometric projection A non-perspective pictorial method of representing a 3D object, containing a true plan, and constructed with the aid of a T-square and a 45-degree set square. It is the simplest metric projection to set up from orthographic drawings.

Cabinet, cavalier projection see *Oblique projection*.

Cad Computer-aided design or, more exactly in the case of 2D systems, computer-aided *drafting*. Computer-*automated* design is not here just yet!

Cam Computer-aided manufacture: all the downstream shopfloor activities, such as *NC* and production planning, which can make use of the part's geometry as it is output from the cad system.

Cadcam Joining the two acronyms does not necessarily ensure integration, although nowadays the two types of system can be run on the same machine.

FEA Finite-element analysis: breaking down a component's geometry into a mesh of simple shapes which can be analysed for stress and thermal properties. FEA programs are very large and are often sent off to a batch numbercruncher for processing. Personal computers (PCs) usually run the pre- and post-processors that build the mesh, and display the results in the form of coloured contour images.

First-angle projection see *Orthographic projection*.

GA General arrangement: these drawings are the key to all other detail, tooling and assembly drawings needed for production, which could run to hundreds and might be at different scales. It is in these that the final layout is decided, dimensions are fixed, ergonomic considerations resolved and the methods of production finalized. All of them are coordinated with reference to the GA.

Isometric projection A non-perspective pictorial method of representing a 3D object, producing a less extreme drawing than the *axonometric projection*. Elevations are constructed using a 30-degree set square, so the "plan" is distorted.

NC Numerical control: as applied to machine tools, this can be DNC (direct numerical control), where the machine is hardwired to the cam system, or CNC (computer numerical control), where the part data is passed physically from the cam system to the machine via paper tape. NC part programming is the method of converting the geometry of a component output from a cad system into an efficient toolpath for the appropriate machine tool to manufacture the part, and verifying that there are no clashes between the tool and the part's fixtures.

Oblique projection A non-perspective pictorial method of representing a 3D object used where the front elevation of the object is of particular importance – in furniture design, for example. The oblique lines emerging from the elevation can be any length: in a cavalier projection they are true length; in a cabinet projection they are half the true length.

Orthographic projection The "engineering drawing" method of representing three dimensions on 2D paper by projecting three adjacent views of an object – a plan and two elevations – on to three orthogonal planes (i.e. at right angles to one another) and then "unfolding" those planes so that they lie on the same plane. First-angle projection has the plan with the elevation of the front face immediately above it and the end elevation to the right. Third-angle projection has the views arranged so that one elevation is placed below the plan, with the end elevation to the left of the first elevation.

Parametric programming An almost automatic method of generating drawings of components having a family resemblance, by first defining a generalized component shape and subsequently inputting specific dimensions.

Perspective A method of introducing systematic distortions into drawings to *symbolize* reality. Objects appear to diminish and converge as their distance from the viewer increases. The horizon is assumed to be infinitely distant, so that parallel lines meet at "vanishing points."

Pixel Short for picture element, which is the size of a dot on a computer display. The resolution (sharpness) of a raster display is measured by the number of pixels horizontally by the number of scan lines vertically, e.g. 1280×1024.

Ray tracing A technique for computing a photographically realistic visualization of an object and its environment by using the laws of optics. Each ray leaving a surface is the sum of varying contributions from three sources: diffusely reflected light; specularly reflected light and transmitted (or refracted) light. Rays are traced back from the viewpoint (shot, in effect, through the pixels of the display's screen), bounced around the scene, and arrive eventually back at the light source. Radiosity is more sophisticated, determining the light energy equilibrium of all the surfaces in a static environment independent of the observer's position.

Scrap view An enlarged close-up of a detail on a drawing requiring particular attention.

Section A slice through a solid object to illustrate a profile or the interior of a part not made obvious by *orthographic projection*. Whole series of sections are needed to represent complex doubly curved shapes, such as car bodies.

Solid modeller A cad system that produces a complete and unambiguous 3D model of the component that can be "weighed" and checked for interferences with other objects.

Spline The computer equivalent to the French curve, but more controllable. The most advanced type commercially available is called nurbs: non-uniform rational B-spline.

Surface modeller A specialized 3D cad module for designing objects with complex doubly curved surfaces, such as those defining turbine blades, automobile bodies and telephone handsets. It is not usually integrated with *wireframe* or *solid modeller* systems.

Third-angle projection see *Orthographic projection*.

Turnkey system A packaged and integrated assembly of hardware, software and support. Turnkey suppliers buy in equipment from manufacturers and re-package the components, perhaps adding some proprietary boards as well as their own software, before passing on the thoroughly tested system to the user.

2½D A simplified version of 3D in which an x, y 2D profile is "extruded" in the z direction to generate a shape with no undercuts.

Wireframe A "transparent" 3D representation of an object – made up of lines and points, but no surfaces.

Further Reading

The history of drawing

Baynes, Ken and Pugh, Francis, *The Art of the Engineer*, Lutterworth Press, Guildford 1981. A lavishly illustrated book, concentrating on the drawings of Victorian engineers and restricted in content to modes of transport.

Booker, Peter J., *A History of Engineering Drawing*, Northgate, London 1979. An authoritative account charting the development of descriptive geometry and engineering drawing from earliest times until the 1960s.

Brett, David, "Drawing and the ideology of industrialization," *Design Issues*, MIT Press, Cambridge, Massachusetts, Vol. III No. 2 (Fall 1986) p.56. A paper on the implications of the way drawing was taught in the 19th century for the appearance of objects today.

Hambly, Maya, *Drawing Instruments: Their History, Purpose and Use for Architectural Drawings*, RIBA Drawings Collection, London 1982. Annotated catalogue of an exhibition of drawing instruments through the ages.

Lambert, Susan, *Drawing: Technique and Purpose*, Victoria and Albert Museum, London 1981. Catalogue of an exhibition examining the role of the drawing in art and design.

Leymarie, Jean et al, *History of an Art: Drawing*, Albert Skira, Geneva 1979. Beautifully illustrated book on the history and role of drawing in art.

Rawson, Philip, *Drawing*, Oxford University Press, London 1969, and *The Art of Drawing: an Instructional Guide*, Macdonald, London 1983. Two books, the second a later version of the first, on the history of the drawing in art, with sections on technique.

Techniques and materials

Beasley, David, *Design Presentation: Layout and Colouring Techniques*, Heinemann, London 1984. An elementary book aimed at craft, design and technology students.

Borgeson, Bet, *The Coloured Pencil: Key Concepts for Handling the Medium*, Watson-Guptill, New York 1983. A book devoted to drawing and rendering in coloured pencils.

Burden, Ernest, *Design Presentation: Techniques for Marketing and Project Proposals*, McGraw Hill 1984. A book aimed at architects but with some useful information for designers.

Camp, Jeffrey, *Draw: How to Master the Art*, André Deutsch, London 1981. A "how to draw" book, based on the idea that copying from the masters is not cheating.

Dell, Fred and Charlesworth, Andy, *The Airbrush Artist's Handbook*, Macdonald, London 1986. A practical guide to accessories, media and maintenance of commercially available airbrushes.

Doblin, Jay, *Perspective: a New System for Designers*, Whitney, New York 1956. A simplified approach to drawing perspectives, aimed at the product designer.

Dubery, Fred and Willats, John, *Perspective and Other Drawing Systems*, Herbert Press, London 1983. A primer for artists and designers on methods for drawing 3D shapes in perspective and the other "metric" forms.

Edwards, Betty, *Drawing on the Right Side of the Brain: How to Unlock your Hidden Artistic Talent*, Fontana/Collins 1979, and *Drawing on the Artist Within: a Guide to Innovation, Invention, Imagination and Creativity*, Collins, London 1987. Two novel books from the Professor of Art at California State University with techniques to stimulate the often underdeveloped visual and perceptual side of the brain.

Engineering Drawing Practice for Schools and Colleges, PP7308:1986 British Standards Institution, London 1980. An abbreviated introduction to the principles and conventions of BS308.

Goetsch, David and Nelson, John, *Technical Drawing and Design*, Delmar, New York 1978. A comprehensive manual of engineering practice to US standards, with a section on computer-assisted design.

Holder, Eberhard, *Design: Darstellungstechniken; Ein Handbuch*, Bauverlag, Wiesbaden und Berlin 1987. A guide to materials and techniques by a practising designer, with plenty of case study material.

Holmes, Clive, *Beginners' Guide to Technical Illustration*, Newnes Technical Books, London 1982. A pocket guide to technical illustration techniques for line work.

Kemnitzer, Ronald B., *Rendering with Markers*, Watson-Guptill, New York 1983. A how-to-do-it book with a strong emphasis on product design.

McHugh, Robert, *Working Drawing Handbook*, Van Nostrand Reinhold, New York 1982. A book aimed at architects but with some useful information for designers.

Martin, Judy, *The Complete Guide to Airbrushing: Technique and Materials*, Thames and Hudson, London 1983. A comprehensive book on airbrushing applications with a strong section on technical illustration.

Maurello, S. Ralph, *The Complete Airbrush Book*, Leon Amiel, New York 1980. A book on the applications and techniques of airbrushing, first published in 1955.

Nelms, Henning, *Thinking with a Pencil*, Barnes and Noble, New York 1964. An idiosyncratic "no skill necessary" how-to-draw book, with lots of tips on cheating.

Owen, Peter and Rollason, Jane, *The Complete Manual of Airbrushing Techniques*, Dorling Kindersley, London 1988. A comprehensive guide to selecting and using an airbrush.

Parker, Maurice, *Manual of British Standards in Engineering Drawing and Design*, BSI/Hutchinson, London 1984. A guide to the use of BS308 in the drawing office.

Powell, Dick, *Presentation Techniques*, Orbis, London 1985. A well illustrated how-to-do-it book on producing presentation drawings by a practising designer.

Powell, Dick and Monahan, Patricia, *Advanced Marker Techniques*, Macdonald Orbis, London 1987. More on markers by a practising designer, with chapters devoted to product and automotive design.

Rhodes, R.S. and Cook, L.B., *Basic Engineering Drawing*, Longman, London 1978. An introduction to engineering drawing practice to BS308.

Smith, Ray, *The Artist's Handbook*, Dorling Kindersley, London 1987. A thorough and comprehensive handbook of materials and techniques for artists, many of which are of use to the designer.

Ungar, Joseph, *Rendering in Mixed Media*, Watson-Guptill, New York 1985. How to create presentation-quality drawings as they are most often done – using a mixture of marker, pencil, pastel and whatever is most appropriate.

Vero, Radu, *Airbrush 2: Concepts for the Advanced Artist*, Watson-Guptill, New York and Columbus Books, London 1985. A thorough and methodical step-by-step guide to airbrushing techniques.

Computer-aided design

Foley, James D. and van Dam, Andries, *Fundamentals of Interactive Computer Graphics*, Addison-Wesley, Reading, Massachusetts 1982. The definitive work, though now becoming dated, on the theory of computer graphics. For serious enthusiasts and computer programmers only.

Lewell, John, *Computer Graphics*, Orbis, London 1985. A clear, accurate and well illustrated book covering all aspects and applications of computer graphics.

Pipes, Alan (ed.), *Computer-aided Architectural Design Futures*, Butterworths, London 1986. Proceedings of a conference with a large section on computer-aided drawing and visualization.

Woodwark, John, *Computing Shape*, Butterworths, London 1986. A practical guide to the ways computers represent shape and form.

Practice

Gorb, Peter (ed.), *Living by Design*, Lund Humphries, London 1978. A book about the UK practice Pentagram. The sections on the working methods of product designer Ken Grange are particularly useful.

Loewy, Raymond, *Industrial Design*, Faber & Faber, London 1979. The role of the industrial designer from the perspective of perhaps the best-known American designer.

Scarzella, Patrizia, *Steel and Style*, Arcadia Edizioni, Milan 1982. A collection of illustrated essays on the designers – Aldo Rossi, Oscar Tusquets Blanca, etc. – who have worked for Alessi.

Design methods

Hanks, Kurt et al, *Design Yourself*, William Kaufmann, Los Altos, California 1977. A "how to be a designer" book, with the emphasis on participation.

Jones, J. Christopher, *Design Methods*, Wiley-Interscience, London 1970. The standard work on design methods and theory.

Lawson, Bryan, *How Designers Think*, Architectural Press, London 1980. A design methods book aimed mainly at architects, with coverage of computer-assisted design.

Thackara, John (ed.), *Design After Modernism*, Thames and Hudson, London 1988. A collection of essays discussing contemporary design issues; includes a paper by Mike Cooley on the effect of cadcam on the role of the designer.

Theil, Philip, *Visual Awareness and Design*, University of Washington Press, Seattle 1981. An introduction to conceptual awareness, perceptual sensitivity and basic design skills.

Periodicals

Drawings by designers are few and far between in the general design magazines such as *Design* and *Blueprint* in the UK, *Ardi* in Spain and *Industrial Design* in the USA. They are more likely to be found in the more architecturally oriented *Architectural Review* in the UK and *Domus* in Italy. There are a growing number of journals devoted to cad, notably *CadCam International* and *3d* (the three "d"s stand for desktop design and documentation), both published monthly in the UK by EMAP, and *Computer Images*, published in the UK by Maclaren. In the USA, *Computer Graphics World*, published by Pennwell in Littleton, Massachusetts, is the source of information on cad systems for product designers. Most European countries have magazines or newsletters published in their own languages devoted to cad, albeit mainly for engineering and architectural applications.

Index

Index